FREE INSTRUCTOR'S COPY

READ AND RESPOND
A Reading Improvement Text

SECOND EDITION

Janet R. Swinton
Spokane Falls Community College

William J. Agopsowicz
San Joaquin Delta College

ROXBURY PUBLISHING COMPANY

NOTE TO INSTRUCTORS

A comprehensive **Instructor's Manual** is available

Library of Congress Card Catalogue Number: 91-067988

READ AND RESPOND

Copyright © 1992 by Roxbury Publishing Company. All rights reserved under International and Pan American Copyright Conventions. No part of this publication may be reproduced in any form or by any means, stored in a retrieval system, or transmitted in any form or by any means, electronic, mechanical, photocopying, recording, or otherwise without prior written permission of the publisher.

Second Edition   10 9 8 7 6 5 4 3 2 1

Manufactured in the United States of America

ISBN 0-935732-35-7

Publisher: Claude Teweles
Editors: Judith Ellis & Ingrid Herman Reese
Assistant Editor: Dawn VanDercreek
Typography and Design: Ingrid Herman Reese
Cover Design: Greg Cammack & Allan Miller

Since this page cannot legibly accommodate all of the copyright notices, the two following pages constitute an extension of the copyright page.

ROXBURY PUBLISHING COMPANY
P.O. Box 491044
Los Angeles, California 90049
(213) 653-1068

COPYRIGHT NOTICES
(Listed in Order)

"How to Read Faster" by Bill Cosby from International Paper's "Power of the Printed Word Program." Copyright © 1985 by International Paper Company. Reprinted by permission of International Paper.

"The Importance of Childhood Memories" by Norman M. Lobsenz. Reprinted with permission from the *Reader's Digest*, November, 1970. Copyright © 1970 by the Reader's Digest Association, Inc.

"Wool...The Living Fiber" adapted from the "Wool Story...From Fleece to Fashion," Section 2, from Pendleton Woolen Mills. Copyright © 1965 by Pendleton Woolen Mills. Used by permission.

"Part-time Jobs/Big-time Money" by JoAnne Alter, from *A Part-time Career for a Full-time You*. Copyright © 1982 by Houghton Mifflin.

"How to Spell" by John Irving from International Paper's "Power of the Printed Word Program." Copyright © 1985 by International Paper Company. Reprinted by permission of International Paper.

"How to Improve Your Vocabulary" by Tony Randall from International Paper's "Power of the Printed Word Program." Copyright © 1985 by International Paper Company. Reprinted by permission of International Paper.

"Revitalize Your Memory" by Mark Golin from *Prevention* magazine. Copyright © 1988, Rodale Press, Inc. All rights reserved. Reprinted by permission of *Prevention*.

"Pressure: How to Keep Going When the Going Gets Tough" by Dan Rather reprinted from *Ladies Home Journal*, April, 1983. Copyright © 1983 by Meredith Corporation. All rights reserved. Reprinted by permission.

"Speedwalk" by Pat Smith from *Mirabella* magazine, September, 1989. Copyright © 1989 by Pat Smith. Reprinted by permission.

"Diet and Exercise Dangers" by Anastasis Toufexis from *Time* magazine, November 2, 1981. Copyright © 1981 by Time, Inc. All rights reserved. Reprinted by permission of *Time*.

"When Staying Thin is a Sickness" by Earl Ubell from *Parade* magazine, October 23, 1983. Copyright © 1983 by Parade Publications. Reprinted by permission of *Parade*.

"Diets of Champs" by Laura Flynn McCarthy from *Harper's Bazaar*, May 1991. Copyright © 1991 by Laura Flynn McCarthy. Reprinted by permission.

"How to Keep Your Legs Young" by Joann Rodgers from *Parade* magazine, April 17, 1983. Copyright © 1983 by Joann Rodgers. Reprinted by permission of *Parade* and the author.

"Facing the Test" by Laura Fraser from *Vogue* magazine, June, 1991. Copyright © 1991 by Laura Fraser. Reprinted by permission.

"Hitting the Road" by David Elkind, Ph.D. Copyright © 1991 by David Elkind. Reprinted from *Parents* magazine by permission.

"Family Pet: For the Birds" by Sheldon L. Gerstenfeld, V.M.D. from *Parents* magazine, October, 1991. Copyright © 1991 by Sheldon L. Gerstenfeld. Reprinted from *Parents* magazine with permission.

"Your Child's Self-Esteem" by Lilian G. Katz from *Parents* magazine, November, 1988. Copyright © 1988 by Gruner + Jahr USA Publishing. Reprinted from *Parents* magazine with permission.

"School Age Parents: The Challenge of Three-Generation Living" by Jeanne Warren Lindsay, from *School Age Parents: The Challenge of Three-Generation Living*. Copyright © 1990 by Morning Glory Press.

"Dealing With the Angry Child" from a National Institute of Mental Health pamphlet. Reprinted by permission.

"The End of Innocence" by Nina Darton from *Newsweek* magazine, Summer, 1991. Copyright © 1991 by Newsweek, Inc. All rights reserved. Reprinted by permission.

"When Animals Open Wide" by Catherine Cremer from *International Wildlife Magazine*, May-June issue, 1982. Copyright © 1982 by the National Wildlife Federation. Reprinted by permission.

"Open for Sourdough, Please" by Eileen and Darwin Lambert from *Reader's Digest*, December 1983. Copyright © 1983 by Eileen and Darwin Lambert. Reprinted by permission of the authors.

"Frank Searle's Patient Stalk of the Beastie" by Lawrence A. Cenotto V, from *Tacoma News Tribune*, March 13, 1983. Copyright © 1983 by Lawrence A. Cenotto V. Reprinted by permission.

"Many Hooked on Strange Tales of Giant Catfish" by John Harold Brunvand from *The Spokesman-Review*, May 13, 1987. Copyright © 1987 by United Media Enterprises. Reprinted by permission of United Features Syndicate, Inc.

"Just Too Beastly for Words" by Jesse Birnbaum from *Time* magazine, June 24, 1991. Copyright © 1991 by Time, Inc.

"Soul of a Hero" from *Time* magazine, January 3, 1983. Copyright © 1983 by Time, Inc. All rights reserved. Reprinted by permission of *Time*.

"Commemorating a Heroic Act" from *Time* magazine, September 14, 1981. Copyright © 1981 by Time, Inc. All rights reserved. Reprinted by permission of *Time*.

"Ly Tong's Long Trek to Freedom" by Anthony Paul. Reprinted with permission from the *Reader's Digest*, June 1984. Copyright © 1984 by The Reader's Digest Association, Inc.

"The Child I Couldn't Forget" by Lisa Strick from *Good Housekeeping* magazine, May 1988. Copyright © 1988 by Lisa Wilson Strick. Reprinted courtesy of *Good Housekeeping*.

"She Leads a Nation" by Hank Whittemore. Reprinted with permission from *Parade* magazine, August 4, 1991. Copyright © 1991. Reprinted by permission of author and author's agent: Scott Meredith Literary Agency, Inc., 845 Third Avenue, New York, New York 10022.

"Food Fight" by David Grogan and Marilyn Balamaci from *PEOPLE Weekly* magazine, June 24, 1991. Copyright © 1991 by Time, Inc. Magazine Co. Reprinted by permission.

"Your Rights as a Crime Victim." Reprinted with permission from *McCall's* magazine. Copyright © 1988 by The New York Times Company.

"I Can't Stop Crying" from *Time* magazine, January 24, 1983. Copyright © 1983 by Time, Inc. All rights reserved. Reprinted by permission of *Time*.

"They've Killed My Daughter Twice!" by Joseph P. Blank. Reprinted with permission from the *Reader's Digest*, January 1981. Copyright © 1981 by the Reader's Digest Association, Inc.

"Battered Women Who Kill: Should They Receive Clemency?" reprinted courtesy of *Glamour* magazine, July, 1991. Copyright © 1991 by Condé Nast Publications, Inc.

"Revenge is the Mother of Invention" from *Time* magazine, January 24, 1983. Copyright © 1983 by Time, Inc. All rights reserved. Reprinted by permission of *Time*.

"Marriages Made to Last" by Jeanette and Robert Lauer from *Psychology Today*, June 1985. Reprinted by permission of *Psychology Today* magazine, Copyright © 1985 APA.

"The Myth of Romantic Love" from *The Road Less Traveled* by M. Scott Peck, M.D. Copyright © 1978 M. Scott Peck, M.D. Reprinted by permission of Simon & Schuster, Inc., New York, New York.

"Why Isn't a Nice Person Like You Married?" by Elsie Bliss. Copyright © 1991 by Elsie Bliss. Reprinted by permission.

"Love and Romance Make a Comeback" by Gabriel García Márquez from *Expreso*, Lima, Peru. Reprinted in *World Press Review*, May, 1991. Copyright 1991 by *World Press Review*, 200 Madison Avenue, New York, NY 10016. Reprinted by permission.

"Women Still Face Long Journey to Sports Fanaticism" by Dave Barry from *The Spokesman-Review*, March 14, 1985. Copyright © 1985 Dave Barry. Reprinted by permission of the author.

"Super Women" by Edward Dolnick excerpted from *Health* magazine, July, 1991. Copyright © 1991 by *Health* magazine. Reprinted by permission.

DEDICATION

At the all-important "after" meetings, there will always be just the five of us. Thanks, Jim, Ed, and Marcia.

ACKNOWLEDGEMENTS

The editors would like to thank the following individuals serving on the Editorial Advisory Board for their valued assistance in evaluating the first edition of *Read and Respond*. Their reviews and editorial comments have greatly strengthened and improved the text.

Alice Almay
Columbus State Community College

Rhea Ashmore
University of Montana

Horace A. Banbury
John Jay College (CUNY)

Isidore H. Becker
Lock Haven University

JoAnn P. Benda
Prince William Sound Community College

Phyllis Beukema
Muskegon Community College

John E. Boyd
Manor Junior College

Jane Brown
Jacksonville State University

JoAnn Carter-Wells
California State University, Fullerton

Donna Corlett
University of Portland

Agnes Crothers
Cayuga County Community College

LaVaughn DeHon
Vincennes University

Mary Alice Diehr
Schoolcraft College

Karen Dunlap
Craven Community College

Mary Dunn
College of Lake County

Margaret W. Fox
Oregon State University

Mary Anne F. Grabarek
Durham Tech Community College

Johnnie Hamrick
Gardner-Webb College

Barbara A. Henry
West Virginia State College

Shula Hirsch
Hofstra University

Billie Hobart
Contra Costa College

Dr. Wendy C. Kasten
University of South Florida at Sarasota

Marsha Konz
University of Wisconsin, Stevens Point

Jim L. Lambrinos
El Paso Community College

Norman C. Machart
Valley City State University

Marlene Meisels
National College of Education

Edwin C. Reeves
Glassboro State University

Clarita M. Reed
Xavier University

Virginia Regelman
Fort Lewis College

Julia Ryden
Rogue Community College

Rita Smilkstein
North Seattle Community College

Jerry W. Thomason
Hannibal-LaGrange College

Maria Valeri-Gold
Georgia State University

Linda R. Walter
Ocean County College

Westa W. Wood
Virginia State University

PREFACE

To the Instructor

We are pleased at the enthusiastic reception to the First Edition of ***Read and Respond***, a combination text/anthology designed to improve reading and writing skills. The Second Edition has been significantly expanded and improved.

The book's approach is unique because students are assessed for comprehension by summary writing rather than objective testing. After summarizing an article, students write a personal response to the article.

The Second Edition offers a variety of useful new features, including

- expanded text and models in Part One to aid classroom instruction in finding the subject, main idea, and major details of an article.

- a new appendix on 1) summarizing narrative essays, 2) summarizing expository essays, and 3) how to read a textbook chapter.

- more detailed instruction to clarify Chapter 5, "Writing a Response," including an easy-to-follow set of questions that serve as a prewriting exercise for short or more developed essays.

- a longer anthology section with many recent articles, including a new section on parenting. Half of these articles are new to the Second Edition. and many of them celebrate cultural diversity.

The design and philosophy of the Second Edition are in keeping with the original. The use of written summaries tests the student's ability to state main points rather than simply recognize them. Furthermore, since the summary and personal response are written in the student's own words, the instructor gains insight into the student's vocabulary and writing ability. Topics of student interest become evident, and the instructor can make recommendations for further reading. In this way, the crucial student-teacher relationship is enhanced, which helps build student self-esteem. Students develop proficiency in reading, writing, and critical thinking.

The exercises in Part One—the instruction section—include convenient ruled lines for student answers. In the new edition, exercise pages are perforated and designed to be removed without affecting instructional material.

Part Two—the anthology—is a collection of 39 articles for students to practice reading, summarizing, and writing responses. These articles, most of which were selected *by students* from the popular press, are grouped by subject, allowing students to choose topics of interest and read several viewpoints on the same subject. The selections are arranged in each section from easiest to most difficult. Every article is preceded by a preview section to help focus the reader's attention and pique curiosity. Definitions of difficult words, in limited context, precede each article.

To the Student

The ability to read well can make your school work and your job easier. It can provide hours of relaxing pleasure. As with other skills, it takes lots of practice to improve your reading ability. A good tennis player stays in practice by hitting tennis balls on a regular basis; a pianist practices piano at least an hour a day; a dancer rehearses for hours each week. In addition to practice, you need a method to help guide you as you improve through practice.

Read and Respond provides you with a step-by-step reading method. You will learn how to state the main idea and details of an article in your own words and how to develop a summary. Your summary then becomes a measure of how much you understand of what you read. You are also given the opportunity to "respond" to the author, that is, to write your personal reaction to the author's ideas. By summarizing what you have read and responding to it, you become a better reader. You will better understand textbooks and enjoy out-of-class reading more. In addition, you will become a better writer by acquiring skill in writing summaries, a necessary step in writing any research paper.

The articles in *Read and Respond* were chosen—primarily by students—from popular magazines and newspapers and were tested in classes for interest, readability, and potential for evoking thoughtful responses. You will see that these non-fiction articles represent a wide variety of styles and topics. It is our hope that you will enjoy working with them.

Janet R. Swinton
William J. Agopsowicz

FREE INSTRUCTOR'S COPY

TABLE OF CONTENTS

PART ONE

CHAPTER ONE: FINDING THE SUBJECT

General and Specific Subjects 4
How to Find the Subject 4
    Model One: Finding the subject of a one-paragraph article
                            Re-entry Students 5
    Exercise One: *The Key to Good Memory* 7
    Model Two: Finding the subject of an article
                                Repairing Your Car 9
    Exercise Two: *Do the Facts Ever Lie?* 11
    Exercise Three: Articles from Part Two 13
Key Points to Remember 15

CHAPTER TWO: FINDING THE MAIN IDEA

Understanding the Main Idea 17
How to Find the Main Idea 18
    Model One: Finding the subject and main idea of a
                              one-paragraph article
                              Driving in Europe 19
    Model Two: Finding the subject and main idea of a
                              one-paragraph article
                              Houseplants 20
    Exercise One: *Daylight Saving Time* 21
                              Taking Tests 22
    Model Three: Finding the subject and main idea of an article
                              The Value of a Speed Reading Course 23
    Exercise Two: *How to Read Faster* 25
    Exercise Three: Articles from Part Two 31
Key Points to Remember 33

CHAPTER THREE: FINDING MAJOR DETAILS

Signal Words 36
    Model One: Identifying signal words and phrases
                             Driving in Europe 37

    Exercise One: *Taking Tests* 39
    Model Two: Identifying major details with the help
                             of signal words
                             How to Preview a Textbook 41
Key Sentences 42
    Model Three: Identifying major details without the help
                             of signal words
                             Washington State's Economy 42
    Exercise Two: *Test Anxiety* 45
    Exercise Three: *Why Take Good Notes?* 47
    Exercise Four: *How to Take Good Notes* 49
Strategies for Longer Articles 51
    Model Four: Identifying major details in an article
                             Improving Your Memory 51
    Model Five: Identifying major details in an article
                             The Importance of Childhood Memories 54
    Exercise Five: *How to Read Faster* 59
    Exercise Six: Articles from Part Two 65
Key Points to Remember 67

CHAPTER FOUR: WRITING A SUMMARY

How to Make an Outline 69
How to Turn Your Outline into a Summary 70
    Model One: Summary of a one-paragraph article
                             How to Preview a Textbook 71
    Model Two: Summary of an article
                             The Shakers 73
    Exercise One: *Repairing Your Car* 75
    Exercise Two: *The Importance of Childhood Memories* 79
    Exercise Three: *Wool...The Living Fiber* 87
    Exercise Four: Articles from Part Two 93
Key Points to Remember 97

CHAPTER FIVE: WRITING A RESPONSE

Recording Your First Reactions 100
Writing the Response 101
    Model One: Two Responses to *Buying a Car* 101
    Model Two: Two Responses to *Discipline* 104
    Exercise One: *How to Read Faster* 107
    Exercise Two: *The Importance of Childhood Memories* 109
    Exercise Three: Articles from Part Two 111
Key Points to Remember 115

PART TWO

SELF-HELP

1. *Part-time Jobs/Big-time Money* 121
   Making money with a part-time job
2. *How to Spell* 125
   Tips from author John Irving on how to spell better
3. *How to Improve Your Vocabulary* 129
   Suggestions from actor Tony Randall on increasing your word power
4. *Revitalize Your Memory* 135
   Suggestions for improving your memory
5. *Pressure: How to Keep Going When the Going Gets Tough* 141
   Dan Rather's personal tips on how to handle pressure

HEALTH AND EXERCISE

6. *Speedwalk* 149
   Effective exercise that is kinder and gentler than running
7. *Diet and Exercise Dangers* 153
   A warning against weekend exercising and quick dieting
8. *When Staying Thin is a Sickness* 157
   Symptoms and treatment for eating disorders such as bulimia
9. *Diets of Champs* 161
   Myths and facts about the diets of successful athletes
10. *How to Keep Your Legs Young* 167
    Exercises to keep your legs looking and feeling young
11. *Facing the Test* 173
    Hidden Dangers of AIDS testing

PARENTING

12. *Hitting the Road* 181
    Advice about teenage driving
13. *Family Pet: For the Birds* 183
    Making a bird feeder
14. *Your Child's Self-Esteem* 187
    Ways to improve your child's self-esteem
15. *School Age Parents: The Challenge of Three-Generation Living* ... 191
    Parents and Grandparents coping with child rearing
16. *Dealing With the Angry Child* 195
    Responding to an aggressive or angry child
17. *The End of Innocence* 201
    What happens when children are exposed to the "secrets" of adulthood too soon

ANIMALS

18. *When Animals Open Wide* 209
    A study of why some animals yawn
19. *Open for Sourdough, Please* 213
    The story of a pet dog named Sourdough
20. *Frank Searle's Patient Stalk of the Beastie* 219
    One man's patient search for the Loch Ness monster
21. *Many Hooked on Strange tales of Giant Catfish* 223
    An urban legend about giant catfish
22. *Just Too Beastly for Words* 227
    The pros and cons of zoos

HEROES

23. *Soul of a Hero* 233
    The story of one man risking his life to save another
24. *Commemorating a Heroic Act* 235
    Heroic actions in a nineteenth century English village
25. *Ly Tong's Long Trek to Freedom* 239
    The story of a Vietnamese prisoner's escape from Vietnam
26. *The Child I Couldn't Forget* 247
    The story of a heroic army nurse who struggles with her memories of a Vietnamese child
27. *She Leads a Nation* 255
    Wilma Mankiller, the first female chief of the Cherokee Indian Nation

28. *Food Fight* 261
    David Kessler's fight for accurate food labeling

THE LAW AND JUSTICE

29. *Your Rights as a Crime Victim* 267
    An attorney's advice for victims of small crimes
30. *I Can't Stop Crying* 273
    The story of a man on death row who may be innocent
31. *They've Killed My Daughter Twice* 275
    A story of the pain and suffering drunk drivers caused one family
32. *Battered Women Who Kill: Should They Receive Clemency?* 281
    Battered women who plead self-defense when they kill
33. *Revenge is the Mother of Invention* 285
    A historical look at how the death sentence has been enforced

THE SEXES

34. *Marriages Made to Last* 291
    Why some marriages are successful
35. *The Myth of Romantic Love* 299
    Why some marriages don't survive
36. *Why Isn't a Nice Person Like You Married?* 303
    A single person talks about the respectability of being single
37. *Love and Romance Make a Comeback* 307
    Gabriel García Márquez's view of the return of love and romance
38. *Women Still Face Long Journey to Sports Fanaticism* 311
    A humorous look at how much more serious men are about sports than women
39. *Super Women* 315
    Ways in which women are superior to men

APPENDICES

Appendix A — Reading Textbooks 321

Appendix B — Reading Narrative and Expository Prose 327

INDEX OF ARTICLES AND PARAGRAPHS 329

PART ONE

Part One consists of five chapters, each containing instruction, models, and exercises. For each chapter, first carefully read the instruction and study the models. Then complete the exercises. The exercises will help you evaluate your understanding of each chapter.

CHAPTER ONE
FINDING THE SUBJECT

After class, Nate and Jennifer were talking about an article Nate had just read.
"What's it about?" Jennifer asked.
"Tests."
"All kinds of tests?"
"It's really just about objective tests," Nate replied.
"True-false, multiple-choice, and all that stuff?"
"No, it's just about multiple-choice tests."
"Hmmm," Jennifer said, "sounds like a boring subject to me."
"Actually I liked it because it gave me some good tips about how to answer multiple-choice questions."
"Oh, when you first said it was about 'tests,' I didn't know what you meant."

To understand what you hear or read, you need to first identify the **subject**. Furthermore, as the above conversation demonstrates, the more specifically the subject is stated, the better your understanding will be. In other words, although "tests" is the general subject of the article Nate read, Jennifer only really understood what it was about when he was more specific.

Because knowing the specific subject is so important to understanding what you read, this first chapter will focus on recognizing and stating the subject. The subject is sometimes called the "topic" or "subject matter," but in this book we will use the term "subject." All three of these terms refer to what the article is about.

The exercises in this chapter will help you to
- identify the subject of an article.
- state the specific subject of an article.

GENERAL AND SPECIFIC SUBJECTS

The subject can be stated in a single word such as *tests, dating,* or *boating.* These terms are all very general; they do not indicate the specific focus. For example, they do not tell what kind of tests or boats. Furthermore, they do not indicate what the author will emphasize about the subject. You do not know if the author tells how to take tests or argues for the importance of tests; you do not know if the author compares dating practices in different cultures or offers hints on how to find the ideal mate.

After you read something, your first approach may be to state the subject generally; however, there is an advantage in going further and identifying the subject more specifically. This will add to your understanding of the article. The conversation that opens this chapter is an example. Once Nate is specific about the subject, Jennifer understands the author's focus (multiple-choice questions) and emphasis (advice on how to answer these questions).

HOW TO FIND THE SUBJECT

The General Subject

To locate the subject of an article, first ask yourself the question, "What is the article about?" By answering it, you will be stating the **general subject**. However, to answer this question, you will need to **preview** the article. Start your preview by reading the title. You will usually find the general subject in the title. You may also get clues to the general subject from other features such as pictures, subtitles, or boldface headings.

The Specific Subject

The title may also provide the **specific subject**. For instance, it is clear from the title "Why We Must Save the Humpback Whale" the type of whale the author is discussing as well as the article's emphasis (reasons for saving this species). However, not all titles are this specific. If the author had entitled the article "Saving the Whales," "The Humpback Whale," or simply "Whales," you would need to look further for more specific information. Continue to preview by reading the first and last paragraphs of the article. If the article is only one paragraph long, read the first and last sentences of that paragraph. This will often be sufficient, but if you still need more information in an article several paragraphs long, read the first sentence of each paragraph.

MODEL ONE: Finding the subject of a one-paragraph article

RE-ENTRY STUDENTS

Re-entry students have a positive effect on college students, instructors, and the community. They are called "re-entry" students because they have been out of school for a period of time and now have come back. No longer are college classes primarily made up of 18- to 20-year-old recent high school graduates. The average age of students in many colleges is closer to 30. Occasionally a student graduates from college for the first time at the age of 70 or even older. For younger students, re-entry students are often models of dedication and hard work. Instructors enjoy the variety of life experiences that these students bring to the classroom. Finally, it might be the community at large that benefits most, for the re-entry students truly exemplify the saying that we are learners all our lives.

What is the article about? (Subject)

The positive effects of re-entry students

Or you might write

Re-entry students' positive effects on others

COMMENTS: The title provides the general subject (re-entry students). You can determine the specific subject by reading the first sentence, which indicates that these students have positive effects on a number of people. As indicated, the specific subject can be stated in more ways than one as long as the phrase accurately states the author's focus and emphasis.

Reading comprehension is greatly improved when you know the specific subject rather than just the general subject. From now on, when we use the term subject we are referring to the specific subject.

6 Read and Respond

Name_____ Class_____ Date_____

EXERCISE ONE

Read the following article and write the subject on the line provided.

THE KEY TO GOOD MEMORY

Good memory depends on how interested you are in what you are trying to remember. If you are interested in baseball, you are likely to remember batting averages, earned run averages, and World Series results. On the other hand, if you are not interested in baseball, you might think you have a poor memory because you cannot remember vital baseball statistics. It is likely that you will remember names of popular recording stars if you are interested enough in them—items that the baseball fan might easily forget. In short, interest is the key to a good memory.

What is the article about? (Subject)

_____

8   *Read and Respond*

MODEL TWO: Finding the subject of an article

REPAIRING YOUR CAR

Good mechanics can save you a lot of money during the lifetime of your car. More importantly, they can save your life. Since good mechanics are so important to car owners, it is helpful to know where to find them. Good mechanics may be found working in a variety of places.

Dealers' service departments specialize in repairs of particular makes of cars, and their mechanics are given special training by the manufacturer. They are the highest paid in the industry. You would be wise to use your dealer while your warranty is in effect.

Independent garages can and often do charge less than a dealer due to lower overhead. Their reliability is largely dependent on the individual in charge. It is a good idea to check out a garage's reputation by questioning local residents and customers if possible.

Specialty shops service one part of the car only: radiators, tires, mufflers, automatic transmissions, ignitions, or brakes. Usually these mechanics are very skilled within their areas of expertise.

Service departments of chain department and discount stores are usually located near large shopping areas. Their mechanics are experienced in making fast, relatively simple repairs and replacements—particularly on popular U.S. cars—but lack training and experience to diagnose complex mechanical problems.

Gasoline stations offer the advantages of a close-in location and conveniently long hours. In addition, their owners are not likely to take advantage of good, regular customers. For routine maintenance and minor repair jobs, you would probably find a neighborhood service station satisfactory.

Automotive diagnostic centers possess highly sophisticated electronic equipment to evaluate the various mechanical systems of a car, diagnose existing problems, and predict future ones. Authentic diagnostic centers are usually not in the repair business themselves. Charges are quite low.

What is the article about? (Subject)
Places to take your car for repair
Or you might write
Different kinds of auto repair shops

COMMENTS: The title, "Repairing Your Car," is a bit misleading. You might think the article offers advice on how to repair your own car. However, by reading the entire first paragraph and the first sentence of the other paragraphs, you realize that the article is about repair shops for your car.

Name_____ Class_____ Date_____

EXERCISE TWO

Read the following article and identify the subject on the line provided.

DO THE FACTS EVER LIE?

In many controversial articles, there is one set of facts, but two different interpretations. The readers of such articles must question both the facts and the interpretations and make up their own minds. Good readers think and read critically; they do not blindly accept someone else's conclusions.

A recent study by the National Center for Health Statistics is a good example of why critical thinking is so important. The study concludes that children in non-smoking households are likely to be healthier than children who live with smokers. The study shows that 4.1 percent of young children in households with smokers were in fair to poor health. Only 2.4 percent of the children never exposed to tobacco smoke were in fair to poor health. However, this conclusion is disputed by the tobacco industry.

The claim by the tobacco industry is that the difference is really one of income levels. In other words, they believe that the study does not take all factors into consideration. It is unfair, they say, to single out smoking as the big cause of the health problems.

The two sides in this dispute are using the same facts, but are interpreting them differently. Therefore, it is up to the readers to question all aspects of the controversy. They need to ask a number of questions: "What is the bias or motive of the tobacco industry in this case?" "Why would a government agency interpret statistics this way?" "How was the study conducted?" "Are there other reasons why these children have poorer health?" These and other questions must be asked in order to make a judgment about such a dispute. Good readers evaluate information; they do not just accept it.

What is the article about? (Subject)

_____

12   Read and Respond

Name_____ Class_____ Date_____

(Do not tear out this page until you have completed Exercise 3 in Chapter Two.)

EXERCISE THREE

Turn to *Part Two* which begins on page 109 of this book.

Identify the subject of the following articles and write them on the lines provided.

1. "Your Rights as a Crime Victim" (p. 267)

   _____

2. "Speedwalk" (p. 149)

   _____

3. "Revitalize Your Memory" (p. 135)

   _____

14   Read and Respond

KEY POINTS TO REMEMBER

- The subject reveals the author's focus and emphasis.

- To understand what you read, you must determine the subject.

- To find the subject, ask the question, "What is the article about?"

- To answer this question, preview by reading the title and looking at other features such as pictures, subtitles, or boldface headings.

- If more information is needed to find the specific subject, read the first and last paragraphs of the article (for a one-paragraph article, read the first and last sentences).

- If necessary, read the first sentence of all other paragraphs.

16 Read and Respond

CHAPTER TWO
FINDING THE MAIN IDEA

One day Jaime saw Eduardo in the reading room of the library. He glanced at the magazine Eduardo was reading and asked, "Why are you reading an article on restoring your old car?"

"Well, it's interesting."

"That's not something I care about. I guess I'm just not mechanical."

"It's not about how to restore old cars," said Eduardo. "It tells stories about people who've restored them. The author's point is that many people restore old cars for their sentimental value."

"Oh, that does sound interesting. Maybe I'll look at it when you're finished."

The subject of the article Eduardo was reading is why people restore old cars. As the conversation illustrates, knowing the subject is helpful, but it does not indicate the main point the author is making about the subject. Several different articles might have the same subject, yet each one could have a different main point. For example, one article might explain why restoring old cars is so expensive. Another might explain the many steps involved in restoring a car.

The exercises in this chapter will help you to

- identify the main idea of an article.
- state the main idea of an article.

UNDERSTANDING THE MAIN IDEA

The **main idea** of an article is the overall point the author makes about the subject.

Students are often confused about what is meant by the "main idea." Some of the confusion might be due to the different labels used for this concept. In an article or an essay, the main idea is usually referred to as the "thesis statement" or simply the "thesis." In a paragraph it is often called the "topic sentence." All of these terms refer to the main point the author wants to get across about the subject.

Some students are also confused about the difference between the main idea and the subject. While the subject reveals what the article is about, it does not indicate the author's main point about that topic. For instance, in Model One on page 5, once you know the subject, you know that the author is writing about re-entry students and that the author is emphasizing the positive effects these students have on others. However, you do not know the extent of these effects until you identify the main idea. This information is in the first sentence: "Re-entry students have a positive effect on college students, instructors, and the community."

The main idea is usually stated in a complete sentence whereas the subject can be stated in a word or a phrase. A phrase can show the focus of an article, but it usually does not show the author's main point. Suppose the subject is "dating practices in different cultures." This phrase reveals the author's focus and emphasis. A number of main points can be made about this subject, but each needs to be written in a complete sentence. For example, "Dating practices vary widely in different cultures," or "One way to learn about different cultures is to study their dating practices," could both be main idea sentences about this subject.

HOW TO FIND THE MAIN IDEA

To find the main idea, ask "What is the author's main point about the subject?" To answer this question, begin by looking at the clues that helped you identify the subject, such as the title, pictures, and headings. For further clues, read the first and last paragraphs of the article (first and last sentences of a one-paragraph article) because authors often state their main idea near the beginning or end. If you find what you think is the main idea, underline it. Then write it in your own words to be sure you understand it.

If you do not find the main idea clearly stated, write it in your own words based on the information you have gathered by previewing. Read the article to see if you are correct. If you are correct, most of the information in the article will in some way describe, explain, or offer examples of the main idea sentence you have written. If most of the information does not relate to your main idea statement, you need to write a new main idea sentence based on your complete reading of the article.

MODEL ONE: Finding the subject and main idea of a one-paragraph article

---

DRIVING IN EUROPE

<u>Driving experiences vary from one European country to the next.</u> For example, in England people drive on the left-hand side of the road. This gets confusing for Americans, especially when they are turning at intersections. On the other hand, the French drive on the right-hand side of the road, but their roads are narrow and many of them wind through small villages. In contrast, Germany has autobahns (freeways) without speed limits. For instance, it is not uncommon for Germans to drive 100 miles an hour or more on autobahns. Finally, in Switzerland the roads are wide and in good condition. But travel on them is often slow because of the many mountain passes.

NOTE: The sentence stating the main idea has been underlined. This format will be used in all the models in Part One.

What is the article about? (Subject)

Driving in Europe

Or you might write

How Europeans drive

What is the author's main point about the subject? (Main Idea)

People who drive in Europe encounter different road conditions from country to country.

Or you might write

Driving experiences are not the same in all countries.

COMMENTS: The subject is a restatement of the title. It shows the author's focus on Europe and emphasis on driving. However, the main idea goes one step further: it reveals that driving experiences differ from one European country to another. In other words, the main idea states something about the subject—in a complete sentence.

MODEL TWO: Finding the subject and main idea of a one-paragraph article

---

HOUSEPLANTS

Houseplants are big business. Most plants are expensive, yet millions are sold each year. One of the reasons for the high volume sold is that many are killed—often by overwatering. It is difficult to kill a plant by underwatering it. Leaves may droop for days, but one good watering will revive the plant. <u>If you overwater a plant, however, the roots will begin to rot, and you will probably lose the plant. Do your plants and your pocketbook a favor—water only when necessary.</u>

What is the article about? (Subject)

Watering houseplants

Or you might write

The care of houseplants

What is the author's main point about the subject? (Main Idea)

Overwatering kills most houseplants.

Or you might write

Water houseplants only when needed.

COMMENTS: The author's general subject (houseplants) is indicated by the title, but the main idea is not. By reading the first line, you probably anticipated that the main idea was the cost of plants. However, the author's main idea (over-watering often kills houseplants) actually comes later in the article. Reading the title and the first and last lines is one way to identify the main idea of an article. But to be sure, read the rest of the article; in the article on houseplants most of the sentences explain the consequences of overwatering.

Name_____ Class_____ Date_____

EXERCISE ONE

Read the following one-paragraph articles and write the subject and main idea in the spaces provided. Remember, if you find a sentence in the paragraph that states the main idea, underline it before you write it in your own words.

DAYLIGHT SAVING TIME

Some people like daylight saving time, but others hate it. Many people enjoy it because it gives them extra daylight hours in the evening to barbecue or go to the park. Others feel that it saves energy and therefore natural resources. However, most farmers do not like it because the morning darkness delays their morning chores. Additionally, some parents oppose it because they worry about their children going to school when it is still dark. The debate continues about the merits of daylight saving time.

What is the article about? (Subject)
_____

What is the author's main point about the subject? (Main Idea)
_____
_____
_____

TAKING TESTS

What is the first thing you do when you take a test? If you are like most students, you probably start by answering the first question, then proceed through the test, answering the rest of the questions in order. You may not know that there are a number of test-taking steps you can complete to boost your grade. The first step is to preview. Spend a few minutes scanning the test to find out how many questions there are and what types of questions are asked (multiple choice, true-false, essay, etc.) Next make a quick plan of how much time to spend on each section of the test. Allow more time for those sections worth the most points. The next step is to begin with the section that is easiest for you. This will insure a few quick, easy points for you and will probably give you a positive feeling that will help get you through the rest of the test. Finally, when you come to questions that you cannot answer or are not sure about, skip them for the time being. After you have finished the rest of the test, you can come back and guess the answers if there is no penalty for guessing.

What is the article about? (Subject)

_____

What is the author's main point about the subject? (Main Idea)

_____
_____
_____

MODEL THREE: Finding the subject and main idea of an article

THE VALUE OF A SPEED READING COURSE

Leon was a typical college student, or a least he thought he was. He got fairly good grades, mostly C's and B's, but his grades began falling when he was swamped with reading assignments. He thought about quitting school, and he walked to the student union building to play pool. Instead, he decided to talk with a counselor. The counselor suggested that Leon take a speed reading course offered through the school's reading lab. <u>Leon followed the advice and learned several skills which helped him improve his reading ability and self-confidence.</u>

First, Leon learned to preview reading material by reading the title and by looking at pictures, charts, headings, or anything else that gave him some sense of the subject and main idea. Then, before he read the article, he would think about the subject to discover what he knew about it. He usually found that he already knew something about the subject matter and sometimes quite a lot. In either case, he found it helpful to briefly think about his own feelings and knowledge of the subject. It not only made the reading material interesting, but he found he understood it better.

Next, Leon developed the ability to vary his reading rate according to the material and his purpose for reading it. For example, Leon realized it does not make sense to speed read poetry or textbooks. Nor does it make sense to speed read material that is to be learned for a test the next day. However, when Leon was reading a novel or an article for pleasure or general information, speed reading techniques saved him a great deal of time.

Leon also learned how to read entire phrases instead of word-by-word. His instructor called this "clustering," and Leon soon found it easy to look at two or three words at a time instead of just one. Since the eyes stop when they focus, the fewer times Leon focused, the faster he read.

24 *Read and Respond*

> Finally, Leon learned not to waste eye movement. Instead of moving his eyes all the way to the end of each line, he practiced making his last eye-stop two or three words from the end of the line. He also learned to focus his eyes two or three words away from the left-hand margin of each new line rather than on the first word of the line.
>
> Leon soon overcame his feeling of being overwhelmed by reading assignments. He realized that he had to determine what type of material he was being asked to read and analyze his purpose for reading it. He then felt free to use speed reading techniques when they were appropriate.

What is the article about? (Subject)

The value of a speed reading course

Or you might write

Skills to improve reading speed

What is the author's main point about the subject? (Main Idea)

Leon learned four skills that helped him read faster.

Or you might write

A reading course will provide skills to improve reading.

COMMENTS: The title usually provides clues to the author's subject. By completing the next step of the preview (reading the first and last paragraphs), you can better determine the subject.

Also, this second step of the preview reveals the author's main point. Remember that it is important to read the entire first and last paragraphs of articles; as in this case, the last sentence of the first paragraph often states the main idea.

Name_____ Class_____ Date_____

EXERCISE TWO

Read the following article and determine the subject and the main idea. In this article the main idea is clearly stated. Underline it. Then write the main idea in your own words, using the spaces provided. (HINT: Sometimes the author uses two sentences to state a main idea. When this is the case, try to combine the two sentences into one of your own.)

HOW TO READ FASTER
By Bill Cosby
"Power of the Printed Word" Program
International Paper Company

When I was a kid in Philadelphia, I must have read every comic book ever published. (There were fewer of them than there are now.)

I zipped through all of them in a couple of days, then reread the good ones until the next issues arrived.

Yes indeed, when I was a kid, the reading game was a snap. But as I got older, my eyeballs must have slowed down or something! I mean, comic books started to pile up faster than my brother Russell and I could read them!

It wasn't until much later, when I was getting my doctorate, I realized it wasn't my eyeballs that were to blame. Thank goodness. They're still moving as well as ever.

The problem is, there's too much to read these days, and too little time to read every word of it.

Now, mind you, I still read comic books. In addition to contracts, novels, and newspapers. Screenplays, tax returns, and correspondence. Even textbooks about how people read. And which techniques help people to read more in less time.

I'll let you in on a little secret. There are hundreds of techniques you could learn to help you read faster. But I know of three that are especially good. And if I can learn them, so can you—and you can put them to use immediately.

They are commonsense, practical ways to get the meaning from printed words quickly and efficiently. So you'll have time to enjoy your comic books, have a good laugh with Mark Twain or a good cry with *War and Peace*. Ready?

Okay. The first two ways can help you get through tons of reading material fast—without reading every word.

They'll give you the overall meaning of what you're reading. And let you cut out an awful lot of unnecessary reading.

1. PREVIEW—IF IT'S LONG AND HARD

Previewing is especially useful for getting a general idea of heavy reading like long magazine articles, business reports, and nonfiction books.

It can give you as much as half the comprehension in as little as one-tenth the time. For example, you should be able to preview eight or ten 100-page reports in an hour. After previewing, you'll be able to decide which reports (or which parts of reports) are worth a closer look.

Here's how to preview: Read the entire first two paragraphs of whatever you've chosen. Next read only the first sentence of each successive paragraph. Then read the entire last two paragraphs.

Previewing doesn't give you all the details. But it does keep you from spending time on things you don't really want—or need—to read.

Notice that previewing gives you a quick, overall view of long unfamiliar material. For short, light reading, there's a better technique.

2. SKIM—IF IT'S SHORT AND SIMPLE

Skimming is a good way to get a general idea of light reading—like the popular magazines or the sports and entertainment sections of the paper.

You should be able to skim a weekly popular magazine or the second section of your daily paper in less than half the time it takes you to read it now.

Skimming is also a great way to review material you've read before.

Here's how to skim: Think of your eyes as magnets. Force them to move fast. Sweep them across each and every line of type. Pick up only a few key words in each line.

Everybody skims differently.

You and I may not pick up exactly the same words when we skim the same piece, but we'll both get a pretty similar idea of what it's all about.

To show you how it works, I circled the words I picked out when I skimmed the following story. Try it. It shouldn't take you more than ten seconds.

My brother Russell thinks monsters live in our bedroom closet at night.

But I told him he is crazy.

"Go and check then," he said.

I didn't want to.

Russell said I was chicken.

"Am not," I said.

"Are so," he said.

So I told him the monsters were going to eat him at midnight. He started to cry. My dad came in and told the monsters to beat it. Then he told us to go to sleep.

"If I hear any more about monsters," he said, "I'll spank you."

We went to sleep fast. And you know something? They never did come back.

Skimming can give you a very good idea of this story in about half the words—and in less than half the time it'd take you to read every word.

So far, you've seen that previewing and skimming can give you a general idea about content—fast. But neither technique can promise more than 50 percent comprehension, because you aren't reading all the words. (Nobody gets something for nothing in the reading game.)

To read faster and understand most—if not all—of what you read, you need to know a third technique.

3. CLUSTER—TO INCREASE SPEED AND COMPREHENSION

Most of us learn how to read by looking at each word in a sentence—one at a time. Like this:

My—brother—Russell—thinks—monsters...

You probably still read this way sometimes, especially when the words are difficult. Or when the words have an extra-special meaning—as in a poem, a Shakespearean play, or a contract. And that's okay.

But word-by-word reading is a rotten way to read faster. It actually cuts down on your speed.

Clustering trains you to look at groups of words instead of one word at a time—to increase your speed enormously. For most of us, clustering is a totally different way of seeing what we read.

Here's how to cluster: Train your eyes to see all the words in clusters of up to three or four words at a glance. Here's how I'd cluster the story we just skimmed:

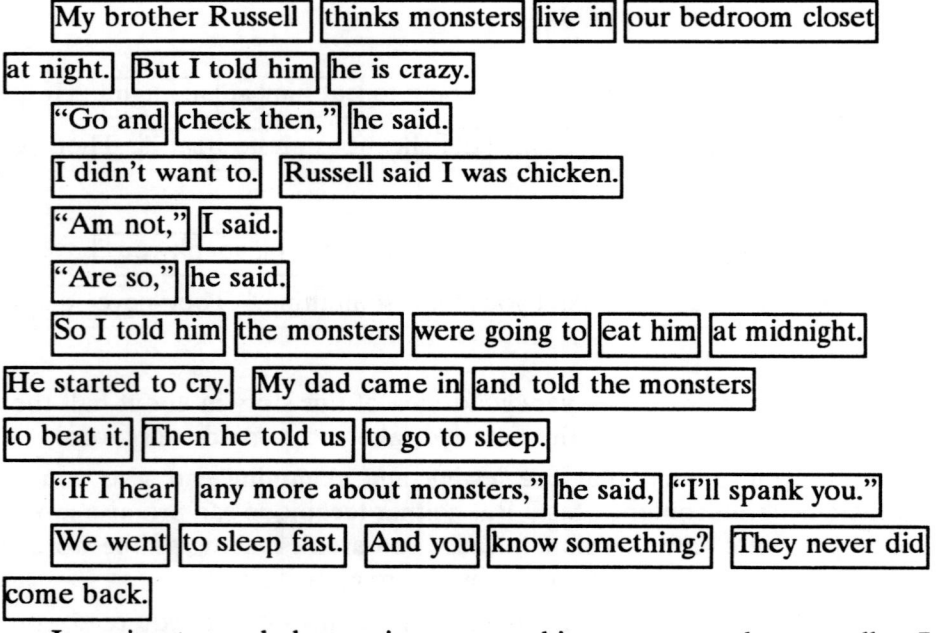

|My brother Russell| |thinks monsters| |live in| |our bedroom closet| |at night.| |But I told him| |he is crazy.|

|"Go and| |check then,"| |he said.|

|I didn't want to.| |Russell said I was chicken.|

|"Am not,"| |I said.|

|"Are so,"| |he said.|

|So I told him| |the monsters| |were going to| |eat him| |at midnight.| |He started to cry.| |My dad came in| |and told the monsters| |to beat it.| |Then he told us| |to go to sleep.|

|"If I hear| |any more about monsters,"| |he said,| |"I'll spank you."|

|We went| |to sleep fast.| |And you| |know something?| |They never did| |come back.|

Learning to read clusters is not something your eyes do naturally. It takes constant practice.

Here's how to go about it: Pick something light to read. Read it as fast as you can. Concentrate on seeing three to four words at once rather than one word at a time. Then reread the piece at your normal speed to see what you missed the first time.

Try a second piece. First cluster, then reread to see what you missed in this one.

When you can read in clusters without missing much the first time, you'll know that your speed has increased. Practice 15 minutes every day and you might pick up the technique in a week or so. (Don't be disappointed if it takes longer. Clustering everything takes time and practice.)

So now you have three ways to help you read faster. <u>Preview</u> to cut down on unnecessary heavy reading. <u>Skim</u> to get a quick, general idea of light reading. And <u>cluster</u> to increase your speed and comprehension.

With enough practice, you'll be able to handle more reading at school or work—and at home—in less time. You should even have enough time to read your favorite comic books—and *War and Peace*!

What is the article about? (Subject)
_____

What is the author's main point about the subject? (Main Idea)
_____
_____

Name_____ Class_____ Date_____

(Do not tear out this page until you have completed Exercise 4 in Chapter Four.)

EXERCISE THREE

At the end of Chapter One you identified the subject of three articles from Part Two of this book. Write the subjects again in the spaces below. Now write the main idea for each article.

Remember to look for a sentence that states the main idea, and if there is one, underline it before you write it in your own words.

#1. What is the article about? (Subject)

_____

What is the author's main point about the subject? (Main Idea)

_____

_____

_____

#2. What is the article about? (Subject)

_____

What is the author's main point about the subject? (Main Idea)

_____

_____

_____

#3. What is the article about? (Subject)

_____

What is the author's main point about the subject? (Main Idea)

_____

_____

_____

32   Read and Respond

KEY POINTS TO REMEMBER

■ The main idea reveals the author's main point about the subject.

■ To understand what you read, you must determine the author's main idea.

■ To find the main idea, ask the question "What is the author's main point about the subject?"

■ To answer this question, preview by reading the title and looking at other features such as pictures, subtitles, or boldface headings; sometimes you will also need to read the first and last paragraphs and the first sentence of all other paragraphs in the article.

■ If you find what you think is the main idea of the article, underline it.

■ Write the main idea in a complete sentence, using your own words.

CHAPTER THREE
FINDING MAJOR DETAILS

Outside the computer lab, Maria asked Kyle about his computer class.

"Aren't you afraid that some day computers will become the masters of humans?"

"No, I don't think it's much of a problem," Kyle answered. "I just read an article about that. The author's point was that people will always be one step ahead of computers."

"Oh really? How does he prove that?"

"He gives two major reasons. First, computers will always need to be programmed by humans. Second, intelligence involves more than just computer facts. A machine doesn't have intuition or feelings."

You have a natural curiosity to understand both an author's point and the reasoning or support for that point. This sense of curiosity should be developed, for it is the key to critical thinking.

In the conversation above, the author uses two **major details** to support the idea that computers will never be the masters of humans. Only by examining the author's logic can you intelligently agree or disagree with this point.

Major details answer the question, "How does the author support the main idea?" Authors use facts, examples, explanations, scientific proof, or combinations of these to support their main idea and make it clear. Major details supply information to support or clarify the main idea or to identify steps in a process.

Usually an author expands on major details with examples, facts or explanations. These are called **minor details.** While minor details can be interesting or informative, they are not usually essential to the understanding or evaluation of the main idea.

The exercises in this chapter will help you to
- identify the major details of an article.
- restate the major details of an article in outline form.

SIGNAL WORDS

Major details are often indicated by **signal words and phrases** (sometimes called **transitions**). For example, the word "finally" usually indicates that the author is about to state the final point. In the sentence you just read, the signal phrase "for example" is used to indicate that an example follows.

The following signal words and phrases are grouped according to their function.

Words that signal time or order of importance:
first	finally	before
in the first place	when	after that
second	then	later on

Words that signal contrast or an opposite point:
however	in contrast	despite
but	by contrast	although
on the contrary	in spite of	nevertheless

Words that signal the conclusion of an idea:
in conclusion	to sum up	finally
therefore	in short	as a result
consequently	in summary	

Words that signal the same or a similar idea:
and	more than that	likewise
furthermore	also	similarly
moreover	in the same manner	

Words that signal causes and effects:
because	due to	consequently
since	therefore	as a result

Words that signal examples:
for example	for instance	to illustrate

A NOTE OF CAUTION: Even though major details are often introduced by signal words and phrases, authors also use them for other purposes. Therefore, you need to read carefully; don't assume that behind every signal word is a major detail.

MODEL ONE: Identifying signal words and phrases

In Chapter Two, you read an article called "Driving in Europe." Read the article again, this time noting the signal words and phrases which indicate major details.

DRIVING IN EUROPE

<u>Driving experiences vary from one European country to the next.</u> **For example**, in England people drive on the left-hand side of the road. This gets confusing for Americans, especially when they are turning at intersections. **On the other hand,** the French drive on the right-hand side of the road, but their roads are narrow and many of them wind through small villages. **In contrast**, Germany has autobahns (freeways) without speed limits. For instance, it is not uncommon for Germans to drive 100 miles an hour or more on autobahns. **Finally**, in Switzerland the roads are wide and in good condition, but travel on them is often slow because of the many mountain passes.

COMMENTS: The signal words and phrases in bold print indicate the four major details in this article. "For instance" is also a signal phrase, but in this article it does not introduce a major detail. It precedes an example (minor detail) of how fast some Germans drive.

Name_____ Class_____ Date_____

EXERCISE ONE

"Taking Tests" is an article you read when you were learning to find the main idea of a one-paragraph article in Chapter Two. Now read it and underline the signal words and phrases.

TAKING TESTS

What is the first thing you do when you take a test? If you are like most students, you probably start by answering the first question, then proceed through the test, answering the rest of the questions in order. You may not know that there are a number of steps you can take to boost your grade. The first step is to preview. Spend a few minutes scanning the test to find out how many questions there are and what types of questions are asked (multiple choice, true-false, essay, etc.). With this information in mind, next make a quick plan of how much time to spend on each section of the test. Allow more time for sections worth the most points. The next step is to begin with the section that is easiest for you. This will insure a few quick, easy points for you and will probably give you a positive feeling that will help get you through the rest of the test. Finally, when you come to questions that you cannot answer or are not sure about, skip them for the time being. After you have finished the rest of the test, you can come back and guess the answers if there is no penalty for guessing.

MODEL TWO: Identifying major details with the help of signal words

---

HOW TO PREVIEW A TEXTBOOK

One of the most helpful things you can do when you begin a new class in college is to preview your textbook. To do this, follow these simple steps. **First**, examine the table of contents. This will quickly tell you how many chapters are in the book and the nature of the material covered. **Second**, read the "To the Student" section or the preface, if there is one, to see how the book is organized and how the author approaches the material. Among other things, this will tell you if the book is practical or theoretical in approach. **Then** examine the copyright date to see how recent the text is. **Finally**, check to see what special features the book contains. For example, is there an index at the back listing important terms and concepts? Is there a glossary where terms are defined? Is the book arranged chapter-by-chapter or alphabetically? Is there an appendix of additional information? Are there summaries at the end of each chapter? By taking just a few minutes to preview your next textbook, you can get more out of your book in a shorter amount of time.

What is the paragraph about? (Subject)

_____

Or you might write

Steps in previewing a textbook

What is the author's main point about the subject? (Main Idea)

Previewing a textbook involves four steps.

Or you might write

There are four steps to previewing a textbook.

How does the author support the main idea? (Major Details)

—read table of contents
—read preface or "To the Student"

42   Read and Respond

— look at copyright date
— look for special features

COMMENTS: The major details in this article are those that name the steps in previewing a book. They are indicated by the signal words *first*, *second*, *then*, and *finally*. The signal phrase *for example* introduces a minor detail (an example of a special feature).

KEY SENTENCES

When you cannot find any signal words or phrases, look for **key sentences** which contain reasons, causes, effects, examples, or steps of a process. Keen in mind that an author can use details to explain or support the main idea of an article without using signal words or phrases.

MODEL THREE: Identifying major details without the help of signal words

---

WASHINGTON STATE'S ECONOMY

The economy of Washington state is likely to remain troubled for many years. The reasons for this are many. The salmon fishing has suffered through several shortened and non-productive seasons. This has affected the inflow of tourist dollars. The lumber industry has never fully recovered from the recession and the mining industry is in trouble because of depressed metal prices. The state has no income tax, relying instead on an array of taxes on alcohol, property, gasoline, and businesses. When times are bad, people do not drive as much and businesses do not thrive. Revenues are simply not adequate to meet increasing costs.

What is the article about? (Subject)
Washington's troubled economy

What is the author's main point about the subject? (Main Idea)
Washington's economy is troubled for many reasons.

How does the author support the main idea? (Major Details)

— salmon fishing poor
— lumber industry down
— mining industry down
— no state income tax

Below is a different way of writing these major details. As you saw in the models in Chapters One and Two, there is no one correct way of stating something as long as the content is correct.

— bad fishing seasons
— decline in lumber sales
— low metal prices hurt mining industry
— dependence on unreliable taxes

COMMENTS: The major details in this article are not marked by signal words or phrases. The major details cover the reasons why the economy is troubled, such as the lack of an income tax and the poor fishing seasons. The fourth and seventh sentences are minor details which explain the previous sentences. The last sentence is a restatement of the main idea and as such serves as a conclusion to this one-paragraph article.

44 Read and Respond

Name_____ Class_____ Date_____

EXERCISE TWO

Read the following article and write the subject, main idea, and major details using the spaces provided. (Remember to underline the author's main idea if it is clearly stated.) Some of the major details are indicated by signal words; to find the others, look for key sentences.

TEST ANXIETY

    Whenever I take a test I get nervous. My hands shake so much I can hardly hold my pen. Also, the palms of my hands get sweaty, and I have to keep wiping them on my pants to keep them dry. My stomach tightens up. It feels as if I have just eaten too much, even when I have an empty stomach. Furthermore, I usually get a headache, sometimes so strong that I can hardly think. I am working to control my nervousness but so far have not had much luck.

What is the article about? (Subject)
_____

What is the author's main point about subject? (Main Idea)
_____
_____

How does the author support the main idea? (Major Details)
_____
_____
_____
_____

Name_____ Class_____ Date_____

EXERCISE THREE

Read the following article and write the subject, main idea, and major details using the spaces provided. (Remember to underline the author's statement of the main idea if it is clearly stated.) Some of the major details are indicated by signal words; to find the others, look for key sentences.

WHY TAKE GOOD NOTES?

Taking good class notes is important for several reasons. First, the process helps you keep your mind on what the instructor is saying. If you are trying to write the important ideas of the lecture, you have to keep your mind focused. Second, notes are a good memory aid. They remind you of future assignments and due dates, and they are invaluable as review sheets before tests. Another good reason for taking notes is that they can help clarify material in your textbook. Sometimes the instructor lectures on the same ideas as those in the textbook reading assignment. Finally, good notes are a record of information that might not be included in your textbook but which your instructor expects you to know.

What is the article about? (Subject)

_____

What is the author's main point about the subject? (Main Idea)

_____
_____

How does the author support the main idea? (Major Details)

_____
_____
_____
_____

48 Read and Respond

Name_____ Class_____ Date_____

EXERCISE FOUR

Read the following article and write the subject, main idea, and major details using the spaces provided. (Remember to underline the author's statement of the main idea if it is clearly stated.) Some of the major details are indicated by signal words; to find the others, look for key sentences.

HOW TO TAKE GOOD NOTES

Taking good class notes involves several steps. The first step is to date and label your notes. This keeps your notes organized. Then if an instructor says that you will be tested on material from the previous two weeks, you will be able to quickly identify what to study. Also, leave plenty of space as you take notes. This allows you to fill in words or ideas you may have missed and still keep your notes neat and readable. Furthermore, you should devise a method for indicating key points. Some people underline these points; others put a star or check beside them; still others indicate them by indenting either the major points or the subpoints. The important thing is not *how* you identify them but that you *do* identify them. Always take notes in your own words. To do this, develop your own shorthand or system of abbreviations so that you can concentrate on listening rather than on writing. Putting ideas in your own words, even in abbreviations, is the only way to be sure you understand the material.

Perhaps the most important step is to get in the habit of editing your notes as soon as possible after class. By doing this you will automatically review the important ideas from class, fill in any information you jotted down in too sketchy a form, and realize what you missed so that you can ask questions later.

What is the article about? (Subject)

_____

50   Read and Respond

What is the author's main point about the subject? (Main Idea)
_____
_____

How does the author support the main idea? (Major Details)
_____
_____
_____
_____
_____

Chapter Three/Finding Major Details 51

STRATEGIES FOR LONGER ARTICLES

So far the models and exercises in this chapter have been one or two paragraphs long. Most articles you will read are much longer, and identifying the main idea and major details usually becomes a greater challenge due to the increased length. Like any other skill, the ability to find major details improves with practice. Here are some suggestions to help you develop this skill.

1. Follow all of the preview steps discussed in Chapters One and Two:
   - read the title.
   - look at pictures, subtitles, and headings.
   - read the first and last paragraphs.
   - read the first sentence of each of the other paragraphs.
2. Divide the article into sections which indicate the introduction, main idea, major details, and conclusion. The sections may consist of one or more paragraphs. Check the main idea of each paragraph to see if it is a major detail of the article. Do not assume that each paragraph contains a major detail.
3. Label each section on the article itself.

MODEL FOUR: Identifying major details in an article.

IMPROVING YOUR MEMORY

Section One:
Introduction

At a party, Nora was introduced to five friends of the host. The host said, "Nora, I'd like you to meet Teresa and her husband Juan. Teresa works at the reading lab with me; I'm sure I've told you about her. And this is Sherry, Alexis, and Maria." Nora said hello to each one and went into the kitchen to find her roommate. A few minutes later, Nora could not remember the names of any of the people she had just met. She complained to her roommate, "I just don't have a good memory."

Main Idea

How is your memory? It is probably only when your memory fails you that you think about it. An occasional lapse is normal. <u>The key to "managing" your memory and improving it is to understand how memory works.</u>

Section Two:
Major Detail

In order to remember something, you need to have sensory input; that is, a sensation is recorded by one of your senses. For example, a plane flies over your house and you hear it, or a cake is burning in the oven and you smell it.

Section Three:
Major Detail

But sensory input is not enough. Your eyes and ears might be seeing and hearing numerous sights and sounds, but you can only focus on a few at any one time. The ones you focus on are the ones you are most likely to remember.

Section Four:
Major Detail

To improve your memory retention, you must consciously *intend* to remember certain sights, sounds, smells, or other stimuli, and then focus on them. For example, at a party like the one Nora attended, you might be introduced to several people. If you feel it is important to remember their names, focus on their names and faces and make an effort to remember them. If necessary, use word associations to help you remember. (For example, to remember Alexis' name, you might associate her with the television character on "Dynasty.") Without the intention to remember, you probably won't retain the name in the first place. Or you may forget it as soon as you hear it because you did not make any special effort to remember.

Section Five:
Major Detail

This conscious effort is not enough for lasting memory, however. You will not remember the sensory input for very long if you do not do something to place it in your long-term memory. You need to review the new information within 24 to 48 hours to remember it over time. Periodic review will ensure that you never forget the information.

Chapter Three/Finding Major Details 53

> **Section Six:**
> **Conclusion**
>
> Improving your memory using this technique is not difficult. Practice it often to improve your retention skills. Pay attention to the input, your intent to remember, and of course, review. You have the power to remember anything you want—if you choose to.

What is the article about? (Subject)

How memory works

What is the author's main point about the subject? (Main Idea)

Everyone has a "good" memory but can improve it by understanding how memory works.

How does the author support the main idea? (Major Details)

- *We receive input via one of the senses.*
- *We focus on certain input.*
- *In order to remember, we must intend to remember.*
- *Reviewing within 24 hours is important.*

COMMENTS: Section One (the first two paragraphs) of this article introduces the subject and states the main idea of the entire article. Sections Two, Three, Four and Five each contain one major detail. Section Six (the conclusion) restates the main idea and major details.

54 Read and Respond

MODEL FIVE: Identifying major details in an article

THE IMPORTANCE OF CHILDHOOD MEMORIES
by Norman M. Lobsenz
from *Reader's Digest*

Section One:
Introduction

Some years ago, when my young wife became desperately ill, I wondered how I would be able to cope with the physical and emotional burden of caring for her. One night, when I was drained of strength and endurance, a long forgotten incident came to mind.

I was about ten years old at the time and my mother was seriously ill. I had gotten up in the middle of the night to get a drink of water. As I passed my parents' bedroom, I saw the light on. I looked inside. My father was sitting in a chair in his bathrobe next to Mother's bed, doing nothing. She was asleep. I rushed into the room.

"What's wrong?" I cried. "Why aren't you asleep?"

Dad soothed me. "Nothing's wrong. I'm just watching over her."

I can't say exactly how, but the memory of that long-ago incident gave me the strength to take up my own burden again. The remembered light and warmth from my parents' room were curiously powerful and my father's words haunted me: "I'm just watching over her." The role I now assumed seemed somehow more bearable, as if a resource has been called from the past or from within.

Section Two:
Main Idea

<u>In moments of psychological jeopardy, such memories often turn out to be the ultimate resources of personality, dark prisms which focus our basic feeling about life.</u> As Sir James Barrie once wrote, "God gives us memory so that we may have roses in December."

Section Three:
Major Detail
Can't predict what makes lasting memories

No parent can ever really know which memory, planted in childhood, will grow to be a rose. Often our most vivid and enduring remembrances are of apparently simple, even trivial things. I did not discover this myself until one bright, leaf-budding spring day when my son Jim and I were putting a fresh coat of paint on the porch railing. We were talking about plans to celebrate his approaching 15th birthday, and I found myself thinking how quickly his childhood had passed.

"What do you remember best?" I asked him.

He answered without a moment's hesitation. "The night we were driving somewhere, just you and me, on a dark road, and you stopped the car and helped me catch fireflies."

Fireflies? I could have thought of a dozen incidents, both pleasant and unpleasant, that might have remained vivid in his mind. But fireflies? I searched my memory—and eventually it came back to me.

I'd been driving cross-country, traveling late to meet a rather tight schedule. I had stopped to clean the windshield, when all at once a cloud of fireflies surrounded us. Jim, who was five years old then, was tremendously excited. He wanted to catch one. I was tired and tense, and anxious to get on to our destination. I was about to tell him that we didn't have time to waste when something changed my mind. In the trunk of the car I found an empty glass jar. Into it we scooped dozens of the insects. And while Jim watched them glow, I told him of the mysterious cold light they carried in their bodies. Finally, we uncapped the jar and let the fireflies blink away into the night.

"Why do you remember that?" I asked. "It doesn't seem terribly important."

"I don't know," he said. "I didn't even know I did remember it until just now." Then a few moments later: "Maybe I do know why. Maybe it was because I didn't think you were going to stop and catch any with me—and you did."

Since that day I have asked many friends to reach back into their childhoods and tell me what they recall with greatest clarity. Almost always they mention similar moments—experiences or incidents not of any great importance. Not crises or trauma or triumphs, but things which, although small in themselves, carry sharp sensations of warmth and joy, or sometimes pain.

One friend I spoke with was the son of an executive who was often away from home. "Do you know what I remember best?" he said to me. "It was the day of the annual school picnic when my usually very dignified father appeared in his shirt-sleeves, sat on the grass with me, ate a box lunch, and then made the longest hit in our softball game. I found out later that he postponed a business trip to Europe to be there." My friend is a man who experiences the world as a busy, serious place but who basically feels all right about it and about himself. His favorite childhood memory is both clue to and cause of his fundamental soundness.

Section Four:
Major Detail: *Parents can help shape memories*

Clearly, the power parents have to shape the memories of their children involves an awesome responsibility. In this respect nothing is trivial. What to a grown-up might seem a casual word or action often is, to a child, the kernel of a significant memory on which he will build. As grownups, we draw on these memories as sources of strength or weakness. Author Willa Cather saw this clearly. "There are those early memories," she wrote. "One cannot get another set; one has only those."

Not long ago, I talked with a woman who has married a young and struggling sculptor. She cheerfully accepted their temporary poverty. "I grew up during the depression," she said. "My dad scrambled from one job to another. But I remembered that each time a job ended, my mother would scrape together enough money to make us an especially good dinner. She used to call them our 'trouble meals.' I know now that they were her way of showing Dad she believed in him, in his ability to fight back. I learned that loving someone is more important than having something.

Section Five
Major Detail
Steps to provide good memories

If childhood memories are so important, what can parents do to help supply their children with a healthy set?

- For one thing, parents should be aware of the importance of the memory-building process. In our adult preoccupation, we tend to think that the "important" experiences our children will have are still in their future. We forget that, to them, childhood is reality rather than merely a preparation for reality. We forget that childhood memories form the adult personality. "What we describe as 'character,' " wrote Sigmund Freud, "is based on the memory traces of our earliest youth."

- Parents can try to find the extra energy, time, or enthusiasm to carry out the small and "insignificant" plan that is so important to a child. The simple act of baking that special batch of cookies or helping to build that model car, even though you are tired or harried, may make an important memory for your youngster.

Conversely, parents can try to guard against the casual disillusionments and needless disappointments which they often unthinkingly inflict on children. I would venture that almost everyone has a memory of an outing canceled or a promise broken without a reason or an explanation. "My father always used to say, 'We'll see,'" one man told me. "I soon learned that what that meant was 'no,' but without any definite reason."

- Parents can think back to their own childhoods and call up their own memories. By remembering the incidents that made important impressions on them, parents can find guideposts to ways in which they can shape the future memories of their own youngsters.

- Finally, parents can, by their own actions and words, communicate emotions as well as experiences to their children. We can give them a memory of courage rather than fear; of strength rather than weakness; of an appetite for adventure rather than a shrinking from new

58 *Read and Respond*

> people and places; of warmth and affection rather than rigidity and coldness. In just such memories are rooted the attitudes and feeling that characterize a person's entire approach to life.

What is the article about? (Subject)
Childhood memories

Or you might write
Why childhood memories are important

What is the author's main point about the subject? (Main Idea)
Childhood memories can help us get through tough times.

Or you might write
In tough times, childhood memories can give us strength.

How does the author support the main idea? (Major Details)
- *Parents can't predict what makes lasting memories*
- *Parents can help shape their children's memories in four ways:*
  1. *be aware of the importance of memory process*
  2. *try to find extra time & energy for children's activities*
  3. *recall own childhood memories*
  4. *share both your emotions & experiences w/children*

COMMENTS: Notice that not every paragraph contains a major detail. For example, Section One (the introduction) is five paragraphs long and Section Three (one long example) is seven paragraphs long.

Name_____ Class_____ Date_____

EXERCISE FIVE

In Chapter Two you read "How to Read Faster" and wrote the subject and main idea using the spaces provided. Now look for the author's statement of the main idea and underline it. Then divide the article into sections, label them, and list the major details in the spaces provided.

HOW TO READ FASTER
By Bill Cosby
"Power of the Printed Word" Program
International Paper Company

When I was a kid in Philadelphia, I must have read every comic book ever published. (There were fewer of them than there are now.)

I zipped through all of them in a couple of days, then reread the good ones until the next issues arrived.

Yes indeed, when I was a kid, the reading game was a snap. But as I got older, my eyeballs must have slowed down or something! I mean, comic books started to pile up faster than my brother Russell and I could read them!

It wasn't until much later, when I was getting my doctorate, I realized it wasn't my eyeballs that were to blame. Thank goodness. They're still moving as well as ever.

The problem is, there's too much to read these days, and too little time to read every word of it.

Now, mind you, I still read comic books. In addition to contracts, novels, and newspapers. Screenplays, tax returns, and correspondence. Even textbooks about how people read. And which techniques help people to read more in less time.

I'll let you in on a little secret. There are hundreds of techniques you could learn to help you read faster. But I know of three that are especially good. And if I can learn them, so can you—and you can put them to use immediately.

They are commonsense, practical ways to get the meaning from printed words quickly and efficiently. So you'll have time to enjoy your comic books, have a good laugh with Mark Twain or a good cry with *War and Peace*. Ready?

Okay. The first two ways can help you get through tons of reading material fast—without reading every word.

They'll give you the overall meaning of what you're reading. And let you cut out an awful lot of unnecessary reading.

1. PREVIEW—IF IT'S LONG AND HARD

Previewing is especially useful for getting a general idea of heavy reading like long magazine articles, business reports, and nonfiction books.

It can give you as much as half the comprehension in as little as one-tenth the time. For example, you should be able to preview eight or ten 100-page reports in an hour. After previewing, you'll be able to decide which reports (or which parts of reports) are worth a closer look.

Here's how to preview: Read the entire first two paragraphs of whatever you've chosen. Next read only the first sentence of each successive paragraph. Then read the entire last two paragraphs.

Previewing doesn't give you all the details. But it does keep you from spending time on things you don't really want—or need—to read.

Notice that previewing gives you a quick, overall view of long unfamiliar material. For short, light reading, there's a better technique.

2. SKIM—IF IT'S SHORT AND SIMPLE

Skimming is a good way to get a general idea of light reading—like the popular magazines or the sports and entertainment sections of the paper.

You should be able to skim a weekly popular magazine or the second section of your daily paper in less than half the time it takes you to read it now.

Skimming is also a great way to review material you've read before.

Here's how to skim: Think of your eyes as magnets. Force them to move fast. Sweep them across each and every line of type. Pick up only a few key words in each line.

Everybody skims differently.

You and I may not pick up exactly the same words when we skim the same piece, but we'll both get a pretty similar idea of what it's all about.

To show you how it works, I circled the words I picked out when I skimmed the following story. Try it. It shouldn't take you more than ten seconds.

My brother Russell thinks monsters live in our bedroom closet at night.

But I told him he is crazy.

"Go and check then," he said.

I didn't want to.

Russell said I was chicken.

"Am not," I said.

"Are so," he said.

So I told him the monsters were going to eat him at midnight. He started to cry. My dad came in and told the monsters to beat it. Then he told us to go to sleep.

"If I hear any more about monsters," he said, "I'll spank you."

We went to sleep fast. And you know something? They never did come back.

Skimming can give you a very good idea of this story in about half the words—and in less than half the time it'd take you to read every word.

So far, you've seen that previewing and skimming can give you a general idea about content—fast. But neither technique can promise more than 50 percent comprehension, because you aren't reading all the words. (Nobody gets something for nothing in the reading game.)

To read faster and understand most—if not all—of what you read, you need to know a third technique.

3. CLUSTER—TO INCREASE SPEED AND COMPREHENSION

Most of us learn how to read by looking at each word in a sentence-one at a time. Like this:

My—brother—Russell—thinks—monsters...

You probably still read this way sometimes, especially when the words are difficult. Or when the words have an extra-special meaning—as in a poem, a Shakespearean play or contract. And that's okay.

But word-by-word reading is a rotten way to read faster. It actually cuts down on your speed.

Clustering trains you to look at groups of words instead of one word at a time—to increase your speed enormously. For most of us, clustering is a totally different way of seeing what we read.

Here's how to cluster: Train your eyes to see all the words in clusters of up to three or four words at a glance. Here's how I'd cluster the story we just skimmed:

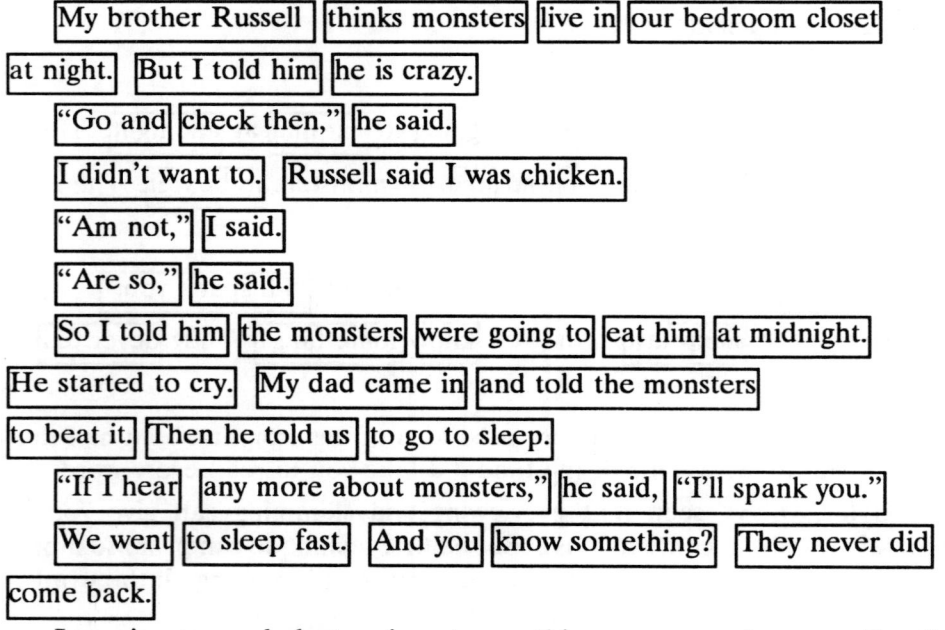

| My brother Russell | thinks monsters | live in | our bedroom closet | at night. | But I told him | he is crazy.

"Go and | check then," | he said.

I didn't want to. | Russell said I was chicken.

"Am not," | I said.

"Are so," | he said.

So I told him | the monsters | were going to | eat him | at midnight. | He started to cry. | My dad came in | and told the monsters | to beat it. | Then he told us | to go to sleep.

"If I hear | any more about monsters," | he said, | "I'll spank you."

We went | to sleep fast. | And you | know something? | They never did | come back.

Learning to read clusters is not something your eyes do naturally. It takes constant practice.

Here's how to go about it: Pick something light to read. Read it as fast as you can. Concentrate on seeing three to four words at once rather than one word at a time. Then reread the piece at your normal speed to see what you missed the first time.

Chapter Three/Finding Major Details 63

> Try a second piece. First cluster, then reread to see what you missed in this one.
>
> When you can read in clusters without missing much the first time, you'll know that your speed has increased. Practice 15 minutes every day and you might pick up the technique in a week or so. (Don't be disappointed if it takes longer. Clustering everything takes time and practice.)
>
> So now you have three ways to help you read faster. <u>Preview</u> to cut down on unnecessary heavy reading. <u>Skim</u> to get a quick, general idea of light reading. And <u>cluster</u> to increase your speed and comprehension.
>
> With enough practice, you'll be able to handle more reading at school or work—and at home—in less time. You should even have enough time to read your favorite comic books—and *War and Peace*!

What is the article about? (Subject)

_____

What is the author's main point about the subject? (Main Idea)

_____

_____

How does the author support the main idea? (Major Details)

_____

_____

_____

_____

_____

_____

_____

Name_____ Class_____ Date_____

(Do not tear out this page until you have completed Exercise 4 in Chapter Four.)

EXERCISE SIX

In Chapter Two, you identified the subject and main idea of three articles from Part Two. Review what you wrote for the subject and main idea of each article, then divide the article into sections. Label the sections, and list the major details in the spaces provided.

#1

_____
_____
_____
_____
_____
_____
_____
_____
_____

#2

_____
_____
_____
_____
_____
_____
_____
_____
_____

#3

KEY POINTS TO REMEMBER

■ Major details support the author's main point; they are essential to your understanding of the main idea and your ability to evaluate it.

■ Major details answer the question, "How does the author support the main idea?"

■ To find major details:
- Preview the article to determine the subject and main idea.
- Use signal words and phrases to help you identify major details.
- Divide longer articles into sections; read the first line of every paragraph to help you determine where to divide the sections.
- Determine the main idea of each section; these are usually the major details of a longer article.

CHAPTER FOUR
WRITING A SUMMARY

"Hey, Lionel, how about a set of tennis?"

"I can't, Shaheen. I've got to write a summary of an article for biology class. It'll take me all afternoon."

"Writing a summary isn't so bad. We learned how to write one in English class. I use summaries all the time in American History. I really understand what I read when I write a summary. It forces me to put the ideas in my own words. I'll show you how and then we'll play a couple of sets."

In a summary, you rewrite, in your own words, an author's main idea and major supporting details. You retell what someone else has written in a shorter version, using your own wording and sentence style.

Knowing how to write a good summary can benefit you in several ways: (1) A written summary allows you to measure your understanding of an article's content according to your background, experience, and reading ability. (2) A summary helps you understand what you read because it forces you to rewrite the text in your own words. (3) Summaries are required in many college courses. (4) Knowing how to write a summary is essential when you have to write a term paper. You have to condense long articles and books by summarizing them before you write your paper. Therefore, if you can write a good summary, you have a clear advantage over students who cannot.

The exercises in this chapter will help you to

- write the subject, main idea, and major details of an article in outline form.
- write a summary of an article from an outline.

HOW TO MAKE AN OUTLINE

The subject, main idea, and major details are the elements of an outline. You have practiced writing these elements separately in Chapters One, Two, and

70 Read and Respond

Three. By listing these together, you create an outline from which you can write a summary. Your outline should include
- the subject (stated in a word or phrase)
- the main idea (stated in a complete sentence)
- a list of major details (stated in phrases)

The following is an outline of the article in Model Three of Chapter Three:

Subject:	Washington's troubled economy.
Main Idea:	Washington's economy is troubled for many reasons.
Major Details:	• Bad fishing season
	• Decline in lumber sales
	• Low metal prices hurt mining industry
	• Dependence on unreliable taxes

HOW TO TURN YOUR OUTLINE INTO A SUMMARY

The outline can be turned into a summary by writing an opening sentence and changing the phrases into complete sentences and adding necessary details.

1. The opening sentence should contain the article's title and author (if given) as well as the author's main idea.

    For example, here are sample openings for summaries of articles you Chapters One, Two, and Three.

    A. Bill Cosby offers three ways to cut down on reading time in "How to Read Faster."

    B. In "The Importance of Childhood Memories," Norman M. Lobsenz describes how childhood memories can help us get through difficult times later in life.

    C. The author of "Repairing Your Car" identifies a number of places to take your car for repair.

    Notice that the verbs in each of these examples are written in the present tense. Here are some other verbs you might use:

    Bill Cosby *explains*...
    Norman Lobsenz *states*...
    The author *discusses*...

Later in the summary you may wish to use the author's name again. Use only the author's last name.

> Cosby also lists...
> Lobsenz further examines...

2. A good summary contains major details of the article.
3. A good summary contains any minor details needed to explain or clarify the major details.
4. A good summary is written primarily in your own words. If you use more than three consecutive words from the article, use quotation marks. You might wish to quote an important phrase or sentence, but your summary should never be a string of quotations.
5. The length of a summary varies. It is generally no longer than one-fourth as long as the original.

MODEL ONE: Summary of a one-paragraph article

Below is an article you read in Chapter Three. Following it are the subject, the main idea, and the major details.

HOW TO PREVIEW A TEXTBOOK

One of the most helpful things you can do when you begin a new class in college is to preview your textbook. To do this, follow these simple steps. **First**, examine the table of contents. This will quickly tell you how many chapters are in the book and the nature of the material covered. **Second**, read the "To the Student" section or the preface, if there is one, to see how the book is organized and how the author approaches the material. Among other things, this will tell you if the book is practical or theoretical in approach. **Then** examine the copyright date to see how recent the text is. **Finally**, check to see what special features the book contains. For example, is there an index at the back listing important terms and concepts? Is there a glossary where terms are defined? Is the book arranged chapter-by-chapter or alphabetically? Is there an appendix of additional information? Are there summaries at the end of each chapter? By taking just a few minutes to preview your next textbook, you can get more out of your book in a shorter amount of time.

OUTLINE

What is the paragraph about? (Subject)

How to preview a textbook

Or you might write

Previewing a textbook

Main Idea:

Previewing a textbook involves four steps.

Major Details:

- *look at table of contents*
- *read any introductory material*
- *check copyright date*
- *look for special features*

The outline consists of the subject, main idea, and major details. It can now be turned into a summary, as in the following model.

SUMMARY

The author of "How to Preview a Textbook" lists four simple steps to preview a textbook. These steps are as follows: 1) look over the table of contents; 2) read any introductory material; 3) check the copyright date; 4) look for special features such as charts, graphs, or chapter summaries.

COMMENTS: No author is given, so the opening sentence states only the title and the main idea. Then the four major details of the paragraph are listed. A brief explanation of what is meant by "special features" is also given, since that detail alone is not clear enough.

MODEL TWO: Summary of an article

Read the following article and the list of the subject, main idea, and major details. Then observe the way this list is turned into a summary.

THE SHAKERS
by Janice Garvin

The Shakers are officially referred to as the United Society of Believers in Christ's Second Appearing. The name Shakers comes from the way they "danced" in the church. They would jump about in an attempt to shake the evil from their bodies. As time went on they started to organize specific dances, believing that God gave them arms and legs to use in worshipping Him. Eager to find time for worship, they continually improved their systems of heating, cooling, lighting, and housekeeping.

The Shakers are famous for their inventions and skill at making furniture. Just a partial list of their inventions is astounding. They invented the clothespin, the flat-sided broom, the waterwheel, and the alarm clock. They created kitchen utensils such as appliances for paring, coring, and quartering apples. They also are credited with the first circular saw, the threshing machine, the pea sheller, and the first aqueduct to carry water directly to the kitchen.

Another invention was a by-product of their herb farms. The Shakers sold medicinal herbs, ointments, and wintergreen lozenges. To sell their wares more efficiently, they created the first mass-produced garden seed distributed in packets.

Many types of furniture we use today are copied from the Shaker's original designs. The Shakers wanted to be comfortable while they worshipped. For example, they made chairs with ladder-type backs, using horizontal rungs instead of vertical ones. They fashioned the first chairs with woven wicker seats and backs. They also built sturdy tables, sewing desks, and cupboards.

Shaker furniture was pleasing to the eye but designed more for function than beauty. The Shaker craftsmen made the first slanted chair backs, which provided more comfort than straight-back chairs. They even devised what they called "tilters" on the back legs of chairs so that when they leaned back in their chairs the legs would not wear down.

74 Read and Respond

> At their peak, the Shakers had a following of over 6,000 people in 24 communities. After the Civil War the order began to decline, but there are still Shaker communities in existence today. The Shakers haven't changed; they still invent time-saving products to give them more time for worshipping God.

OUTLINE

Subject: *Shakers' inventions and furniture*

Main Idea: *The Shakers are good inventors and craftsmen.*

Major Details:
- *inventions such as kitchen utensils & tools*
- *mass produced seed packets*
- *furniture whose design has been copied*
- *functional innovations*

SUMMARY

In "The Shakers," Janice Garvin describes how the Shakers were both exceptional inventors and furniture craftsmen. They invented many useful kitchen utensils, tools, and machinery that are standard household items today. They mass-produced and marketed the first seed packets to sell the herbs they grew. Garvin also explains that the Shakers built furniture with design and functional comfort in mind, much of which was later admired and copied by other craftsmen.

COMMENTS: The first sentence of the summary identifies the title, author, and main idea of the article. Separate sentences are written for each of the first two major details, including necessary explanation. The last two major details are combined in the last sentence of the summary. Notice that neither the main idea nor the major details are written in the exact words used by the author in the article.

EXERCISE ONE

In Chapter One, you read "Repairing Your Car." Look at the article again and read the outline that follows it. Using this outline, write a summary of the article.

REPAIRING YOUR CAR

Good mechanics can save you a lot of money during the life time of your car. More important, they can save your life. Since good mechanics are so important to car owners, it is helpful to know where to find them. <u>Good mechanics may be found working in a variety of places.</u>

Dealers' service departments specialize in repairs of particular makes of cars, and their mechanics are given special training by the manufacturer. They are the highest paid in the industry. You would be wise to use your dealer while your warranty is in effect.

Independent garages can and often do charge less than a dealer due to lower overhead. Their reliability is largely dependent on the individual in charge. It is a good idea to check out a garage's reputation by questioning local residents and customers if possible.

Specialty shops service one part of the car only: radiators, tires, mufflers, automatic transmissions, ignitions, or brakes. Usually these mechanics are very skilled within their areas of expertise.

Service departments of chain department and discount stores are usually located near large shopping areas. Their mechanics are experienced in making fast, relatively simple repairs and replacements, particularly on popular U.S. cars—but lack training and experience to diagnose complex mechanical problems.

Gasoline stations offer the advantages of a close-in location and conveniently long hours. In addition, their owners are not likely to take advantage of good, regular customers. For routine maintenance and minor repair jobs, you would probably find a neighborhood service station satisfactory.

Automotive diagnostic centers possess highly sophisticated electronic equipment to evaluate the various mechanical systems of a car, diagnose existing problems, and predict future ones. Authentic diagnostic centers are usually not in the repair business themselves. Charges are quite low.

Chapter Four/Writing a Summary 77

Name_____ Class_____ Date_____

EXERCISE ONE *(continued)*

OUTLINE

What is the article about? (Subject)
Places to take your car for repair

What is the author's main point about the subject? (Main idea)
You can find a good mechanic at a number of places.
Or you might write
There are a number of places to take your car for repair.

How does the author support the main idea? (Major details)
- *dealer service depts. good for warranty work*
- *independent garages charge less but should be checked*
- *specialty shops for just one type of repair*
- *discount & dept. stores convenient for minor repairs*
- *gas stations open long hours — best for routine work*
- *automotive diagnostic centers only for diagnosing*

COMMENTS: Notice that details about each of these locations are provided. You might consider these details minor; however, a list of repair places without this information would neither help you understand the article nor summarize it.

SUMMARY

_____
_____
_____
_____
_____

78 *Read and Respond*

EXERCISE TWO

In Chapter Three, you read "The Importance of Childhood Memories" and studied the model of its subject, main idea, and major details. Read the article and outline again, then write a summary of the article.

THE IMPORTANCE OF CHILDHOOD MEMORIES
by Norman M. Lobsenz
from *Reader's Digest*

Section One: Introduction

Some years ago, when my young wife became desperately ill, I wondered how I would be able to cope with the physical and emotional burden of caring for her. One night, when I was drained of strength and endurance, a long forgotten incident came to mind.

I was about ten years old at the time and my mother was seriously ill. I had gotten up in the middle of the night to get a drink of water. As I passed my parents' bedroom, I saw the light on. I looked inside. My father was sitting in a chair in his bathrobe next to Mother's bed, doing nothing. She was asleep. I rushed into the room.

"What's wrong?" I cried. "Why aren't you asleep?"

Dad soothed me. "Nothing's wrong. I'm just watching over her."

I can't say exactly how, but the memory of that long-ago incident gave me the strength to take up my own burden again. The remembered light and warmth from my parents' room were curiously powerful and my father's words haunted me: "I'm just watching over her." The role I now assumed seemed somehow more bearable, as if a resource has been called from the past or from within.

Section Two: Main Idea

<u>In moments of psychological jeopardy, such memories often turn out to be the ultimate resources of personality, dark prisms which focus our basic feeling about life.</u> As Sir James Barrie once wrote, "God gives us memory so that we may have roses in December."

Section Three:
Major Detail
Can't predict what makes lasting memories

No parent can ever really know which memory, planted in childhood, will grow to be a rose. Often our most vivid and enduring remembrances are of apparently simple, even trivial things. I did not discover this myself until one bright, leaf-budding spring day when my son Jim and I were putting a fresh coat of paint on the porch railing. We were talking about plans to celebrate his approaching 15th birthday, and I found myself thinking how quickly his childhood had passed.

"What do you remember best?" I asked him.

He answered without a moment's hesitation. "The night we were driving somewhere, just you and me, on a dark road, and you stopped the car and helped me catch fireflies."

Fireflies? I could have thought of a dozen incidents, both pleasant and unpleasant, that might have remained vivid in his mind. But fireflies? I searched my memory—and eventually it came back to me.

I'd been driving cross-country, traveling late to meet a rather tight schedule. I had stopped to clean the windshield, when all at once a cloud of fireflies surrounded us. Jim, who was five years old then, was tremendously excited. He wanted to catch one. I was tired and tense, and anxious to get on to our destination. I was about to tell him that we didn't have time to waste when something changed my mind. In the trunk of the car I found an empty glass jar. Into it we scooped dozens of the insects. And while Jim watched them glow, I told him of the mysterious cold light they carried in their bodies. Finally, we uncapped the jar and let the fireflies blink away into the night.

"Why do you remember that?" I asked. "It doesn't seem terribly important."

"I don't know," he said. "I didn't even know I did remember it until just now." Then a few moments later: "Maybe I do know why. Maybe it was because I didn't think you were going to stop and catch any with me—and you did."

Since that day I have asked many friends to reach back into their childhoods and tell me what they recall with greatest clarity. Almost always they mention similar moments—experiences or incidents not of any great importance. Not crises or trauma or triumphs, but things which although small in themselves carry sharp sensations of warmth and joy, or sometimes pain.

One friend I spoke with was the son of an executive who was often away from home. "Do you know what I remember best?" he said to me. "It was the day of the annual school picnic when my usually very dignified father appeared in his shirt-sleeves, sat on the grass with me, ate a box lunch, and then made the longest hit in our softball game. I found out later that he postponed a business trip to Europe to be there." My friend is a man who experiences the world as a busy, serious place but who basically feels all right about it and about himself. His favorite childhood memory is both clue to and cause of his fundamental soundness.

Section Four:
Major Detail:
Parents can help shape memories

Clearly, the power parents have to shape the memories of their children involves an awesome responsibility. In this respect nothing is trivial. What to a grown-up might seem a casual word or action often is, to a child, the kernel of a significant memory on which he will build. As grownups, we draw on these memories as sources of strength or weakness. Author Willa Cather saw this clearly. "There are those early memories," she wrote. "One cannot get another set; one has only those."

Not long ago, I talked with a woman who has married a young and struggling sculptor. She cheerfully accepted their temporary poverty. "I grew up during the depression," she said. "My dad scrambled from one job to another. But I remembered that each time a job ended, my mother would scrape together enough money to make us an especially good dinner. She used to call them our 'trouble meals.' I know now that loving someone was far more important than having something."

Section Five
Major Detail
Steps to provide good memories

If childhood memories are so important, what can parents do to help supply their children with a healthy set?

• For one thing, parents should be aware of the importance of the memory-building process. In our adult preoccupation, we tend to think that the "important" experiences our children will have are still in their future. We forget that, to them, childhood is reality rather than merely a preparation for reality. We forget that childhood memories form the adult personality. "What we describe as 'character,' " wrote Sigmund Freud, "is based on the memory traces of our earliest youth."

• Parents can try to find the extra energy, time, or enthusiasm to carry out the small and "insignificant" plan that is so important to a child. The simple act of baking that special batch of cookies or helping to build that model car, even though you are tired or harried, may make an important memory for your youngster.

Conversely, parents can try to guard against the casual disillusionments and needless disappointments which they often unthinkingly inflict on children. I would venture that almost everyone has a memory of an outing canceled or a promise broken without a reason or an explanation. "My father always used to say, 'We'll see,'" one man told me. "I soon learned that what that meant was 'no,' but without any definite reason."

• Parents can think back to their own childhoods and call up their own memories. By remembering the incidents that made important impressions on them, parents can find guideposts to ways in which they can shape the future memories of their own youngsters.

- Finally, parents can by their own actions and words communicate emotions as well as experiences to their children. We can give them a memory of courage rather than fear; of strength rather than weakness; of an appetite for adventure rather than a shrinking from new people and places; of warmth and affection rather than rigidity and coldness. In just such memories are rooted the attitudes and feelings that characterize a person's entire approach to life.

84 *Read and Respond*

Chapter Four/Writing a Summary **85**

Name_____ Class_____ Date_____

EXERCISE TWO *(continued)*

OUTLINE

What is the article about? (Subject)
Childhood memories

Or you might write
Why childhood memories are important

What is the author's main point about the subject? (Main Idea)
Childhood memories can help us get through tough times.

Or you might write
In tough times, childhood memories can give us strength.

How does the author support the main idea? (Major Details)
- Parents can't predict what makes memories
- Parents can help shape their children's memories in four ways:
  1. be aware of the importance of memory process
  2. try to find extra time & energy for children's activities
  3. recall own childhood memories
  4. share both your emotions & experiences w/ children

SUMMARY

_____

_____

EXERCISE THREE

For the article in this exercise, and for most of the remaining articles in this book, you will be given a preview question or statement to help guide your reading. Also, some of the difficult words in the article will be defined before you begin reading. If the meaning of a word is not clear from its brief definition, look the word up in a dictionary before you read the article.

STEPS TO FOLLOW:

1. <u>Preview question or statement.</u> Before reading "Wool...the Living Fiber," read and think about the title. Do you like to wear wool clothes or use wool blankets? If not, is it because you find it "scratchy" or too warm? If you do like it, why?

2. <u>Study the vocabulary.</u>

    cross-breeding "...by careful **crossbreeding** of sheep..."
    Meaning: mating different breeds to get desirable traits from each

    intricate "...**intricate** in its chemical composition..."
    Meaning: complex, complicated

    follicles "...grow out of the inner **follicles** in the skin..."
    Meaning: small glands or sacs in the body used for excretion or secretion. Hair grows from follicles.

    forages "...as the sheep **forages** for food..."
    Meaning: hunt or search for food

    affinity "...molecules have an **affinity** for one another."
    Meaning: natural attraction or connection

    nonflammable "Wool is also completely **nonflammable**."
    Meaning: not easily lit; will not burn rapidly if lit

3. Read the article.

4. Divide the article into sections and label the sections.

5. Outline the article. The subject and main idea are written for you. Fill in the major details.

6. Turn your complete outline into a summary.

WOOL...THE LIVING FIBER
by Joseph Plaidly
from Pendleton Woolen Mills pamphlet

For centuries man has gratefully accepted the protective qualities of wool. By the careful crossbreeding of sheep, he has developed fibers of different lengths, diameters, and various degrees of softness and crispness.

Wool is almost custom-made by nature to fit the needs of man. In its processing and manufacture, man takes up where sheep left off. But while new processes and treatments have made wool more versatile in its uses, man has not improved the fiber itself. <u>Wool has a number of characteristics that make it an ideal material.</u>

Wool is the only fiber possessing a natural crimp, or wave. It is the crimp which gives wool its resiliency and vitality. Wool can be stretched to 50 percent of its length and returned to its original dimension without damage. It can be twisted out of shape and subjected to repeated strain under dry or wet conditions. The crimps will always return to their original positions.

The outer scaly covering of wool sheds water, making it naturally rain-resistant. The protein cortex, on the contrary, readily absorbs moisture. Like a sponge, wool can absorb up to 30 percent of its weight in water or body vapor without becoming damp. This quality also enables woolen clothing to absorb normal perspiration. Wool provides the most warmth with the least weight. This is due to the millions of air spaces enclosed within its compression-resistant structure. In clothing, wool acts as a shield against cold and hot air. It regulates the loss or gain of heat and keeps the body at its normal temperature.

Wool is the most naturally wrinkle-resistant of all fibers. Its spindle-shaped molecules have an affinity for one another and a determination to remain folded together in their normal arrangement. Wrinkles caused by body movements during wear or compression in a suitcase displace and stretch the material. When the wool relaxes, it corrects any displacement and returns to its original position, eliminating the wrinkle.

Wool takes dye completely, permanently, and beautifully. Striking evidence can be observed in the dye kettles. When wool is dyed, the dye in the liquid agent is completely absorbed, leaving behind only a clear solution in the kettles after the wool is removed.

Wool resists fading from sunlight, atmospheric impurities, and perspiration. It maintains its natural luster for years of service and wear. Even after wool has been worn for many years, it can be shredded back into fiber to be spun and woven into new fabrics. The recovery and re-use of wool in low-price fabrics is an industry of its own.

Wool is also nonflammable. Fire insurance companies recommend the use of wool blankets, rugs, or coats to extinguish flames. Practically all laboratory or industrial activity involving highly flammable materials requires that wool blankets be made available to extinguish small fires or ignited clothing. Wool, unless it is in continued direct contact with flame, will extinguish any fire. The denser the weave and the greater the weight of a wool fabric, the less likely it is even to char due to its smaller oxygen content.

Another property of wool is its lack of static. Static attracts dirt from the air and imbeds it in fabrics. This quality makes wool the easiest of all fabrics to keep clean. Freedom from static permits woolen fabrics to hang and drape in natural lines, unlike materials woven from artificial fabrics or blends.

Finally, wool is a living fiber, intricate in its chemical composition and physical structure. It is composed of cells that grow out of the inner follicles in the skin of sheep. Wool forms within the protection of a wax-like substance called "wool grease" which protects the fibers as the sheep forages for food. The fiber also contains suint, the salts of perspiration. In the first step of processing, the wool grease, or suint, and other foreign matter adhering to the fiber, are removed. Refinement of the wool grease produces lanolin, the base of beauty preparations and the perfect carrier for medicinal ointments. The lanolin and its by-products are also used as a rust preventive.

Name_____ Class_____ Date_____

EXERCISE THREE *(continued)*

OUTLINE

Subject:
Characteristics of wool

Main Idea:
Wool's characteristics make it excellent material.

Major Details:

_____
_____
_____
_____
_____
_____
_____
_____
_____
_____

SUMMARY

_____
_____
_____
_____
_____
_____

Name_____ Class_____ Date_____

EXERCISE FOUR

In Chapter Three you completed an outline for three articles in Part Two. Now write a summary of each of these articles from your outlines.

SUMMARY OF ARTICLE #1

SUMMARY OF ARTICLE #2

SUMMARY OF ARTICLE #3

KEY POINTS TO REMEMBER

■ A summary is a condensed version of something you have read, written in your own words.

■ To write a good summary:
- Outline the subject, main idea, and major details.
- Include the title, author, and main idea of the article in your opening sentence.
- Write the major details in sentence form, adding minor details when necessary.
- Write the author's ideas in your own words; if you use the author's exact words, be sure to use quotation marks.

CHAPTER FIVE
WRITING A RESPONSE

Marge and Leon were discussing graduation requirements at their college.

"What do you think about that professor who wants every student to have two years of a foreign language to graduate?"

"I really haven't thought much about it, Marge. You don't think it's a good idea?"

"Of course not. Think of all the extra time it would take for us to graduate."

"I suppose so. But speaking two languages could have some real advantages later on. Who knows—maybe you'll have a chance to go to Japan or Germany or Mexico someday. It would help if you knew how to speak the language. It's also possible that knowing Spanish or Japanese or any other language could help you get a job or help you in your job."

A response is an answer or reply. In the conversation above, Marge and Leon have different responses to the idea of requiring two years of foreign language study to graduate from college. Any time you talk with others, you usually respond in some fashion to their thoughts and ideas. In a similar sense, whenever you read, a conversation takes place between you and the author. The author says something to you in writing and, in response, you think certain thoughts. The writer probably will not hear or read your response, but *active* reading requires an interaction between reader and author. In fact, this interaction is what makes reading fun. You are now to practice responding to what you read.

The exercises in this chapter will help you to

- note your initial reactions to an article.
- write a response to an article.

Read and Respond

Your first response to something you have read is probably a combination of thoughts and feelings. An author may have presented an opinion that bothers or pleases you, or he or she may have just presented you with new information. Your response to what you read is personal and unique and will be based on your education and life experiences, including your cultural heritage, ethnic origin, gender, age, and political views.

Because a response is personal, it cannot be evaluated for accuracy the way a summary can. Responses are judged in terms of the effort put into them. If you make a good effort to get in touch with your thoughts and feelings about the ideas in an article, you will gain understanding about the subject as well as yourself. By writing your responses, you can share these ideas and your reactions to them with others. In this way, you are completing the circle we call "communication." Although it may not be easy at first, you will soon feel more comfortable about sharing your ideas in writing.

RECORDING YOUR FIRST REACTIONS

Before you write a response to an article, record your first thoughts and feelings. This pre-writing or brainstorming activity allows you to organize your thinking before you write. To record your thoughts and feelings, ask yourself a series of questions about the article as well as your own feelings.

Questions about your **feelings**:

- Are my feelings positive or negative about this subject? Why?
- Are my feelings strong about this subject?

Questions about **the article**:

- What is it about this article that made me feel this way?
- Has the author presented mostly facts or opinions?
- Is the author qualified to write on this subject?
- In what kind of publication was this article printed?

Questions about **how this relates to you**:

- How does the information relate to my own knowledge of the subject?
- How can I use the information I have read?
- Can I add *my* experience and perspective on this subject to help others understand it?

The answers to these questions can be written in either quick notes or complete sentences. The important thing is to identify your initial thoughts and feelings about the ideas and opinions you read.

WRITING THE RESPONSE

Some guidelines may help you shape your writing.

1. Be clear about your opinion. Be sure to include a sentence somewhere in your response that says whether your reaction is negative or positive.

2. Explain your feelings. General terms such as "interesting," "helpful," or "frightening" are fine to use, but try to explain how or why you used such a word to describe your feelings.

3. It is appropriate to use personal pronouns, such as "I," "me," "we," or "us" in this type of writing.

4. Make a personal connection between what you've read and your own experience. Ask how this new information adds to or changes how you act and relate to your surroundings.

MODEL ONE: Two responses to "Buying a New Car"

BUYING A NEW CAR

Some people do not think about the real price of owning and operating a car. Gas mileage, for example, is overrated. Since the price of gas skyrocketed, many people have bought small, foreign cars that get 30 to 40 miles per gallon. That's certainly more economical than a big car that gets 15 miles per gallon. But what does it really cost to get good mileage?

First, consider that foreign cars are expensive. A new "economical" import can cost $14,000 or more. If you finance it over four years, the interest might cost you another $2,000. The license fee can run as high as several hundred dollars depending on the state you live in, and the insurance can run into the thousands.

> Buying an American car is also expensive. However, there are two important differences. First, repairs and parts on foreign cars are usually more costly than on American autos. A simple tail light assembly for a Volvo costs $115. Second, because American cars are usually cheaper to repair, a used American car in good shape is often a better value than a used imported car. Maybe instead of buying a new imported car for $14,000 to $16,000, you could buy a three-year-old American car for $8,000 and still have reliable transportation. The point is, you need to consider all costs, not just the cost of gas.

Response #1

First reactions: agree; not really strong;
gas might only cost $600 - $1,200 per year
mostly opinion - 1 fact
Car shopping
I know quite a bit about other areas of cars.
I've had both foreign and American cars.
Some repairs are enormous.

Response: I agree with the author of "Buying Cars" in some ways, but not in others. I consider more than just the cost of a car. I admit I'm impressed by performance, safety and styling, too.

I definitely agree with the author about overrating gas mileage. If you drive about 14,000 miles a year and your car gets 30 miles a gallon, you'll spend about $600 in

gas — a savings of only $600 over a car that gets a mere 15 m.p.g.
    Most of this article is opinion except the price of the Volvo part. I don't know who the author is, but he/she seems to know quite a bit about cars. I will keep this information in mind when I go car shopping, and I probably will be looking for a newer car next year.

Response #2

First reactions: I tend to agree with this author, but I don't have strong feelings about the subject.
— I see that there are many costs to a car (in addition to the purchase price.)
— Don't know anything about author or source.
— I owned a Subaru & was always shocked at the cost of repairs and parts.
— Subaru experience vs. experiences w/ American-made car; most auto repair places unfamiliar w/ foreign cars.

Response: I agree with the author, but I don't have strong feelings. I see that there are many factors to consider when buying a car besides the car's m.p.g. I have recently owned a Subaru & now own an American-made car. Even though I got better mileage with my Subaru, it was costing me a lot of money to drive it — parts and repair work were expensive. The repair *shops I took it to were not as familiar w/ foreign cars, so I wasted a lot of money.*

COMMENTS: The writers wrote down their first reactions based on the questions listed earlier in this chapter. In the response, most of the items from their notes are mentioned, but not in any particular order. Each writer responds to the article with a different focus because each has unique interests and background.

MODEL TWO: Two responses to "Discipline"

DISCIPLINE

Discipline is a touchy subject for many parents and children. Dozens of books have been written on the subject, all claiming to offer the best approach on how and when to discipline children. As the mother of an eight-year-old and a five-year-old, I have read many such books and tried many of the methods, but have yet to find an effective way of getting my children to behave the way I would like.

First there is the "spare the rod and spoil the child" approach. Advocates of this philosophy say we should correct our children by giving them a swift, firm swat when they misbehave. The problem with this approach is that when I tried it, my children started copying me, giving each other swift swats.

Next I tried the "reasoning" approach. When my four-year-old son tried out his new set of crayons on the wall in his room, I explained at great length that crayons were for paper only and how important it was to keep the walls in his room clean. The next day he colored the walls in his sister's room.

I think I have finally found a method that works. My kids behave better if they are working towards a promised reward at the end of the day, rather than trying to avoid punishment. I call this the "chart" approach. I've posted a list of Do's and Don'ts on the refrigerator for them, and they get a sticker when they perform appropriately. After they've earned 10 stickers, they get a treat or special privilege. Now if I can just figure out a way to afford all the treats I owe them!

Response #1

First reactions: I agree with this mother!
I have tried these different approaches.
Author is qualified to write on this topic on the basis of personal experiences.
However, I find rewards don't always work either — not the way I was raised.

Response: I can easily identify with this mother. As a parent, I know that discipline is one of the most challenging aspects of raising children, and I frequently read articles and books on this topic. I think that the author is believable because she speaks from personal experience. I also like her sense of humor, which she shows at the end of each type of discipline.

Unlike the author, I have not yet found a discipline method that I'm satisfied with. The reward system is good, but I don't always have the patience to follow through with it. Also, because of the way I was raised, I tend to discipline with punishments and consequences instead of rewards.

Response #2

First reactions: — I'm a guy with no kids; no strong feelings about this subject.
— It sounds reasonable & she obviously has experience as a mother.
— Author uses personal examples which are like facts — she then presents own opinion
— No real use for this information now, but who knows — I might have kids someday.

Response: I don't really have strong opinions on this subject because I'm a young, unmarried man without children. However, this woman seems reasonable, & she's obviously experienced. I like the personal examples the author uses — I suppose they actually are facts. She also states her opinion about discipline methods. Even though I'm not too interested in this subject now, I might be in the future. Some beautiful woman may snag me, and who knows? We could be trying to discipline some "little ones." If this happens, I'll read every book I can on the subject.

COMMENTS: From the second response you can see how you do not have to relate directly to the experience described in the article. The writer of this response is not a parent, but nevertheless has ideas and feelings about the subject. Also, note that both writers felt that the author was qualified to write on the subject. You don't always have to know the author's name or professional qualifications to make this type of judgment.

Name_____ Class_____ Date_____

EXERCISE ONE

In Chapter Two on page 25, you read "How to Read Faster" by Bill Cosby. Reread the article, then write your first reactions and response in the space provided.

First reactions: _____

_____
_____
_____
_____
_____
_____
_____
_____
_____

Response: _____

_____
_____
_____
_____
_____
_____
_____
_____
_____
_____

Name_____ Class_____ Date_____

EXERCISE TWO

On page 79 in Chapter Four, you read and summarized "The Importance of Childhood Memories." Read your summary and write a response to it below.

First reactions: _____

_____
_____
_____
_____
_____
_____
_____
_____
_____

Response: _____

_____
_____
_____
_____
_____
_____
_____
_____
_____
_____
_____

Name_____ Class_____ Date_____

EXERCISE THREE

Write your first reactions and responses to the three articles in summarized in Exercise Four on page 93 of Chapter Four.

Article #1

First reactions: _____

_____
_____
_____
_____
_____
_____
_____
_____
_____

Response: _____

_____
_____
_____
_____
_____
_____
_____
_____
_____
_____
_____
_____

112   Read and Respond

Article #2

First reactions: _____

Response: _____

___

___

___

___

___

___

___

___

___

___

___

___

___

___

Article #3

First reactions: ___

___

___

___

___

___

___

___

___

___

Response: ___

___

___

114   Read and Respond

KEY POINTS TO REMEMBER

- A response is an answer or reply to what you have read which allows you to explore your feelings and thoughts about a subject and share them with others.

- To write a response:
    - Ask yourself questions about the author and the subject as well as your own feelings about the article and how the subject relates to you.
    - Record your answers to these questions in note form.
    - Using your notes as a guide, write your opinion and explain it as clearly as you can.

PART TWO

For each of the articles in Part Two, follow these steps in order:

1. *Preview the article*
2. *Study the vocabulary*
3. *Read the article*
4. *Write a summary*
5. *Write your personal response*

1. Preview: Before reading the article, think about the title. Then read the questions or statements preceding the article. Thinking about these ideas for a few moments will help you focus on the subject of the article. In your reading outside this book, try to ask your own questions or think briefly about the subject before you begin reading. Reading "actively" will help you read for comprehension.

2. Study the vocabulary: In the short introduction to each article, note the vocabulary words in bold type and the parts of sentences in quotation marks. This shows how the words are used in the article. Study the meaning of the word. When you read the words in the article, you will most likely remember their meanings.

If you come across a word in the article that you do not know which has not been defined for you, try to figure out the meaning from the surrounding words. This is the best way to understand the meaning of new words—by seeing them used "in context." If you still cannot figure out the meaning, consult a dictionary. But we offer this bit of advice: Looking up words in a dictionary is slow and breaks the flow of thought when you are reading. Although you sometimes have to use a dictionary, you should do so only if the word is crucial to the author's meaning.

3. Read the article: Remember to read for the main idea and the major details which support the main idea. Try not to get bogged down with details, facts, and figures. Notice the details, but realize that you are trying to understand the author's main points so you can summarize and respond to them. When you read textbooks for a different purpose, such as taking a multiple choice test, you need to study and memorize details (see Appendix A); however, for much of your reading, you gain more from understanding the main points.

4. Write a summary: Summaries will vary in length. Remember, a summary is written mostly in your own words and is generally no longer than one-fourth the length of the article. Rather than count the words, ask your teacher to help you determine if you have included the main idea and major details.

5. Write your personal response: The response is one of the most rewarding parts of the reading process. You get a chance to talk back, in effect, to the author. Once you have understood the author's point and the support for the point, you can get in your "two cents" worth.

From time to time you may want to reread these directions for review and to make sure you are following all the steps.

1. SELF-HELP

You read advice in a variety of places. In fact, the book you are now reading attempts to advise you on how to improve your reading comprehension. There are books which explain how to do most anything: repair, build, or decorate things; travel, budget, and plan events; even how to grow old gracefully.

One of the benefits of reading is that we can gain the advice and wisdom of experts without having to meet them. Gaining practical knowledge this way can save us both time and money.

The articles in this section offer advice on how to improve your vocabulary, spelling, and memory, how to handle pressure, and how to earn decent pay for part-time work.

1. PART-TIME JOBS/BIG-TIME MONEY
from *A Part-time Career for a Full-time You*
by JoAnne Alter

> A part-time job may fit our lifestyles—if we can just make enough money at it. Especially for a parent with young children, the author has some interesting comments on this subject.
>
> **prorated** — "...salary and all company benefits were **prorated** to reflect her new schedule."
> *Meaning:* divided or distributed according to a schedule
>
> **deteriorated** — "...Lark and Thomas's marriage **deteriorated** over the next several years..."
> *Meaning:* fell apart
>
> **paralegal** — "...a brand-new field that promised all these benefits: **paralegal** work."
> *Meaning:* work assisting a lawyer, such as the work of a legal clerk.

If you have training in a field where your skills are in demand, there are plenty of employers who will hire you part time. Here are some fields that offer top-paying part-time schedules today—and how two women made the part-time solution work for them.

The Proven Performer

Christine Danner of Ross, California, started her career in the early 1970s as a secretary for the Bank of America in San Francisco. She was soon promoted, however, and eventually became the director of personnel for the bank's computer division.

At the end of 1983 Christine and her husband, Eric Lindner, adopted twin baby girls. Christine asked for, and was granted, an unpaid leave of absence. "At that time my boss and I didn't determine how long my leave was going to be," Christine says. "But he did say he was open to discussing any arrangement to get me to return."

When her daughters were 10 months old, Christine was ready to return to work, but not full time. When she met with her boss, she learned that the division of which she had been personnel manager was being relocated to another part of the state. "I knew those people; I thought I could help with the relocation on a part-time basis," Christine says. "So I suggested I be hired as an internal consultant."

They agreed on a 25-hour work-week schedule, which included days in the office and time at home. Christine's previous salary and all company benefits were prorated to reflect her new schedule.

The relocation project took eight months. Then in 1985, after taking several other temporary jobs, Christine was asked to be in charge of personnel development for the bank's human resources department. She was delighted, but cautious. "I asked my boss what his objectives were; then I wrote down my ideas on how best to structure the job," she says. "He wanted me to work full time. But we finally agreed on three 10-hour days a week."

Four years later Christine says the arrangement still works well: "I make a point of being flexible. I'm available by phone day or night. And I never miss a meeting."

Establish a Track Record

Christine Danner was able to negotiate a part-time schedule for several reasons: First, she was clearly an employee any boss would want to keep. "I had established a track record," she says. "I was a self-starter who got things done—and done on time. There was no question about my dependability."

In discussing a new position, Christine wisely focused on the company's needs, not her own. She learned her boss's goals, then wrote a proposal detailing how she would accomplish them. She emphasized her willingness to take phone calls at home and put in extra time when necessary. She also stressed the advantages to her boss of not having to find and train someone else. Explains Christine, "I basically said, 'Look what you've already invested in me. I've been with the bank for years. I have skills, a lot of varied experience, and dedication to the job.'"

The Talented Newcomer

Like Christine Danner, Lark McGuire of Newton Centre, Massachusetts, is also a mother of two. But unlike Christine, Lark is a single mother who made her career change during a very difficult time—while she was going through a divorce.

Lark had worked as an elementary-school teacher in Connecticut until she and her husband, Thomas, and their newborn son, Lee, moved to Boston in 1976. In 1978 their daughter, Meghan, was born. Unfortunately, Lark and Thomas's marriage deteriorated over the next several years, and Lark realized she would have to go back to work. Teaching positions were scarce, however, and she was determined to work part time.

"I couldn't imagine leaving my kids until 6 or 6:30 each day after what they'd been through," she says. "I also wanted to work in a challenging field, but not one that would take four years of training for me to enter."

On the advice of her brother-in-law, an attorney, Lark investigated a brand-new field that promised all of these benefits: paralegal work. She enrolled in a program at a local college, choosing to take classes part time and at night. Her ex-husband or a baby sitter would watch the children while she attended classes.

Peddling Her Skills

In 1983, armed with a certificate and a newspaper, Lark began to look for a job. But being at the forefront of a new field, she discovered there weren't any ads under the heading *paralegal*. "The term was still so new that most people didn't know what a paralegal was," she says.

She did see one interesting ad for a legal secretary, which was what many law firms still called any employee who assisted lawyers. The ad was placed by three attorneys who had just opened a practice specializing in worker's compensation and labor law. Lark knew she was overqualified for the job they were advertising, but she recognized that this position had real potential." I decided to answer the ad just to get in the door," she recalls. "I said to myself, 'These guys are just starting out. So am I. We can grow together."

She told the partner who interviewed her that she only wanted to work 20 hours a week. He was clearly happy to have found someone with her training and did not see this as a problem. They agreed she would work four hours a day, five days a week, at a starting salary of $6,000 a year.

Since 1983, the law firm has grown considerably, and as Lark predicted, she has grown with it. She now works 30 hours a week, and the partners plan to put her in charge of the entire paralegal department this spring. She's also toying with the idea of becoming a lawyer when her children are both in high school. In the meantime, she plans to continue working part time.

Is Lark's walk-right-in success unusual? Not necessarily. Today it's possible for anyone with the training and skills needed to fill a high demand job to find a good part-time position.

Word count: 1023

2. HOW TO SPELL
by John Irving
from "Power of the Printed Word" Program
International Paper Company

> Are you a good speller? Chances are your answer is "no." For many people, spelling is not easy, so if you answered "no" to the above question you have plenty of company. However, in the following article, author John Irving offers some advice that you may find helpful.
>
> **intimidate**   "If you'd like to **intimidate** yourself..."
> *Meaning:* to frighten and discourage

Let's begin with the bad news.

If you're a bad speller, you probably think you always will be. There are exceptions to every spelling rule, and the rules themselves are easy to forget. George Bernard Shaw demonstrated how ridiculous some rules are. By following the rules, he said, we could spell *fish* this way: *ghoti*. The "f" as it sounds in enou*gh*, the "i" as it sounds in w*o*men, and the "sh" as it sounds in fic*ti*on.

With such rules to follow, no one should feel stupid for being a bad speller. But there are ways to improve. Start by acknowledging the mess that English spelling is in—but have sympathy: English spelling changed with foreign influences. Chaucer wrote "geese," but "guess," imported earlier by the Norman invaders, finally replaced it . Most early printers in England came from Holland; they brought "ghost" and "gherkin" with them.

If you'd like to intimidate yourself—and remain a bad speller forever—just try to remember the 13 different ways the sound "sh" can be written.

*sh*oe   suspi*ci*on
*s*ugar   naus*e*ous
o*ce*an   con*sc*ious
i*ss*ue   *ch*aperone

na*t*ion mansion
sc*h*ist fu*ch*sia

Now the Good News

The good news is that 90 percent of all writing consists of 1,000 basic words. There is, also, a method to most English spelling and a great number of how-to-spell books. Remarkably, all these books propose learning the same rules! Not surprisingly, most of these books are humorless.

Just keep this in mind: If you're familiar with the words you use, you'll probably spell them correctly—and you shouldn't be writing words you're unfamiliar with anyway. Use a word—out loud, and more than once—before you try writing it, and make sure that you know what it means before you use it. This means you'll have to look it up in a dictionary, where you'll not only learn what it means, but you'll see how it's spelled. Choose a dictionary you enjoy browsing in, and guard it as you would a diary. You wouldn't lend a diary, would you?

A Tip on Looking It Up

Beside every word I look up in my dictionary, I make a mark. Beside every word I look up more than once, I write a note to myself—about WHY I looked it up. I have looked up "strictly" 14 times since 1965. I prefer to spell it with a K—as in "stric*k*tly." I have looked up "ubiquitous" a dozen times. I can't remember what it means.

Another good way to use your dictionary: When you have to look up a word, for any reason, learn—and learn to *spell*—a *new* word at the same time. It can be any useful word on the same page as the word you looked up. Put the date beside this new word and see how quickly, or in what way, you forget it. Eventually, you'll learn it.

Almost as important as knowing what a word means (in order to spell it) is knowing how it's pronounced. It's gover*n*ment, not goverment. It's Feb*ru*ary, not Febuary. And if you know that *anti-* means against, you should know how to spell *anti*dote and *anti*biotic and *anti*freeze. If you know that *ante-* means before, you shouldn't have trouble spelling *ante*chamber or *ante*cedent.

Some Rules, Exceptions and Two Tricks

I don't have room to touch on *all* the rules here. It would take a book to do that. But I can share a few rules that help me most. Some spelling problems that seem hard are really easy. What about *-ary* or *-ery*? Just remember that there are only six common words in English that end in *-ery*. Memorize them, and feel fairly secure that all the rest end in *-ary*:

cemetery   monastery
millinery   confectionery
distillery   stationery (as in paper)

Here's another easy rule. Only four words end in *-efy*. Most people misspell them with *-ify*, which is usually correct. Just memorize these too, and use *-ify* for all the rest:

stupefy   putrefy
liquefy   rarefy

As a former bad speller, I have learned a few valuable tricks. Any good how-to-spell book will teach you more than these two, but these two are my favorites. Of the 800,000 words in the English language, the most frequently misspelled is *alright*; just remember that *alright* is *all* wrong, would you? That's how you know you should write *all* right.

The other trick is for the truly worst spellers. I mean those of you who spell so badly that you can't get close enough to the right way to spell a word in order to even FIND it in the dictionary. The word you're looking up is there, of course, but you won't find it the way you're trying to spell it. What to do is look up a synonym—another word that means the same thing. Chances are good that you'll find the word you're looking for under the definition of the synonym.

Demon Words and Bugbears

Everyone has a few demon words—words that never look right, even when they're spelled correctly. Three of my demons are *medieval, ecstasy,* and *rhythm*. I have learned to hate these words, but I have not learned to spell them; I have to look them up every time.

And everyone has a spelling rule that's a bugbear—it's either too difficult to learn or it's impossible to remember. My personal bugbear among the rules is the one governing whether you add *-able* or *-ible*. I can teach it to you, but I can't remember it myself.

You add *-able* to a full word: adapt, adaptable; work, workable. You add *-able* to words that end in *e*—just remember to drop the final *e*: love, lovable. But if the word ends in two *e*'s, like agree, you keep them both: agreeable.

You add *-ible* if the base is not a full word that can stand on its own: credible, tangible, horrible, terrible. You add *-ible* if the root ends in *-ns*: responsible. You add *-ible* if the root word ends in *-miss*: permissible. You add *-ible* if the root word ends in a soft *c* (but remember to drop the final *e*!): force, forcible.

Got that? I don't have it, and I was introduced to that rule in prep school; with that rule, I still learn one word at a time.

Poor President Jackson

You must remember that it is permiss*ible* for spelling to drive you crazy. Spelling had this effect on Andrew Jackson, who once blew his stack while trying to write a Presidential paper. "It's a damn poor mind that can think of only one way to spell a word!" the President cried.

When you have trouble, think of poor Andrew Jackson and know that you're not alone.

What's Really Important

And remember what's really important about good writing is not good spelling. If you spell badly but write well, you should hold your head up. As the poet T.S. Eliot recommended, "Write for as large and miscellaneous an audience as possible—and don't be overly concerned if you can't spell 'miscellaneous.' " Also remember that you can spell correctly and write well and still be misunderstood. Hold your head up about that, too. As good old G.C. Lichtenberg said, "A book is a mirror: if an ass peers into it, you can't expect an apostle to look out"—whether you spell "apostle" correctly or not.

Word count: 1228

3. HOW TO IMPROVE YOUR VOCABULARY
by Tony Randall
from "Power of the Printed Word" Program
International Paper Company

> How often are you puzzled by the meaning of words when you try to read? When you write, do you sometimes struggle to come up with just the right word to express your thought? Tony Randall, an actor and comedian, offers some hints to improve your vocabulary.
>
> **stuffed shirt**   "Careful—you don't want them to think you're a **stuffed shirt**."
> *Meaning:* one who is too formal
>
> **Aristophanes**   "**Aristophanes** said..."
> *Meaning:* an ancient Greek writer of comic plays

Words can make us laugh, cry, go to war, fall in love. Rudyard Kipling called words the most powerful drug of mankind. If they are, I'm a hopeless addict—and I hope to get you hooked, too!

Whether you're still in school or you head up a corporation, the better command you have of words, the better chance you have of saying exactly what you mean, of understanding what others mean—and of getting what you want in the world.

English is the richest language—with the largest vocabulary on earth. Over 1,000,000 words!

You can express shades of meaning that aren't even *possible* in other languages. (For example, you can differentiate between "sky" and "heaven." The French, Italians and Spanish cannot.)

Yet, the average adult has a vocabulary of only 30,000 to 60,000 words. Imagine what we're missing!

Here are five pointers that help me learn—and remember—whole *families* of words at a time.

They may not *look* easy—and won't be at first. But, if you stick with them, you'll find they *work*!

What's the first thing to do when you see a word you don't know?

1. Try to guess the meaning of the word from the way it's used.

You can often get at least *part* of a meaning—just from how it's used in a sentence.

That's why it's so important to read as much as you can—different *kinds* of things, magazines, books, newspapers you don't normally read. The more you *expose* yourself to new words, the more words you'll pick up *just by seeing how they're used.*

For instance, say you run across the word "manacle": "The manacles had been on John's wrists for 30 years. Only one person had a key—his wife." You have a good *idea* of what "manacles" are—just from the context of the sentence.

But let's find out *exactly* what the word means and where it comes from. The only way to do this, and to build an extensive vocabulary *fast*, is to go to the dictionary. (How lucky, you *can*—Shakespeare *couldn't*. There *wasn't* an English dictionary in his day!)

So you go to the dictionary. (NOTE: Don't let dictionary abbreviations put you off. The front tells you what they mean, and even has a guide to pronunciation.)

2. Look it up.

Here's the definition for "manacle" in *The American Heritage Dictionary of the English Language.*

man-a-cle n. Usually plural.
1. A device for confining the hands, usually consisting of two metal rings that are fastened about the wrists and joined by a metal chain; a handcuff. 2. Anything that confines or restrains. *-tr.v.* **manacled, -cling, -cles.**
1. To restrain with manacles. 2. To confine or restrain as if with manacles; shackle; fetter. (*Middle English manicle,* from Old French, from Latin *manicula,* little hand, handle, diminutive of *manus,* hand. See **man-** in Appendix.*)

The first definition fits here: A device for confining the hands, usually consisting of two metal rings that are fastened about the wrists and joined by a metal chain; a handcuff.

Well, that's what you *thought* it meant. But what's the idea *behind* the word? What are the roots? To really understand a word, you need to know.

Here's where the detective work—and the *fun*—begins.

3. Dig the meaning out by the roots.

The root is the basic part of the word—its heritage, its origin. (Most of our roots come from Latin and Greek words at least 2,000 years old—which come from even earlier Indo-European tongues!)

Learning the roots 1) helps us *remember* words, 2) gives us a deeper understanding of the words we *already know*, and 3) allows us to pick up whole families of *new* words at a time. That's why learning the root is the *most important part of going to the dictionary.*

Notice the root of "manacle" is *manus* (Latin) meaning "hand."

Well, that makes sense. Now, other words with this root, *man*, start to make sense too.

Take *man*ual-something done "by hand" (*man*ual labor) or a "handbook." And *man*age—to "handle" something (as a *man*ager). When you e*man*cipate someone, you're taking him "from the hands of" someone else.

When you *man*ufacture something, you "make it by hand" (in its original meaning).

And when you finish your first novel, your publisher will see your—originally "handwritten"—*man*uscript.

Imagine! A whole new world opens up—just from one simple root!

The root gives the *basic* clue to the meaning of a word. But there's another important clue that runs a close second—the *prefix.*

4. Get the powerful prefixes under your belt.

A prefix is the part that's sometimes attached to the front of a word. Like—well, *pre*fix! There aren't many—less than 100 major prefixes—and you'll learn them in no time at all just by becoming more aware of the meanings of words you already know. Here are a few. (Some of the "How-to" vocabulary-building books will give you the others.)

PREFIX		MEANING	EXAMPLES	
(Latin)	(Greek)			(Literal sense)
com, con	sym, syn	with, very	conform	(form with)
co, col, cor	syl	together	sympathy	(feeling with)
in, im	a, an	not,	innocent	(not wicked)
il, ir		without	amorphous	(without form)
contra	anti	against	contravene	(come against)
counter	ant	opposite	antidote	(give against)

Now, see how the *prefix* (along with the context) helps you get the meaning of the italicized words:

- "If you're going to be my witness, your story must *cor*roborate my story." (The literal meaning of *corroborate* is "strength together.")
- "You told me one thing—now you tell me another. Don't *con*tradict yourself." (The literal meaning of *contradict* is "say against.")
- "Oh, that snake's not poisonous. It's a completely *in*nocuous little garden snake." (The literal meaning of *innocuous* is "not harmful.")

Now you've got some new words. What are you going to do with them?

5. Put your new words to work at once.

Use them several times the first day you learn them. Say them out loud! Write them in sentences.

Should you "use" them on *friends*? Careful—you don't want them to think you're a stuffed shirt. (It depends on the situation. You *know* when a word sounds natural—and when it sounds stuffy.)

How about your *enemies*? You have my blessing. Ask one of them if he's read that article on pneumonoultramicroscopicsilicovolcanoconiosis. (You really can find it in the dictionary.) Now, you're one up on him.

So what do you do to improve you vocabulary?

Remember: 1) Try to guess the meaning of the word from the way it's used. 2) Look it up. 3) Dig the meaning out by the roots. 4) Get the powerful prefixes under your belt. 5) Put your new words to work at once.

That's all there is to it—you're off on your treasure hunt.

Now, do you see why I love words so much?

Aristophanes said, "By words, the mind is excited and the spirit elated." It's as true today as it was when he said it in Athens—*2,400 years ago!*

I hope you're now like me—hooked on words forever.

Word count: 1163

4. REVITALIZE YOUR MEMORY
by Mark Golin
from Prevention

Memory is very important, but few people work to improve it. Can memory be improved? The author thinks so, and he offers suggestions for help in this area.

commodity "...keep this important **commodity** from declining..."
Meaning: anything useful

encode "Since we didn't **encode** it firmly in our memory..."
Meaning: to put a message into

ponderous "To put this **ponderous** statement into everyday clothes..."
Meaning: Something to be seriously considered

cohesive "...difficult to organize into a **cohesive** whole..."
Meaning: something that will stick or hold together

flamboyant "...the more **flamboyant** the image, the better you'll remember it."
Meaning: very elaborate and showy, colorful

accrue "...note the other benefits that will **accrue**."
Meaning: to increase or add up; accumulate

Memory. People tend to think of it as the ability to dredge up the name of that mustached man they met in a Parisian pet shop 25 years ago. But in reality, we use our memory every minute of the day for everything we do. We use it every time we speak a word, drive a car, brush our teeth or shop for groceries.

Given the importance of memory, it's hard to understand why we do so little to keep this important commodity from declining as we get older. Maybe it's because we don't think there's anything we *can* do about it. But in fact, the regeneration of a fading memory is well within most people's power.

"Many of the everyday lapses we experience are more the fault of our poor memory techniques than of any physical problem with the brain," says Robin West, Ph.D., University of Florida psychologist and author of *Memory Fitness Over Forty* (Triad Publishing, 1985). "Given the use of good techniques, practice and daily mental stimulation, there's no reason why you can't improve your memory substantially.

Keeping your memory in top form is similar to keeping your body in shape. But instead of brisk morning strolls, you need to turn the task of memorizing into a creative adventure that makes your mind work up a healthy sweat. Here's how to set up your own memory training program.

Attenn-shun!

Start by memorizing a little one-liner penned by English writer Samuel Johnson: "The art of memory is the art of attention." When we can't remember a piece of information, frequently it's because we never really paid enough attention to it in the first place. Since we didn't encode it firmly in our memory, it's no surprise that it's not there when we look for it.

Taking the attention theme one step further, in 1890, psychologist William James wrote, "Habit diminishes the conscious attention with which our acts are performed." To put this ponderous statement into everyday clothes, try to remember in detail the sign above the first gas station that you pass on the way to the grocery store or work. Don't feel bad if you can't. Even though you pass it every day, chances are you never really see it. "People commonly turn off their minds when they are performing habitual actions," says Dr. West. "When you are in an 'automatic pilot mode,' new information has no way of encoding itself in your mind."

The way to combat automatic-pilot syndrome is to practice the fine art of observation—consciously pay attention to details that make an object or circumstance unique. Dr. West suggests starting with a magazine photo of a person. Look at the photo, then close the magazine. List the features in the photo. What color were the eyes? What shape was the nose? What about hairstyle and clothing? Was there anything in the background? Having made a list, go back to the photo and study it for two details you missed. Then start again. Do this until you've managed to list every aspect down to the most minute.

Another way to practice observation during the day is to think of a common item that you see regularly. It could be a fountain pen, a building you walk by, or a tile floor. Before you actually come across the item again, ask yourself some questions about it. What is it made of? How many windows? What color? If you can't answer the questions immediately, take a moment when confronted by the object to look for the answers.

With practice, observation can become second nature. The way you look at things changes as you focus in on details. And the attention you pay to detail makes each object unique enough that it will stand out in your mind and be easily encoded into your memory.

Off Automatic Pilot

Now you can apply your newfound powers of observation to your behavior. How many times have you left the house only to wonder 10 minutes later if you locked the front door? "To overcome an automatic-pilot behavior like this, you need to either change the pattern of your action or find something concerning this routine action that is new and unusual," says Dr. West.

If you're right-handed, for example, you could lock the front door with your left hand. Or, as you lock the door, note the sound of the lawn mower coming from your neighbor's yard. Twenty minutes later, as you're driving along wondering whether you locked the front door, you'll remember the lawn mower and then remember that you locked the door while listening to that sound.

Making Things Meaningful

Memory and learning are not far apart, notes Dr. West. When we learn, we take random information and arrange it in a manner that has meaning to us.

As we concentrate and note specific details, they become encoded in our memory. But many things we wish to remember, such as lists of items, phone numbers, dates and random facts, are difficult to organize into a cohesive whole because they have no order or inherent meaning. Rather than remembering one thing that naturally flows into another, we try to remember many different pieces of information that have no connection.

A better way—and the secret of most memory techniques—involves organizing those small pieces of material into larger groups, giving the items a context we can understand and making the information unique in our own minds.

"Many times, it's hard to draw a line of understanding between a word and its meaning," says Dr. West. "You might be hard put to remember that the medical prefix *blepharo-* refers to the eyelids, for example, because it provides no clues. But you can take the sound of the word and incorporate it into this sentence: I'd *bl*ink if I saw a *pharaoh*. The sentence reminds you of the word and blink suggests eyelid."

To remember an address, such as 1225 Turner Street, you might say to yourself, "I *turn*ed my life around on *Christmas*," (12/25). Can't seem to remember that there are 5,280 feet in a mile? Think of "5 tomatoes": 5, 2 *(to)*, 8 *(mat)*, 0 *(oes)*.

Interactive Imagery

Here's a good memory technique to practice at the supermarket. Suppose you have six items you need to pick up. To use mental imagery, picture the six items in your mind. Maybe they'd be on a shelf or lined up at the checkout counter, but the six items would be inactive.

Interactive imagery goes one step further, in that you picture a sequence of action events that include the items you want to remember. That way, when you're at the store, you can just replay the image in your mind like a video. It may sound confusing, but let's give it a whirl using a typical grocery list: milk, bread, celery, pepper, apples, and cucumbers. Keep in mind, the more flamboyant the image, the better you'll remember it.

Walking through the woods you come to the bank of a white river of milk. To make your journey easier you decide to sail down the river and do so on a raft made of a large slice of bread. The long green steering oar you're using is actually an enormous celery stalk. The weather starts to turn bad and soon dense flakes of black snow (pepper) and huge red hailstones (apples) begin to fall. Things go from bad to worse as your bread raft sails out to a milk sea where an enemy submarine is waiting. The sub fires and you see a cucumber torpedo heading straight for you.

Now close your eyes and try very hard to actually see yourself in the story. Once you have seen the image, try testing yourself and see if you remember all six items by replaying your mental video. Try again five days from now.

This technique can also be applied to other tasks, such as remembering names. "When I want people to remember my name," says Dr. West, "I have them picture a robin flying west. To connect the name to my person, I ask them to include my most memorable feature, long hair, in the image. The end result is a mental image of a robin flying west with long hair streaming behind it in the wind. When they see my long hair, it triggers the image that contains my name, Robin West."

If you are thinking that this is an awful lot of trouble just to remember a few things, note the other benefits that will accrue. "Storing information in a rich, elaborate form is the secret of sharp recall," says psychologist Endel Tulving, Ph.D., of the University of Toronto.

The process of making information rich and elaborate is also one of the finest ways to stimulate yourself intellectually. Your mind needs this stimulation to stay sharp just as your heart needs aerobic exercise to stay strong. And you may just find that tailoring information into sayings and images can be quite an entertaining way to stay in mental shape.

Finally, if you don't exercise your memory, you will begin to lose it. There's little doubt about that, experts agree. Most of the time, the process can be reversed, but why not start to recharge your memory now and enjoy it to the fullest?

Word count: 1548

140   Read and Respond

5. PRESSURE: HOW TO KEEP GOING WHEN THE GOING GETS TOUGH
by Dan Rather
from *Ladies Home Journal*

> What pressures are you under in your job or in your personal life? How do you handle them? Compare your methods with those of Dan Rather, news anchorman for CBS.
>
> **decisive** — "...the fear at the **decisive** moment..."
> *Meaning:* important, critical
>
> **sustained** — "...when you're under **sustained** pressure..."
> *Meaning:* continual, long-lasting
>
> **appraisal** — "...the support and honest **appraisal** of your family and friends."
> *Meaning:* judgment, rating
>
> **perspective** — "They're always there with encouragement and **perspective**..."
> *Meaning:* viewpoint
>
> **contagion** — "...we can catch their courage as if by **contagion**."
> *Meaning:* to easily spread or influence
>
> **coalesce** — "Pressure makes everything **coalesce**."
> *Meaning:* come together

When CBS first announced its choice of a successor for Walter Cronkite, managing editor and anchorman of the *CBS Evening News*, a columnist wrote, "Dan Rather is about to step into more pressure than anyone on television has ever known." I laughed.

Like so much else in those days, his warning seemed overstated, overdramatized. It still does. But now, two years later, I think of what he said and I know exactly what he meant. I don't claim to have been under the most pressure ever, but the past two years were a tough learning experience. Even though I was prepared for it. Even though I thought I knew a few things about pressure.

When I took over for Walter Cronkite, the sudden but intermittent pressures of my reporter's life turned into the sustained pressure of the anchorman's. I love my job, and things have eased up considerably, but I'd be lying if I said it wasn't tough in the beginning. My hair even started to turn gray.

There I was, taking the place of one of the few people in this country whose face and voice are recognized by everyone. Naturally, in the beginning, millions of people tuned in merely to compare. The critics reviewed everything: my hair, my sweater, my pacing, my seriousness and sense of humor: "He smiles too much!" "Why doesn't he smile?" "He's dyeing his hair!" "No, he *stopped* dyeing his hair!" Some of this struck me—and must have struck listeners and readers—as ridiculous. Sometimes I laughed. Other times I got annoyed. And, yes, sometimes the first faint edges of insecurity crept in.

But pressure, I know, is a part of life, not only for me but for everyone. We all perform, and we all hope for approval: The mother bringing the roast to the table and wondering, "Will they like it?" The businessman giving a presentation. The kid just out of college going for an interview. The reporter speaking live on television. We're all under pressure, which I think of as the fear that at the decisive moment you won't come through, and you'll let yourself down.

Now when people remark to me that the pressure on my job must be enormous, I laugh and say "Yes, but..." Yes, but what about the salesperson with a quota to meet? And the cop on the beat? And, yes, but you should have seen my parents hustling and hoping to meet the rent and see that their kids didn't go without. That was pressure too. It was during the Depression, and everyone was under strain. Most people took it pretty well. It was part of the culture, a culture that said, "Hey, I can take it."

Looking back again at my first year as *CBS Evening News* anchorman, I see it was a crazy time. The Silly Season. It's pretty much over now, but it has taught me a few things. Like how important The List is.

It's a list of things to remember when times get difficult. Things that I've found useful over the years. I don't offer it as pearls of wisdom. It's just what's worked for me personally.

It starts with a philosophical approach: Don't be crushed if you fail. If you allow yourself to be crushed, if you indulge yourself that way, then you'll never put yourself in a pressure situation, and you'll never grow.

If you do fail, go back over what happened. Think of everything, including the moment things started to go bad, and why. Figure it out. Practice. Try again. Now the list:

- *Don't change your life radically when you're under sustained pressure or know you're about to be.* Don't force yourself to adjust to new people or habits. Don't buy a new house. As T.S. Eliot said, "There will be time, there will be time...for a hundred visions and revisions." A pressure situation isn't the right time. Wait until things calm down.

- *You can't survive pressure without the support and honest appraisal of your family and friends.* Embrace their help when they offer it. Ask for it if they don't.

I always need someone I can be totally frank with, someone who won't accept "tough day" as an honest expression of why I look so beat. I also need someone who'll be totally frank with me. I rely on my wife, Jean, my two children and a small but solid group of friends. They're always there with encouragement and perspective, and they remind me that they have problems of their own.

Jean, for instance, said at the time of the shooting of the President, "You're under pressure, that's true. But the doctors working on the President are under even more. So is the mother on welfare trying to make her kid turn out right. And so are our two friends back home who are ill." Then, with a slight smile: "And remember, there are nine hundred million Chinese out there who don't care what your reporting and broadcasting are like."

A related point: Read history. The biographer Jackson Bate has observed that when we read the lives of the great, we can catch their courage as if by contagion. I think it's true. Read about Lincoln's terrible depressions and Eugene O'Neill's terrible rages and Samuel Johnson's insomnia. Know your betters and take heart from their fears...and their triumphs in spite of those fears.

- *Get as much information as possible about what to expect before the pressure starts.* Walter Cronkite was superb in his counsel. He said,

"Don't be afraid of your weaknesses, and don't expect miracles." And Eric Sevareid wrote me a magnificent letter predicting what my problems would be and giving advice on how to deal with them.

He told me the job would put new strains on my friendships...and it did. He told me to watch out for time-wasters. When I was a reporter I was a moving target—"Sorry, I'm on my way to Managua." But as an anchorman I'd be a *sitting* target. When the time-wasters descended, I was prepared.

• *Keep your objectives in mind.* After Eric's letter I did an important thing. On three pieces of paper I wrote the question: "Is what you're doing now helping the broadcast?" I put one copy in my billfold, one in my pocket and one in my desk. Now and then, in a meeting or whatever, I'll open the desk and look at that paper, remembering Eric's warning. I don't mean to be cold about it—life is life and fun is fun—but it has proved a useful reminder.

• *Keep it all in perspective.* No matter what kind of pressure you're under, the sun will still come up in the morning. I'll give you an exaggerated case of how to maintain perspective—one that makes the point.

An executive I know is frequently under pressure to perform well and please his many bosses—who do not always make it clear what it is he should do to please them. Every now and then it gets to him. And when it does he puts his feet up on his desk and reviews what they can't do. He says to himself, "Hey, they can't kill me. They can't take away my wife and kids. They can't steal my friends. All they can do is take away my paycheck. Okay. If they do that, I'll get another one."

Then he calms down. Sometimes I think the scope of his fears is not quite sane. But his way of handling them is.

• *Do things that help you relax.* I listen to music to calm myself down and to pump myself up: "The 1812 Overture" or the song "Even Bravest Hearts May Swell." "Will the Circle Be Unbroken" is another favorite of mine when the heat is on. Now and then I'll hum or remember the words of a hymn from childhood. I don't remember if I learned it in Sunday School or at my mother's knee. I feel I was born knowing it. Its old gospel words bring me back in more ways than one. It's "Safe Am I," and the words are:

> Safe am I
> Safe am I
> In the hollow
> Of His hand.
>
> No ill can harm me
> No foe alarm me
> In the hollow
> Of His hand.

As I said, it brings me back in more ways than one. Which brings me to the next point.

● *Have faith.* Realize you need something to believe in—something bigger than yourself, beyond yourself. Whether it's God or Buddha or that there's a higher logic in life—whatever it is, just about everyone needs it. I don't mean to sound "born again"—I'm not—but it's hard to go through life without the steadying effects of someone's hand on your shoulder.

Nearly last, and not only not least but maybe I should have put it at the top:

● *To take pressure you've got to have peasant stamina.* Think of Millet's painting "The Man With The Hoe." There he is, resigned, slogging on despite the elements, despite the meager returns. He's forging on.

To forge on like that, physical exercise is essential. It distracts your mind. I couldn't handle pressure without running and occasionally playing basketball. Also, your mother was right: Nutrition counts. Breakfast counts. Without it, by midmorning you're not good for much of anything.

Don't turn to alcohol to handle pressure. It gives the illusion of control, but *only* the illusion. The next day it takes its toll, leaving your body—and your mind—weaker and jumpier.

● *Finally, remember to use pressure.* When interviewing the winner of Wimbledon, or the guy in the World Series who made the game-saving catch, a reporter never asks, "How did you ever do it under all that pressure?" The reporter knows what the player knows: Pressure *helped* him do it. Pressure served as the spur and the challenge. Pressure makes everything coalesce; without that concentrated moment, hitting your peak is not possible.

Word count: 1669

2. HEALTH AND EXERCISE

Today, many newspapers, books, and magazines feature articles about health. Some promote vitamin supplements; others tell you that these supplements are a waste of money. Some promote exercise while still others warn of its dangers. No doubt all claim to tell the truth, even as they contradict each other. This often results in widespread confusion among health-conscious individuals. On such an important subject as your health, you will probably want to read and think critically before following advice.

In this section you will read several articles on diet and exercise, and even one concerning the possible problems with AIDS testing.

6. SPEEDWALK
by Pat Smith
from Mirabella

> Today many people want to keep fit, but what exercise is best? For some of us, walking, not running, may be the answer.
>
> **simultaneously** "...that uses more muscles **simultaneously**..."
> *Meaning:* at the same time
>
> **synchronization** "...you should reduce your speed and get back into **synchronization**."
> *Meaning:* at the same time and in a state of balance and harmony
>
> **reluctant** "A former **reluctant** runner with bad knees..."
> *Meaning:* not eager; hesitant

I may never walk the same way again and for good reason. Since I met Casey Meyers, the former runner and author of *Aerobic Walking* (Random House), walking has become more than a way of getting there; it's now a way of exercising.

I've always wanted to believe that walking ten minutes could be just as beneficial as running ten minutes and that for overall muscle toning, there was no better way to invest thirty minutes than walking. I wanted to believe that the most natural of human activities was also the best.

Casey Meyers told me what I wanted to hear and more. In 1984, Meyers, a fitness runner, suffered severe knee damage. Recently retired and with time to spare, he began a quest for an alternative to running.

"I was looking for an exercise that was highly effective, injury free, natural, and sustainable," he says. So he started walking in the rolling countryside surrounding his home near St. Joseph, Missouri. He read works by physical anthropologist C. Owen Lovejoy, who says we are physiologically programmed to walk as much as our prehistoric ancestors did. Meyers also interviewed race walkers, including the only American ever to win an Olympic medal in the 50-kilometer (31.1 miles) event. He talked with doctors, trainers, zoologists; studied college physiology textbooks and popular running magazines. And he kept walking, faster and faster. And the faster he walked, the easier it became to sustain the pace.

After a year, Meyer's treadmill stress tests, performed at the famed Cooper Clinic in Dallas, charted him as superior for a male thirty years of age or younger. He was fifty-nine at the time.

Meyers came to the conclusion that there isn't any other single exercise, not even cross-country skiing, that uses more muscles simultaneously in a rhythmic movement, is so injury free, and can burn more energy at a higher rate than walking. He's convinced that walking as an aerobic exercise has been grossly underrated and underutilized when compared to running. "We've been brainwashed and oversold a bill of goods about running, a track and field event that has turned into a mass exercise. But our bodies just can't take running over the long term. They break down," he says.

Now Meyers walks three miles in thirty-three minutes, five days a week. He holds monthly clinics at the Cooper Center In-Residence Program and teaches the gospel at other clinics around the country.

"Walking is posture, technique, rhythm, and speed. If you lose the first three, you should reduce your speed and get back into synchronization."

The use of speed is what makes aerobic walking more effective than running. A person moving at twelve to thirteen minutes per mile burns more calories walking than running because at that speed running is the more efficient gait.

"If a walker and a jogger exercise side-by-side at an eleven-minute-per-mile pace, the walker will burn more calories, use more oxygen, and have a higher heart rate than the jogger," Meyers says.

I fit the stereotype of most people at his clinics. A former reluctant runner with bad knees, I have tried most everything aerobic, sometimes only once. I told Meyers I wanted to get fit but I didn't want it to take much of my time.

He told me to walk, but not the way I was used to walking. All my life people have said I walk too fast, but Meyers called my normal walk, about a twenty-minute mile, a stroll. He proceeded to show me how to get a lot for my investment. His rules are simple.

- Stand straight up, shoulders back, head level, and chin up. The shoulders should be directly over the hips.
- Bend arms to form 90-degree angles at the elbows. This shortens the pendulum of the arm swing so you can increase the frequency of the swing. Vigorous arm swinging is essential to increase your pace.
- Walk loosely and rhythmically.

I did. My arm on the forward swing crossed the center of my rib cage, while the arm on the backswing came back to where my wrist brushed the side seams of my shorts. When I moved my arms faster, I walked faster. When I broke the angle of my arms, I slowed down. When I looked down, I didn't walk as straight and my shoulders felt stiff. The more I thought about what I was doing, the better I did, and the faster I walked.

Although Meyers said I would need to increase my intensity level to receive optimum aerobic benefit, I felt good in this natural, rhythmic gait. I wasn't pounding the ground as I did when I jogged (or lumbering, as I sometimes did when I got tired), but rather mechanically, methodically picking up my feet and placing them down, one by one. It wasn't difficult.

His other words of wisdom were to monitor my heart rate and work to be in aerobic training range (65 to 85 percent of maximum heart rate for most people). "Just listen to your heart. It will tell you if you are walking too slowly or too fast."

Word count: 857

7. DIET AND EXERCISE DANGERS
by Anastasis Toufexis
from *Time*

> Note that the title mentions both diet and exercise. Both are considered necessary to good health. Have you thought carefully about your diet and exercise habits? What works best for you and what hasn't seemed to work? Millions of dollars are made today on diet and exercise books and products. How can you know what is best for you?
>
> **neophyte**   "...if the athlete is a **neophyte** or weekend warrior..."
> *Meaning:* beginner

All the instruments and experts agree that there are often painful pitfalls on the rigorous road to glowing health. Pick up a racket, and you run the risk of a sprained ankle, twisted knee or tennis elbow. Condition your heart by pumping over hill and dale on a racing bike with low-slung handle bars, and you can come up with chronic low back pain. Play softball and be prepared for torn knee ligaments and broken fingers.

Though many different sports put a strain on the same parts of the body and result in the same injuries, some produce their own peculiar ills. Golfers get twinges of golfer's elbow. Swimmer's shoulder may catch up with anybody who favors the butterfly stroke. There is even something known as "duck laceration syndrome" that strikes high-flyers who slam the ball through the basket, hitting their hands against the hoop.

At its best, exercise—particularly regular exercise—is good for the heart rate, blood pressure, respiration and metabolism. Says Jim Barnard, research cardiologist at UCLA: "It's similar to tuning up your car's engine to make the car run more efficiently." Vigorous physical effort helps release tension too. But it can also do a lot of damage, especially if the athlete is a neophyte or weekend warrior, both of whom tend to try to do too much too soon.

The trouble usually starts when sudden demands are made on an unconditioned body. In tennis and basketball, the knees and ankles must accommodate quick stops and starts and lightning changes of direction. In jogging, the athlete's feet typically strike the ground 800 to 1,000 times a mile, with an impact equivalent to about three times the body's weight. The shock jolts the entire skeleton. Statistically, at least, everyone of the nearly 30 million runners in the United States can expect some ailment.

Besides forcing their bodies to perform beyond their capabilities, many people have the Spartan belief that exercise will do no good unless it is pursued until the body aches. Says Gilbert Gleim of Lenox Hill Hospital's Institute of Sports Medicine in Manhattan: "If you're training to be healthy, exercise should never hurt." A few simple precautions, sports specialists point out, can prevent many injuries. Choose an appropriate sport for your weight and body build and always do warming-up and cooling-down exercises.

Diet poses a whole set of different hazards, especially the quickie weight-losing schemes that separate United States dieters from a few pounds each year. Among the current "in" diets are the Pritikin, the Atkins, and the Beverly Hills Diet. Nutrition experts insist that many fad diets are not really diets at all but bizarre and temporary ways of depriving the subject of adequate nutrition.

The problem, of course, is that nobody can (or should) stick to such diets for a long time. Fads fail because they do not offer a diet people can live with. And that, actually, is a blessing. Most people do not stay on such diets long enough to do themselves any physical damage. But more than 80% of people who do lose weight by dieting tend to gain it back within a year.

Fad diets are usually based on some nutritional fallacy. Of the current popular regimes, the one that comes closest to being nutritionally acceptable is a low-fat diet recommended by Nathan Pritikin, somewhat similar to the one that people in underdeveloped countries follow out of necessity. Pritikin, 66, founder of the Pritikin Longevity Center in Santa Monica, California, is a self-taught nutritionist.* He forbids all fats, salt and sugar, oils, most processed foods and dairy products, and discourages the use of tobacco, caffeine, sugar and salt substitutes and even vitamins. Devotees eat mainly fresh fruits, vegetables and whole-grain breads, hoping Pritikin is correct when he claims that the diet curbs heart disease, diabetes, and hypertension. Doctors say more testing is needed to substantiate such claims. They also say the Pritikin Diet is unnecessarily restrictive, especially for healthy people. Says nutritionist Myron Winick of the Institute of Human Nutrition at Columbia University: "If you follow it, you almost can't eat in a restaurant."

The diets that get the poorest medical marks are two very popular ones—Atkins and Beverly Hills. The first, conceived by Dr. Robert Atkins, 51, restricts carbohydrates but allows unlimited consumption of meat and fat. Says nutritionist Nancy Tiger of Boston's Beth Israel Hospital: "You can eat as much bacon, fresh sausage and those kinds of things as you want. They're high in cholesterol and saturated fat. Not good in terms of heart disease."

The Beverly Hills Diet is the creation of Californian Judy Mazel, 37, an aspiring actress until she became a nutritional guru. Mazel allows only fruit the first ten days—as much as five pounds of grapes a day—and no meat, poultry or fish until day 19. Some doctors say the book should be listed under fiction. A leading nutrition expert says, "If you went to a bookstore and bought a history book that said the Declaration of Independence was signed in 1827 or World War I began in 1905, you'd be pretty angry." If followed too long, the Beverly Hills Diet may lead to diarrhea, and although medical evidence is scant, doctors warn of other complications.

Many physicians shake their heads at the public's gullibility about diets. As Psychiatrist Albert Stunkard of the University of Pennsylvania points out, "The only way to lose weight is to make really big changes in your life-style."

---

*Editor's Note: Nathan Pritikin died in 1985. The Pritikin Longevity Center is still in existence.

Word count: 925

8. WHEN STAYING THIN IS A SICKNESS
by Earl Ubell
from *Parade*

Most of us know or have heard of someone who has an eating disorder. What are the causes and symptoms? How are they cured? What are your thoughts about these dangerous disorders?

kleptomania "...a third of our patients have **kleptomania** too..."
Meaning: a strong impulse to steal

binge "...Gayle would **binge** on food..."
Meaning: to do something to excess, in this case to overeat

purge "...vomiting or using laxatives to **purge**..."
Meaning: to get rid of

prone to "...but they are **prone** to such ailments..."
Meaning: likely to get

    She could be your closest friend. Your co-worker. Even your wife or your sister. And you wouldn't know that a terrible disease had gripped both her mind and body, threatening her very life.

    But she would know.

    Gayle Cappelluti, 29, of Brooklyn, New York, knew that something was terribly wrong with her each time she shut herself away in her room to eat.

    "I'd have a whole pizza—one of the big ones. And a couple of pounds of candy and more cookies," recalls Gayle, an elementary school teacher. "Then I'd telephone a Chinese take-out restaurant and order $30 worth of food.

    "It was like being in a dream. I didn't think of anything. I'd just eat all night long."

Yet Gayle never gained much weight. At 5 feet 4½ inches, she weighed 109 pounds. And that was the second part of her guilty secret: Gayle vomited all of the food she ate.

"I'd do it many times a day," she says. "I'd try not to think about what I was doing. But when I did, I hated myself. 'Ugh,' I'd think, how could you do a thing like this?"

Until recently, few doctors considered it an illness when people like Gayle would binge on food and then throw it up or take laxatives. Today, the affliction is called bulimia (from the Greek word meaning "ox hunger") or, simply, the "binge-purge disease."

Physicians and psychologists now rank bulimia as a major physical and mental health problem. Studies reveal bulimia in five to 20 percent of female students aged 13 to 23. Dr. Harrison G. Pope Jr. of McLean Hospital in Belmont, Massachusetts, says estimates show that only one man in 20 is bulimic but as many as 7 million women, aged 10 to 52, are trapped at some point in their lives in the binge-purge syndrome. Jane Fonda says she was bulimic as a teenager.

You may be bulimic and hide it from yourself. Here are some of the signs: 1) eating huge amounts of food; 2) vomiting or using laxatives to purge; 3) hiding your binges from others; 4) trying to control your weight by binging and purging; and 5) feeling out of control once you start eating.

Bulimics may maintain normal body weight and look healthy, but they are prone to such ailments as swollen salivary glands, an inflamed pancreas and gallbladder problems. Constant vomiting harms the stomach and food pipe, or esophagus. Stomach acid coming up into the mouth erodes tooth enamel. I saw a bulimic with so much enamel gone, only tiny stubs of teeth remained.

At its worst bulimia can kill. Purging empties the body of potassium; this makes the heart irritable and prone to stop. Estimated death rate for severe bulimics is one to 10 percent. Some bulimics spend up to $300 a week on food. They isolate themselves at work and at home, even from their spouses. Sometimes they cannot work and lose their jobs.

Bulimia is related to anorexia nervosa, a condition in which patients refuse to eat anything at all and waste away.

Dr. C. Phillip Wilson of Columbia University's College of Physicians and Surgeons in New York City calls anorexia nervosa and bulimia two sides of the same coin because both are rooted in the fear of becoming fat. Every bulimic I spoke to confessed that fear. "Even at 100 pounds, I felt fat," Gayle Cappelluti said. She weighs 120 now.

Nobody knows why the binge-purge syndrome snares mostly women. Dr. Pope and Dr. James I. Hudson, also of McLean Hospital, call bulimia a form of a major depressive disorder. Says Dr. Pope, "Among our bulimic patients, 80 percent suffer from major depressive or manic depressive illnesses."

Dr. B. Timothy Walsh of Columbia University's College of Physicians and Surgeons reports success with anti-depressant drugs. "Bulimics not only stop binging and purging," he says. "For the first time, they feel better."

One of Pope's patients, Sheri Swanson, 34, bulimic since she was 18, says she hid the problem from everyone: "It's so shameful." All treatments failed until Pope prescribed an anti-depressant drug, desipramine. Sheri noticed a difference right away. She says, "This oppressive cloud was lifted. Within a matter of weeks, the binging was gone. It was astonishing."

Studies also show that bulimic women have other psychological disturbances. Up to a third have attempted suicide. Bulimics tend to abuse alcohol and street drugs. "We think a third of our patients have kleptomania too," says Pope. "Imagine a middle-class woman who can buy anything she wants yet steals a bottle of perfume."

Treatment for bulimia varies. Daniel Baker, Ph.D., director of the eating disorder program at University Hospital of the University of Nebraska Medical Center, Omaha, trains bulimics to turn away from food and to build self-esteem.

Associates for Bulimia and Related Disorders, a group of psychologists in New York City, teaches clients to turn to other people rather than to food. Says Ellen Schor, Ph.D., a co-director, "We tell them: 'You have a food addiction. Food has been your secret lover, your confidant and worst enemy. If you go on like this you will never get close to people.'" In groups, patients are taught the facts about bulimia, urged to keep diaries and to make contracts with themselves to change. Co-director Judith Brisman, Ph.D., reports that every year, a third of the group no longer binges and another third cut their gorging by half.

When all else fails, Dr. Katherine Halmi of Cornell University Medical College in White Plains, New York, hospitalizes her patients for an average of three months. Hospitalization keeps the bulimic away from food; in serious cases, it can save the person's life. Step by step, patients are taught to eat normally. At $370 a day, the cost for three months would come to about $33,000.

Aided by group meetings at the American Anorexia/Bulimia Association in Teaneck, New Jersey, Gayle Cappelluti today is a recovered bulimic. She has remarried and expects a second child.

Word count: 987

9. DIETS OF CHAMPS
by Laura Flynn McCarthy
from *Harper's Bazaar*

> What do athletes eat and drink in order to maintain strength and stamina? Are food supplements necessary? Some people probably have false ideas about this subject. Check your knowledge in this area against the ideas in the article.
>
> **hyperthermia** — "One major reason people drop out of athletic events is **hyperthermia**..."
> *Meaning:* overheating
>
> **dehydrate** — "...instead of caffeine-laden sodas that will cause you to **dehydrate**."
> *Meaning:* lose water or fluid
>
> **electrolyte** — "...probably need an **electrolyte** replacement drink."
> *Meaning:* an essential chemical in the body
>
> **shunted** — "...blood is **shunted** away from the brain and the heart."
> *Meaning:* to move aside or onto another course
>
> **regimen** — "If you create a good mix of foods in your ordinary **regimen**..."
> *Meaning:* a procedure or system
>
> **glycogen** — "...then you can actually reload depleted muscle **glycogen** stores faster..."
> *Meaning:* a necessary carbohydrate in the body

Nutritional myths and general food malarkey, as everyone knows, are basics of dieting. But it's in the area of athletic performance and food—i.e., eating for energy—that misconceptions, today, fully abound. Why? Because we're all looking for an edge: the right way to fuel our particular fitness regimen, be that the pro circuit or simply highly competitive Saturday tennis. Food faddism has almost become an athletic badge of honor. Fitness fans toss off terms like fluid intake and carb loading with, seemingly, knowledgeable abandon. They invest heftily in high-performance drinks and sports vitamins. They even—pro players and

Olympic hopefuls alike—hire on today's new specialist—the sports nutritionist—to help them develop a way to eat for success.

And, often, it all adds up to a lot of well-intentioned effort gone wrong.

Bazaar went to six experts in the field and asked them about what's really a diet of champs. And these docs of champs, in response, have plenty to say about the ways in which we're all eating right—and wrong.

Myth 1: Calories are calories. It doesn't matter where they come from.

Regarding weight loss, a calorie is, ultimately, a calorie—whether it takes the form of whole grain pasta or chocolate syrup. One calorie becomes significantly different from another, however, when it comes to sports performance. What's important is where those calories come from and how efficiently the body burns them as energy.

Explains Nancy Clark, M.S., R.D., nutritionist for SportsMedicine in Brookline, Massachusetts, who's counseled almost everyone from the Boston Celtics to Olympic figure skater Kitty Carruthers, "Carbohydrates are needed to fuel the muscles. If you have cereal, banana, and juice for breakfast, that's a high-carb meal that will still give your muscles energy at 5 P.M., when you work out. If you skip breakfast and end up eating a bag of chips later on, that's basically grease. Fatty foods are more likely to be turned into body fat than burned off during exercise. Those fats will fill your stomach, but they won't necessarily fuel your muscles."

Myth 2: Athletes' bodies require special nutritional supplements during training.

"The biggest mistake women athletes make," states Nancy Clark, "is just getting too hungry—restricting themselves too much. Everything deteriorates—willpower, motivation, performance. Some take supplements; what they need is good food, instead. If you take a multivitamin, there may be 10 or 15 different nutrients in there. But there are 50 components in food you need. It's very naive to count on a pill to compensate for lousy eating habits. Sports supplements are no different from ordinary vitamin supplements. That's just a marketing tool."

Myth 3: Protein builds strong bodies.

Says Nancy Clark, "The old idea is that if you have a steak for dinner, you'll have bigger biceps by breakfast. That's just not true. Extra protein in your diet does not make your muscles bigger. Exercise builds muscles. And to have enough energy to exercise, you need carbohydrates—cereals, fruits, breads, pastas, and potatoes. A body-builder should eat the same high-carbohydrate diet a marathoner follows."

Myth 4: Our bodies tell us exactly what we need. When we need fluids, we feel thirsty.

Says Gail Butterfield, Ph.D., R.D., director of nutrition studies at the Palo Alto V.A. Medical Center, "Most of us consume only about 50-60 percent of the fluid we need. Studies have shown that. Our thirst mechanisms just don't keep up with the need for fluid. For most of us who exercise moderately, that's probably not a problem. But if you exercise in heat or train for long periods of time, it's a critical concern. One major reason people drop out of athletic events is hyperthermia, caused by a lack of fluids."

Her Rx: "Drink plenty of water throughout the day instead of caffeine-laden sodas that will cause you to dehydrate. There are a lot of sports drinks on the market; they're all fine. For most of us, water will do just as well. People who lose large amounts of fluid—those who do ultra-endurance types of exercise like long-distance running—probably need an electrolyte replacement drink."

Myth 5: A quart of fluid, at the end of a workout, is all your body requires.

Says Peter J. Bruno, M.D., internist for the New York Knicks and the New York Rangers, "We recommend two glasses of water before you start working out; half a glass every 15 minutes during a workout and a couple of glasses afterward. Don't wait until you get dehydrated. If you feel thirsty, you're already dehydrated."

Myth 6: What matters, in the end, is body weight. Lighter athletes are faster.

Says Cecilia Fileti, R.D., spokesperson for the American Dietetic Association, who has worked with runners, competitive tennis players and gymnasts, "When studies were done on women runners in a 10-kilometer trial, the best performers were not necessarily the thinnest ones. Genetics and training were more important factors. Some athletes think that high-volume training will improve their performance. Most research, in fact, shows that isn't where it's at. When you compare women who are doing high-volume training to women who work out 20 minutes a day, three times a week, those sometimes-athletes end up being in good shape. Among U.S. swimmers, one study concluded that rest was a better investment than overtraining. The more an athlete trains, the more calories are burned. If you're not compensating for that by making sure you have the appropriate diet mix and sufficient calories, you're going to get into problems. We see that particularly in sports that emphasize being slim and trim—such as figure skating and gymnastics."

Myth 7: A good carb-loading meal just before the game is the athlete's answer.

Says Kenneth Cooper, M.D., founder and president of the Aerobics Center in Dallas, "For about 90 minutes after eating, blood is shunted away from the brain and the heart. That's what makes you feel sleepy after a heavy meal. That's why, regardless of age, sex or physical condition, we advise people against vigorous physical activity immediately after eating. If you've got an athletic competition coming up, you should have a fairly light meal at least an hour and a half ahead of time. Limit yourself to carbohydrates and liquids. Where carbohydrate-loading in the days before an event has proven to have substantial benefits is with long-distance events—over 10 miles of running, for example. But that's a very specific endurance situation."

Myth 8: Caffeine boosts metabolism and has been shown to 'up' performance.

Says Dr. Cooper: "Theoretically, a cup of coffee preceding an event might improve performance. But that's a very dangerous recommendation. We've known for years that if people have a cup of coffee before their stress test, it tends to make the heart very irritable. It may skip beats; the person gets lightheaded. Caffeine consumption immediately preceding an athletic event is dangerous and should not be done. Even one cup of coffee."

Myth 9: Before a big meet is when you really need some dietary changes.

Says Dr. Bruno, "Whatever you decide you want to eat during normal workouts and practice sessions, that's the food you should stick to. Competition time is not the moment to experiment. If you create a good mix of foods in your ordinary regimen, it will give you everything you need for an event."

Myth 10: What you eat after exercising doesn't matter; replacing fluids is the key.

Says Jackie Berning, M.S., R.D., nutrition consultant to The United States Swimming Team and to the University of Colorado, "It's been found that if you eat a good source of carbohydrates within 30 minutes of exercise, then you can actually reload depleted muscle glycogen stores faster than if you wait two hours to eat after exercising. The hard part is that many athletes don't have an appetite after a strenuous workout. The ideal would be to grab a banana and drink a cup of Gatorlode; then have a balanced meal a few hours later. This is crucial to anybody who's doing more than once-a-day workouts or somebody who trains on a day-to-day basis. It's making sure that you've got the energy to go out and exercise the day after."

Word count: 1373

10. HOW TO KEEP YOUR LEGS YOUNG
by Joann Rodgers
from *Parade*

Our legs are something we take for granted, but they could be the first parts of our bodies to give us problems as we get older. Read this article to find ways to keep this from happening.

nethermost "...our **nethermost** apparatus begins to fail..."
Meaning: lowest, farthest down the list in terms of importance

apparatus "...our nethermost **apparatus** begins to fail..."
Meaning: mechanism; device

balk "As both men and women round the young-adult bend...the legs **balk**."
Meaning: stop and refuse to move or act

heft "...they must withstand forces many times the body's **heft**..."
Meaning: weight, heaviness

culled "Some tips on leg exercises, **culled** from the advice of specialists..."
Meaning: collected, gathered

mania "Such mileage **mania** often leads to injury..."
Meaning: craziness

regimen "Handball...can be part of your **regimen** into the 50s and beyond..."
Meaning: routine

Legs, darn them, are the first of our equipment to outlive our fantasies of youthful vigor. At the very time when wisdom, wit and experience peak, our nethermost apparatus begins to fail, giving the lie to our prowess and the wobbles to our will.

As both men and women round the young-adult bend and head toward middle age, the legs balk. Knees lock, thighs slump, joints stiffen and muscles ache in mute protest.

"No question about it, the legs go first," complains Gabe Mirkin, 47, a physician, author, competitive runner and world class expert on legs. "Twenty years ago, I could easily run 100 miles a week, and now I'm happy if I can do 25. The coordination is still there. The brain sends the right signals. But the legs don't listen as well."

We can't, of course, stop the march of time. But the good news is that regular and rigorous exercise begun at any age can mount an impressive holding action.

Why do the legs go first? Legs are the body's major weight-bearing organs. Housing the largest, longest and strongest of the adult's joints and 206 bones, they must withstand forces many times the body's heft for hours at a time.

In youth, the thigh bone alone can support a compact car. Cable-like muscles that allow us to leap stairs or turn on a dime are always tensed to fight gravity and maintain tone. But for each decade over 20, if we are inactive, we can expect to lose up to five percent of the muscle tissue. Beyond 30, the heart's blood-pumping ability may decline, cutting oxygen supply to muscles of the calves and feet. At the same time, a reduced supply of calcium softens and shrinks bones, diminishing toughness and range of motion. By 80, says Dr. Nathan Shock, a government specialist on aging, muscle strength may fall to about 55 percent of what it was at age 25.

Yet experts insist the situation isn't hopeless. "It's something of a fallacy to say the legs go first," says Robert Porter, the head of the sports medicine clinic at Dartmouth College in Hanover, New Hampshire, a hotbed of running in the East. "With exercise, your endurance and ability to perform decline noticeably less per decade. If we maintain muscle tone and fitness, our legs should be able to perform 80 percent of the capability we had at age 20 as we enter middle age."

And it's never too late to start. Studies of elderly people show that exercise significantly increases their muscle and bone strength and slows the loss of muscle tissue. Exercise that emphasizes motion can prevent the locking of even the worst arthritic joints that normally occurs through disuse.

So begin today. Some tips on leg exercises, culled from the advice of specialists and their patients, follow. A word of caution, however: The exercises will not make lean, mean marathon runners out of potbellied desk pilots or give slack-thighed matrons pin-up limbs.

What they will do is tone and strengthen your personal transportation; help ward off the complications of arthritis; and fight fat, cramps, sprains, breaks, aches and other ills of middle-aged hips, thighs, calves, ankles, feet and toes. Not least of all, they will extend your enjoyment of sports, dancing and the out doors to the end of your life.

Getting started. If you are launching a first or new assault on what Shakespeare called the "decreasing legs" of age, have a checkup that includes hips, knees and feet as well as the heart and lungs. Then, buy the right sport shoes—at least $35 to $45 in a reputable specialty store.

Which exercise is best? The answer will vary with individual interests, climate, time and resources.

Many sports—and even common activities like walking up steps, two at a time—offer excellent conditioning. Jogging, walking and running increase lung power and lower-body strength while reducing fat and blood pressure. But don't overdo it. "Running," says Dr. Mirkin, "is the most dangerous sport known for legs. You quickly build tolerance and need more distance to get the high it produces." Such mileage mania often leads to injury, he adds.

Handball, tennis (singles), squash, racquetball and skiing (downhill and cross-country) can be part of your regimen into the 50s and beyond, but only if you are one of the long-term fit. "I play a lot more doubles than I used to," says a 60-year-old bank officer. "I get as much kick out of the mental game now as I used to get out of the tougher physical game. And the running I do during matches keeps my legs as strong."

Of all solid exercise, swimming is probably the safest, especially for arthritis victims and those with foot problems. Arthritis puts unusual stress on joints, so even walking may put too much strain on them. For almost everyone else, however, experts agree that brisk walking is the best overall leg-strengthening exercise. In addition to being safe, it offers aerobic benefits to the heart and lungs and gets the walker out of doors for at least part of the year. "Anything you can accomplish running you can accomplish walking," says Dr. Saul Haskell, a sports medicine specialist in Chicago. "It just takes a little longer."

How much exercise how often? Injuries to the knee and other parts of the leg almost always occur in men and women who overtrain, skip warm-ups or try to "play through" pain.

A hard workout often causes a certain amount of muscle swelling and microscopic damage, and healing takes 48 hours even in those who are fit. Never, therefore, use the same muscle groups hard every day. Specialists advise even professional athletes to follow a "hard-easy-hard-easy" workout schedule. Alternate running days, for instance, with cycling or swimming. Stretch muscles gently between workouts. If you bicycle, stretch the muscles above the knee and at the calf. If you run, stretch the calf, hamstring (at the back of the upper leg), inner thigh and lower back muscles. If you jog, do a two-minute jog-walk routine, increasing the running time week by week. Jog no more than three days a week.

Pay strict attention to warm-ups and cool-downs. Thomas Jefferson advised "not less than two hours a day" devoted to exercise. To keep legs fit, however, 45 minutes to an hour a day will do, not including warm-up periods.

Protect the back and knee. Always include lower back stretching exercises before tennis, skiing and racquetball. Sit-ups, which develop abdominal muscles, will help the back and legs too.

To strengthen knees, work on the muscles that pull them, especially if the foot rolls inward. (The lower legs may then twist one way, forcing the knee joint in the opposite direction.) Wearing shoes with good arch support, stand straight, pull the kneecap up an inch or so, hold the position for a 10-count and relax. Repeat several times a day.

Don't cramp your style. Learn to distinguish the types of leg cramps. Those that strike the calf muscle in the middle of the night are exaggerated muscle tendon reflexes. Stretching and massage will work these out. Cramps that begin soon after you start exercise may be serious. Have a checkup before continuing. Cramps after an hour of exercise, especially in heat, usually mean dehydration. Drink a cup of cool water every 15 minutes during exertion.

For women only. Women are more vulnerable to knee and foot injuries, in part because of ill-fitting shoes, but also because of their wider pelvic bones and stance. Building up thigh and calf muscles is an excellent preventive measure.

Dr. Stanley Cohen, who plans physical therapy for disabled patients at Sinai Hospital in Baltimore, says the combination of bad arches, pointy-toed shoes, and high heels can strain the knees, aggravate arthritis and make it too painful to exercise. Women who wear high heels often have Achilles' tendons that are never stretched enough for running in flat shoes. Try foam wedges in sport shoes to slightly elevate the heels.

Exercise those veins away. Varicose veins, a painful swelling in leg veins, occur when flow valves in the circulatory system allow blood to pool there. Standing still encourages the process. To prevent them, "move, move, move," advises Mirkin. "Leg muscles can function as a second heart. When you relax the muscles, the veins fill. When you contract or move them, they empty." Thus, running, walking, skating and cycling are also therapeutic.

How long before results? In a healthy adult, almost-daily leg exercises will begin to strengthen and tighten the super-structure within weeks. Noticeable differences can be expected after several months. Within a year, you are on your way to maximum strength.

A few months ago, a friend and I watched our teenage sons working out before a soccer match. Their legs pumped tirelessly up and down the field for half-an-hour without a break. Running with them was their coach, a man in his mid-50s and a grandfather. "No problem," he shrugged when asked how he kept up with youths a quarter his age. "I just keep the legs moving, and they take care of the rest of me."

Word count: 1537

11. FACING THE TEST
by Laura Fraser
from *Vogue*

> AIDS is certainly frightening, but so is AIDS testing—even if the test is negative. Who will see the results? What are your options concerning testing sites? These questions are addressed in this article.
>
> **bolt**   "I prepared to **bolt**."
> *Meaning:* leave quickly
>
> **anonymous**   "...would have kept my results **anonymous**..."
> *Meaning:* unknown; secret
>
> **discreet**   "Talk things over with your physician to be sure he or she will be **discreet**—"
> *Meaning:* confidential; kept from public knowledge
>
> **subtle**   "Sometimes HIV testing is done with a patient's consent but with **subtle** coercion."
> *Meaning:* not obvious; indirect
>
> **coercion**   "Sometimes HIV testing is done with a patient's consent but with subtle **coercion**."
> *Meaning:* force or pressure

    The thought of having an HIV test hadn't crossed my mind until my new boyfriend suggested, or rather, insisted, I get myself checked out. I was surprised, and even offended. People like me don't get AIDS, I argued. But he knew better; he'd watched a dear friend slowly waste away from AIDS and understood that no one who has sex is safe from the virus.

    I agreed to the test—what could it hurt?—and made an appointment at Planned Parenthood, the first place I could think of. Before the test, the counselor assured me that given my history (more than one relationship, but no needle users or bisexuals in the bunch as far as I knew), there wasn't much likelihood I was positive. I was probably one of the worried well who regularly troop through Planned Parenthood for their peace of mind. I rolled up my sleeve to have my blood drawn.

The days waiting for results were filled with nagging memories of what I'd done in the late seventies. What if I *was* positive? Would my individual health insurance policy cover the cost of my treatment? I had no idea. How would I support myself if I was sick? Could I tell my friends. Could I handle the news?

Three days later, my counselor walked me into her office, sat down slowly, and said, "You're negative." It was all over. I prepared to bolt.

But not so fast. First, she wanted to make sure I understood exactly what the results meant. No HIV antibodies had shown up in my blood, but that didn't mean I hadn't been exposed—it takes around six months for antibodies to appear. In other words, I shouldn't have unprotected sex with my partner until we had another round of tests in six months—until we knew that neither of us had had unsafe sex in the past half year. The counselor pressed me further. If I was planning on having unprotected sex with my partner, was I sure I could trust him not to have any flings? She kept me there until she seemed sure that I wouldn't do anything foolish because of my HIV-negative status.

I walked out of the clinic lucky—and not just because I was HIV negative. Unwittingly, I'd chosen a good testing center, one that provided sensitive thorough counseling before and after the test. And had I been positive, the Planned Parenthood in my state would have kept my results anonymous and given me referrals for treatment. As uncomfortable as the experience was, it was a best-case scenario.

Being tested for HIV makes more sense than ever before; new drug treatments are helping people with AIDS live longer, fuller lives, and the earlier the treatment is started, the better. With women now the fastest-growing segment of the population diagnosed with AIDS, doctors and public health officials are urging more and more women to consider testing.

The official message is that HIV testing is easy, confidential, and necessary. But it's not that simple. Not all testing situations include counseling and follow up care. Not all tests are anonymous—or even voluntary. Finding out your HIV status before you are prepared can be devastating; having someone else find out can be much worse.

Consider these cases:

Sandra*, a professional in her thirties, decided to be tested and made an appointment with her private physician. She was accustomed to dealing with her own doctor, and she didn't believe the care would be as good at an anonymous-testing site. Sandra was assured that the test result would be confidential. But *confidential* doesn't mean *secret*. Her test, which was positive, was billed to her insurance company. Then the results made their way to her employer's desk. She wasn't fired, but she suffered great anxiety over the fact that her employer—and who else?—knew about her HIV status.

Beth*, who was married, applied for health insurance and was told she had to take an HIV test first. She tested positive and was denied coverage.

Charlene*, a twenty-nine-year-old Washington, D.C., woman, went to her obstetrician for a pregnancy test and was told that an HIV test was standard procedure. A nurse called her later to say she was pregnant *and* HIV positive. Her physician advised her to have an abortion but didn't tell her that the chances of her baby being infected with HIV were between 25 and 30 percent. Charlene agreed to end the pregnancy, but it took her several weeks to find a clinic willing to perform an abortion on an HIV-positive woman.

In Florida, Katherine* donated blood, unaware that it would be tested for HIV and traced back to her. She opened a letter from the blood bank while driving her car; she was positive.

Every one of these women needed to know her HIV status in order to get the best possible treatment. But testing—particularly involuntary testing—can have serious implications. Women have lost jobs, partners, housing, and employment when the results of their HIV tests were revealed.

"There's a balancing act going on here," says Leslie Wolfe, executive director of the Center for Women Policy Studies in Washington, D.C. "You have to go into testing with your eyes open about the fact that society isn't as advanced as we'd like it to be."

---

*These names have been changed.

For now, AIDS experts say, the only sure way women can avoid these problems is with anonymous testing. Many women feel reassured when a doctor says their test results will be kept confidential. But *anonymous* and *confidential* can be misleading terms, and in this case they aren't the same. *Confidential* information can be shared with insurers, employers, other doctors, and sometimes partners. "We all know that medical records are of limited confidentiality," says Anke Erhardt, a psychologist and director of the HIV Center for Clinical and Behavioral Studies in New York City. Talk things over with your physician to be sure he or she will be discreet—some will bill an HIV test simply as a diagnostic test, for example—or find an anonymous-testing site. *Anonymous* means that your results will be filed only under a number, not your name; no one will be able to trace results back to you.

Anonymous testing is not always easy to find, however. Fifteen states guarantee your anonymity and hold doctors criminally and civilly liable for revealing test results. Seven states have no such requirements, and policies vary among hospitals and clinics. Four states require testing centers to report some names to health officials (for example, those of infected nurses and doctors); seventeen states report names to the health department but have at least one anonymous-testing site available. In Alabama, Alaska, Arizona, Idaho, Minnesota, North Dakota, South Carolina, and South Dakota, the results of all HIV tests are reported, by name, to the health department. Some of these states merely keep statistics; others trace and notify partners. In twenty-seven states, the results of your test may be given to a partner without your permission or notification. With all the variation, it's important to understand the ground rules before you have blood drawn.

Some AIDS tests are hard to avoid; many hospitals and clinics routinely run an HIV test whenever a patient has other blood work done. Many more test newborns for HIV (if a baby is HIV positive, the mother is sure to be). A study of hospital HIV-testing policies conducted by Charles E. Lewis of the University of California in Los Angeles and sociologist Kathleen Montgomery of the University of California in Riverside found that of 471 hospitals with a testing policy, 12 percent require HIV tests on some or all patients, 69 percent require that test results appear in patients' records, and 17 percent allow HIV testing without a patient-consent form. "It would be nice if you could ask what your blood is going to be tested for," says Leslie Wolfe, "but often you're not in a position to do that."

Sometimes HIV testing is done with a patient's consent but under subtle coercion. When Robin*, a thirty-four-year-old San Francisco woman, went to her obstetrician for prenatal care, she was told an HIV test was routine. "The nurse practitioner urged me to have the test; she said everyone did it," recalls Robin, whose results were negative. "No one counseled me about it at all. It was coercive because it was all so casual."

AIDS experts recommend that no HIV test ever be given without counseling. "Testing without it is virtually useless," says Elizabeth Cooper of the American Civil Liberties Union AIDS Project. "One of the most important things about being tested is finding out not if you're positive or negative but what those results really mean."

A woman who tests negative but isn't counseled is likely to walk out the door assuming that she no longer needs to practice safer sex. A pregnant woman who tests positive may not be given enough information to make a decision about abortion. A woman who tests positive and isn't referred to a treatment program or a support group may assume that there's no hope for her. S. Denise Rouse of the DC Women's Council on AIDS says too many women are "dumped"—given only a phone number of a public hospital—after testing. "HIV-positive women die faster than HIV-positive men," she says, "because they're not getting the care they need."

HIV-positive women also die faster because they don't find out about their infection soon enough to get early treatment. The only way to find out is to be tested.

But you shouldn't just walk into a clinic and rely on luck, as I did. And you can't assume that you'll be able to avoid a test indefinitely. Before you roll up your sleeve, you have to know what the consequences of an HIV test will be for you—positive or negative.

Word count: 1662

178   Read and Respond

3. PARENTING

Parenting may be the toughest job you will ever love. Being a parent was never easy, but in today's world it often seems overwhelming. What is the best method of disciplining a child? How can you develop a child's self-esteem? How do you handle a full-time job while juggling full-time parenting? How can you best raise a child if you are a single parent? These and many other questions trouble today's parents.

In this section you will read articles about building self-esteem in a child, how to deal with an angry child, and how to help children understand and appreciate nature. You will also read about an all-important ritual of the American teenager: going for that first driver's license.

12. HITTING THE ROAD
by David Elkind, Ph.D.
from *Parents*

> It is every teenager's dream and most parents' nightmare: getting a driver's license. What should parents and teens discuss about this important matter? It is a serious concern, and you may find this author's advice helpful.
>
> **bar mitzvah** "Along with confirmation or a **bar** or **bas mitzvah**, a
> **bas mitzvah** sweet-sixteen party,..."
> *Meaning:* Jewish ceremony celebrating a child's reaching the age of religious responsibility. (Bar is for males, bas for females.)
>
> **drastically** "...the insurance rates go up quite **drastically**."
> *Meaning:* sharply; steeply
>
> **chauffeuring** "...**chauffeuring** their younger brothers and sisters..."
> *Meaning:* driving for someone else

Getting a driver's license is an important milestone of maturity for a teenager. Along with confirmation or a bar or bas mitzvah, a sweet-sixteen party, and a work permit, a driver's license signals that the teenager has taken a major step toward adulthood. Such markers give young people a sense of direction—of where they have been, where they are now, and where they are going.

Preliminary Talks

Even before a teenager applies for his driver's license, you should discuss a number of practical considerations associated with driving. Perhaps most important is finances. Teenagers need to be reminded that when a young person is listed on an insurance plan as a driver of the family car, the insurance rates go up quite drastically. They also must realize that if they get a ticket for a moving violation, insurance costs will rise even more steeply. If a young person is going to use the car regularly, particularly to go to and from a job, he should be expected to contribute to the car's upkeep and insurance. Even if the teen uses the car only on a limited basis, you should agree about who is to pay for the gas, oil, car wash, and so on. (This sort of discussion is especially important if the teenager is given a hand-me-down car or purchases one on his own.)

Establish Guidelines

It is also important for you to set general guidelines for the use of the family car. Teenagers must be told to plan for when they wish to use the car. They cannot expect to have it available at a moment's notice. They should also be expected to assume some family driving chores: for example, chauffeuring their younger brothers and sisters, shopping, and picking up elderly relatives. Parents, on the other hand, must be sensitive to teenagers' needs and obligations. They should try not to go back on a promise made to the teenager about when he can use the car.

Most teenagers *are* responsible drivers. The formation of SADD (Students Against Driving Drunk) is just one example of their sense of responsibility. Nevertheless, a few kids do abuse their driving privileges. They may take too many other young people in the car, drive recklessly, or drink and drive. If a teenager abuses the right to drive, he should be grounded, quickly and firmly. How long a young person's driving privileges are suspended will depend upon just how reckless he has been. Teenagers must learn that along with the freedom to drive comes responsibility.

On the other hand, it is important for us as parents not to overreact if a responsible teenager gets a ticket or has a minor accident. More often than not, this is much more frightening to the youngster than to us and will teach him to be more cautious in the future. Driving a car is part of modern adult life, and teenagers who drive responsibly are accepting some of the conditions of being an adult. Although it may be sad for us to see them grow up so soon, it is also a relief to surrender the job of chauffeuring them around.

Word count: 527

13. FAMILY PET: FOR THE BIRDS
by Sheldon L. Gerstenfeld, V.M.D.
from *Parents*

Teaching a child about nature and animals need not require a great deal of money and time. A bird feeder can be installed quite easily. The author describes the process in this article.

suet	"Or drill several large holes, at one-inch intervals, in a log for **suet** and birdseed." *Meaning:* white beef fat
predators	"And be sure that trees, bushes, or other cover is available to protect the birds from **predators** and inclement weather. *Meaning:* animals that live by eating other animals
inclement weather	"...protect the birds from predators and **inclement weather**." *Meaning:* bad weather

---

When it comes to learning about nature, your children's own backyard or windowsill may be their most valuable study aid. By installing a bird feeder this autumn, you can provide your family with a unique glimpse at some of nature's most beautiful creatures.

Easy Ways to Start

Bird feeders and other supplies can be purchased at hardware stores and garden centers. Or you and your children may decide that you want to make your own feeder. Remember: Whether you decide to make a feeder or to buy one, the most important feature is that it keeps the seeds dry. If you'd like to place one right outside your children's window, mount a shallow tray or horizontal board on the windowsill, and then drill drainage holes for rain.

Another easy method of making a feeder is to hang a large plastic bottle, right side up, from a backyard tree. Cut a hole in the side of the bottle about two inches from the bottom. Birds can perch on the edge of the hole to feed on the seeds you've generously stored in the bottom. The size of the hole will determine to some extent the size of your visitors. Or drill several large holes, at one-inch intervals, in a log for suet and birdseed. Hang the log from a tree and wait for your guests.

Finding the Right Spot

Place the feeder so that it is visible from a window where your children can watch the birds feed without disturbing them. And be sure that trees, bushes, or other cover is available to protect the birds from predators and inclement weather.

To find the best location for your feeder, have your children note where the birds land when they first arrive. Where do they fly when disturbed? Where do they spend most of their time? Several small feeders will prevent overcrowding or domination by one or two large birds. Many birds are primarily ground feeders, so sprinkle the area around the feeder with seeds too.

Selecting the Proper Cuisine

Wild-birdseed mixture is the least expensive and most widely available blend. It is usually cheaper when purchased in large quantities from seed stores rather than in small quantities at grocery stores. Sunflower seeds will attract cardinals, titmice, chickadees, house finches, and nuthatches. Finches also flip for a delicacy called Niger seeds, whereas insect eaters, such as woodpeckers, prefer suet—the dry, white, hard beef fat available from your butcher. As a treat, put a suet-peanut butter or suet-cheese spread mixture in your feeder.

Unwelcome Visitors

There are a few creatures other than birds that might want to stop by for a bite. Although hanging your feeder from a tree will discourage field mice and other earthbound rodents from feeding, you will need to buy devices to foil squirrels, chipmunks, and other "social climbers." On the other hand, chipmunks, squirrels, and other creatures can also be enjoyable subjects for study, and you may decide to welcome them.

Don't be discouraged if your feeder isn't an instant hit with the neighborhood flock. Your guests may take a couple of weeks to accept the feeder. Once they do, be a considerate host—remember that after you've attracted birds to your feeder, they will come to depend on your generosity. Don't allow the seeds to pile up and get moldy. Sprinkle fresh seeds when necessary.

Enjoying the Birds

Feeding birds is an inexpensive and educational activity for the entire family. You may want to take pictures and start a nature photo album. Read up on birds. My favorite books are *The Audubon Society Field Guide to North American Birds* (Knopf), all of Roger Tory Peterson's field guides (Houghton Mifflin), and *The Backyard Bird Watcher: The Classic Guide to Enjoying Wild Birds Outside Your Back Door*, by George H. Harrison (Simon and Schuster). Most important, don't forget the peace of simply bird-watching.

Word count: 650

14. YOUR CHILD'S SELF-ESTEEM
by Lilian G. Katz
from *Parents*

> Self-esteem, the liking or acceptance of ourselves as we are, is recognized today as extremely important for mental health and achievement. The author of this article suggests some ways to develop and improve self-esteem in children.
>
> **dilemma**   "With an eye toward helping parents with this **dilemma**..."
> *Meaning:* puzzle; difficult decision
>
> **optimum**   "...the **optimum** level of self-esteem seems to be..."
> *Meaning:* ideal; best
>
> **fluctuations**   "...the normal **fluctuations** in feelings of confidence, pride and competence."
> *Meaning:* variations; ups and downs

The idea that children should feel good about themselves is, remarkably, a relatively modern one. Only one or two generations ago, praise was withheld from children for fear that youngsters might become conceited or "swell-headed." These days, however, it often seems that we err to the other extreme, and many children are in danger of becoming too self-conscious and eager for praise.

It's not so difficult to understand how praising a child's efforts can positively affect his self-esteem, and parents may need little guidance in this regard. But parents may be less clear about how they can affect a child's feelings about himself in other ways. With an eye toward helping parents with this dilemma, I've outlined some ideas below that you may want to consider as you think about developing a healthy sense of self-esteem in your children.

An individual's self-esteem is the result of evaluations by one's self and others. For young children, the greatest influences on self-esteem—high and low—are others' evaluations, especially those of people closest to the child. The basis for self-esteem in childhood is the feeling of being loved and accepted, particularly by someone the child can look up to. This is one reason that parental support means so much to children and has such an extraordinary effect on their self-esteem.

Remember that it is not desirable to have excessive self-esteem. Indeed, an excessively high degree of self-esteem, confidence, or assurance might cause a person to be insensitive to others' reactions and feelings about him. Though it is difficult to know precisely where the level is, the optimum level of self-esteem seems to be that which allows for the normal fluctuations in feelings of confidence, pride, and competence. The actual complexities of life are sufficient that all children (and adults) encounter situations in which it is realistic to have little confidence, hurt pride, or insufficient competence. Children can be helped by adults to accept the fact that such difficult situations are inevitable. They are also temporary, and in the scheme of things, they are only a small portion of the range of experiences they'll have in life.

Self-esteem varies from one interpersonal situation to another. Children do not have to be accepted or loved by everyone they encounter. Parents can help a child cope with occasions of rejection or indifference by reassuring her that Mom's and Dad's own acceptance of the youngster has not been shaken.

Self-esteem is not acquired all at once early in life to last forever and be present in all situations. A child may feel confident and accepted at home but the opposite in the neighborhood or preschool. Adults can generally avoid those situations in which their self-esteem is likely to take a beating, but children are limited to situations adults provide for them. They have few skills or resources for avoiding situations in which their self-assurance will be threatened. Parents should be aware that in some instances inappropriate behavior on the part of their child may be a signal that the child perceives the particular circumstance as threatening to his self-confidence.

Self-esteem is measured against certain criteria, typically acquired within the family. The criteria against which we are evaluated vary among families, ethnic groups, and neighborhoods. They also vary for boys and girls—more so in some communities than in others. In some families or groups esteem is based on physical beauty, in others on intelligence, athleticism, or toughness. Your child will need help in meeting your standards on those criteria. Whatever criteria for being an acceptable person make sense in your family, support your child's effort to meet them, but reassure her that, no matter what, she is loved and always belongs to the family.

Word count: 635

15. SCHOOL AGE PARENTS: THE CHALLENGE OF THREE-GENERATION LIVING
by Jeanne Warren Lindsay
an excerpt from the book of the same name
from *Forecast*

> Every hour of every day, 116 American teenagers become pregnant. That is 2,795 teenagers each day, one million each year. The author describes how parents and grandparents cope with the demands of child rearing.
>
> **drastic**   "There is no way to have a baby in the house without **drastic** changes occurring..."
> *Meaning:* major; large; severe
>
> **three-generational family**   "Practical tasks must be considered for the **three-generational** family."
> *Meaning:* family consisting of grandparent, parent, and child.

For parents of pregnant and parenting teenagers, the term "grandparents-too-soon" is an apt description. Mother is more likely to be single than married, and she probably is not yet financially or emotionally ready to live by herself and take full responsibility for her child.

If an unmarried teenage mother chooses to parent her child, her parents are likely to be deeply involved. There is no way to have a baby in the house without drastic changes occurring in that house.

Fewer than 40 percent of teenage mothers are married to the fathers of their babies by the time of childbirth.

If the baby's father is no longer involved with the young mother, decisions must still be made concerning his contact with the baby and the financial support he will provide. If an adoption plan is made, his signature is needed for the adoption papers.

Generally, the marriage decision should be made as separately from the pregnancy as possible. Many pregnant teens have wisely told me, "Getting married because I'm pregnant wouldn't work. Two wrongs don't make a right."

This can be a difficult concept for parents who feel strongly that marriage is a necessary part of having children.

Practical tasks must be considered for the three-generational family. If adoption is not the choice, where will the baby sleep? Will the young mother breastfeed or bottle feed? Will she continue in school? Is there child care at her school? Must she get a job to support her baby?

Who will actually care for the baby—get up at night, feed him, change him, rock him? Most of us would agree that ideally the young parent will take care of the child. She needs to bond with her child, and the child needs to be very sure exactly which woman in the household is her mother and which one is the grandmother.

Young parents and their parents need to communicate their needs clearly to each other. Preferably before the baby is born, they need to talk about how much babysitting the grandparents are willing to do. Will the teen parent go out every Friday night and expect her parents to babysit?

Working out agreements with each family member as to who does which household tasks would be helpful for most families. In fact, an informal written contract developed before the baby is born could prevent some unpleasantness later.

Will the young mother continue to do her share of non-baby-related tasks such as vacuuming, dusting, cooking, cleaning the kitchen, and handling clutter in the family areas?

Resentment surfaced again and again as parents talked about their frustrations with daughters who left diapers and bottles in the living room and toys all over the house. This is the kind of day-to-day resentment that can build into much bigger problems.

While consideration of the child's emotional, psychological, and physical needs is of primary importance in all parenting issues, there are widely varying, but still appropriate methods of dealing with these issues. Grandparents and teen parents need to remember that more than one way of dealing with a child may be all right. Generally, consistency in child rearing is better for the child, and if the grandparents can respect the young parent's wishes in matters of discipline, feeding, sleep, etc., the child will probably be the winner.

"I thought my life was over." It's a common refrain from teenage mothers—and their parents. For many women, pregnant before 18, life will be a series of hardships, a life of poverty, of attempts to cope with too many children and too few resources. But it doesn't have to be this way.

Some teenage mothers, while actively parenting their children, finish high school, go on to college or job training, then get a job. They may marry their child's father when the time seems right, or they may marry someone else, or they may remain single. The important fact is that teenage mothers can lead happy, fulfilling lives.

Word count: 665

16. DEALING WITH THE ANGRY CHILD
from a National Institute of Mental Health pamphlet

> Specific suggestions for handling aggressive and angry behaviors in children are explored in this article. The goal is to accept and channel the emotions rather than suppress them.
>
> **defiance**   "Angry **defiance** may also be associated with feelings of dependency..."
> *Meaning:* resistance or challenge; lack of cooperation
>
> **impulsive**   "...or other **impulsive** show of affection."
> *Meaning:* not thought out; based on feeling
>
> **sarcasm**   "However, it is important to distinguish between face-saving humor and **sarcasm** or teasing ridicule."
> *Meaning:* mocking, often by saying the opposite of what is meant
>
> **conscientiousness**   "Good discipline includes creating an atmosphere of quiet firmness, clarity, and **conscientiousness**..."
> *Meaning:* state of being careful and thinking out one's responses

Handling children's anger can be puzzling, draining, and distressing for adults. In fact, one of the major problems in dealing with anger in children is the angry feelings that are often stirred up in us. It has been said that we as parents, teachers, counselors, and administrators need to remind ourselves that we were not always taught how to deal with anger as a fact of life during our own childhood. We were led to believe that to be angry was to be bad, and we were often made to feel guilty for expressing anger.

It will be easier to deal with children's anger if we get rid of this notion. Our goal is not to repress or destroy angry feelings in children—or in ourselves—but rather to accept the feelings and to help channel and direct them to constructive ends.

Parents and teachers must allow children to feel *all* their feelings. Adult skills can then be directed toward showing children acceptable ways of expressing their feelings. Strong feelings cannot be denied, and angry outbursts should not always be viewed as a sign of serious problems; they should be recognized and treated with respect.

To respond effectively to overly aggressive behavior in children we need to have some ideas about what may have triggered an outburst. Anger may be a defense to avoid painful feelings; it may be associated with failure, low self-esteem, and feelings of isolation; or it may be related to anxiety about situations over which the child has no control.

Angry defiance may also be associated with feelings of dependency, and anger may be associated with sadness and depression. In childhood, anger and sadness are very close to one another and it is important to remember that much of what an adult experiences as sadness is expressed by a child as anger.

Before we look at specific ways to manage aggressive and angry outbursts, several points should be highlighted:

• We should distinguish between anger and aggression. Anger is a temporary emotional state caused by frustration; aggression is often an attempt to hurt a person or to destroy property.

• Anger and aggression do not have to be dirty words. In other words, in looking at aggressive behavior in children, we must be careful to distinguish between behavior that indicates emotional problems and behavior that is normal.

In dealing with angry children, other actions should be motivated by the need to protect and to teach, not by a desire to punish. Parents and teachers should show a child that they accept his or her feelings, while suggesting other ways to express the feelings. An adult might say, for example, "Let me tell you what some children would do in a situation like this...." It is not enough to tell children what behaviors we find unacceptable. We must teach them acceptable ways of coping. Also, ways must be found to communicate what we expect of them. Contrary to popular opinion, punishment is not the most effective way to communicate to children what we expect of them.

Responding to the Angry Child

Some of the following suggestions for dealing with the angry child were taken from *The Aggressive Child* by Fritz Redl and David Wineman. They should be considered helpful ideas and not be seen as a "bag of tricks."

Catch the child being good. Tell the child what behaviors please you. Respond to positive efforts and reinforce good behavior. An observing and sensitive parent will find countless opportunities during the day to make such comments as, "I like the way you come in for dinner without being reminded"; "I appreciate your hanging up your clothes even though you were in a hurry to get out to play"; "You were really patient while I was on the phone"; "I'm glad you shared your snack with your sister"; "I like the way you're able to think of others"; and "Thank you for telling the truth about what really happened."

Similarly, teachers can positively reinforce good behavior with statements like, "I know it was difficult for you to wait your turn, and I'm pleased that you could do it"; "Thanks for sitting in your seat quietly"; "You were thoughtful in offering to help Johnny with his spelling"; "You worked hard on that project, and I admire your effort."

Deliberately ignore inappropriate behavior that can be tolerated. This doesn't mean that you should ignore the child, just the behavior. The "ignoring" has to be planned and consistent. Even though this behavior may be tolerated, the child must recognize that it is inappropriate.

Provide physical outlets and other alternatives. It is important for children to have opportunities for physical exercise and movement, both at home and at school.

Manipulate the surroundings. Aggressive behavior can be encouraged by placing children in tough, tempting situations. We should try to plan the surroundings so that certain things are less apt to happen. Stop a "problem" activity and substitute, temporarily, a more desirable one. Sometimes rules and regulations, as well as physical space, may be too confining.

Use closeness and touching. Move physically closer to the child to curb his or her angry impulse. Young children are often calmed by having an adult nearby.

Express interest in the child's activities. Children naturally try to involve adults in what they are doing, and the adult is often annoyed at being bothered. Very young children (and children who are emotionally deprived) seem to need much more adult involvement in their interests. A child about to use a toy or tool in a destructive way is sometimes easily stopped by an adult who expresses interest in having it shown to him. An outburst from a older child struggling with a difficult reading selection can be prevented by a caring adult who moves near the child to say, "Show me which words are giving you trouble."

Be ready to show affection. Sometimes all that is needed for any angry child to regain control is a sudden hug or other impulsive show of affection. Children with serious emotional problems, however, may have trouble accepting affection.

Ease tension through humor. Kidding the child out of a temper tantrum or outburst offers the child an opportunity to "save face." However, it is important to distinguish between face-saving humor and sarcasm or teasing ridicule.

Appeal directly to the child. Tell him or her how you feel and ask for consideration. For example, a parent or teacher may gain a child's cooperation by saying, "I know that noise you're making doesn't usually bother me, but today I've got a headache, so could you find something else you'd enjoy doing?"

Explain situations. Help the child understand the cause of a stressful situation. We often fail to realize how easily young children can begin to react properly once they understand the cause of their frustration.

Use physical restraint. Occasionally a child may lose control so completely that he has to be physically restrained or removed from the scene to prevent him from hurting himself or others. This may also "save face" for the child. Physical restraint or removal from the scene should not be viewed by the child as punishment but as a means of saying, "You can't do that." In such situations, an adult cannot afford to lose his or her temper, and unfriendly remarks by other children should not be tolerated.

Encourage children to see their strengths as well as their weaknesses. Help them to see that they can reach their goals.

Use promises and rewards. Promises of future pleasure can be used both to start and to stop behavior. This approach should not be compared with bribery. We must know what the child likes—what brings him pleasure—and we must deliver on our promises.

Say "NO!" Limits should be clearly explained and enforced. Children should be free to function within those limits.

Tell the child that you accept his or her angry feelings, but offer other suggestions for expressing them. Teach children to put their angry feelings into words, rather than fists.

Build a positive self-image. Encourage children to see themselves as valued and valuable people.

Use punishment cautiously. There is a fine line between punishment that is hostile toward a child and punishment that is educational.

Model appropriate behavior. Parents and teachers should be aware of the powerful influence of their actions on a child's or group's behavior.

Teach children to express themselves verbally. Talking helps a child have control and thus reduces acting out behavior. Encourage the child to say, for example, "I don't like your taking my pencil. I don't feel like sharing just now."

The Role of Discipline

Good discipline includes creating an atmosphere of quiet firmness, clarity, and conscientiousness, while using reasoning. Bad discipline involves punishment which is unduly harsh and inappropriate, and it is often associated with verbal ridicule and attacks on the child's integrity.

As one fourth grade teacher put it: "One of the most important goals we strive for as parents, educators, and mental health professionals is to help children develop respect for themselves and others." While arriving at this goal takes years of patient practice, it is a vital process in which parents, teachers, and all caring adults can play a crucial and exciting role. In order to accomplish this, we must see children as worthy human beings and be sincere in dealing with them.

Word count: 1562

17. THE END OF INNOCENCE
by Nina Darton
from *Newsweek*

The author suggests that many youngsters are being robbed of childhood by being exposed too early to the "secrets" of adulthood.

sophistication   "Our preadolescent's level of sexual **sophistication** is high..."
Meaning: awareness

nostalgic   "...is becoming a **nostalgic** luxury..."
Meaning: longing for the past

assimilate   "...in stages so they could **assimilate** them."
Meaning: to absorb or digest

venality   "...children have full access to the **venality**, incompetence, errors and corruption of adults."
Meaning: openness to bribery or corruption

promiscuously   "They are not behaving **promiscuously**..."
Meaning: in a casual, random manner

vamps   "The teenage **vamps** on the soaps..."
Meaning: women who plot to seduce men

vet   "The choice is ours whether we attempt to help children vet what they hear..."
Meaning: check accuracy of; verify

innate   "...let their **innate** and very strong sexual impulses make sense of it for themselves."
Meaning: inborn; natural; not acquired

intuitively   "Most parents know this **intuitively**—"
Meaning: naturally; without thinking

repercussions   "...deal with the different aspects and **repercussions** of sex."
Meaning: indirect effects

vigilant   "It's the parents who need to be more **vigilant**."
Meaning: watchful; aware

cognitive   "...children's language ability far outstrips their **cognitive** ability."
Meaning: ability to know or comprehend

A 16-year-old Houston girl was baby-sitting for two boys, 6 and 9 years old. The kids were glued to the George Michael "I Want Your Sex" video on MTV. Singing along, the boys came to the words "sex with you alone." The younger one looked a little puzzled. "What's that thing when it isn't alone, when lots of people do it?" he asked. "A borney?" "No, his brother shot back contemptuously. "You're so dumb. It's an orgy." Even the babysitter—who thinks of herself as "pretty sexy," has already "had sex" with one boyfriend and "fooled around" with several others—was shocked. "At that age, I never even heard of anything like that," she said. "I didn't know about that stuff until at least sixth grade."

Parents who probably never learned about "that stuff" until considerably later might be taken aback, but sexual awareness is no longer a sign of the end of childhood. Long before kids reach puberty, they know a lot more about sex than children did 25 years ago. How could they avoid it? They watch sex slaves interviewed on "Geraldo," sing along to "Me So Horny" on the radio, and go in droves to see movies like "Pretty Woman," last year's blockbuster about sex for sale. "Our pre-adolescent's level of sexual sophistication is high because of the world kids are living in and the tremendous access they have to that world," says Debra Haffner, executive director of the Sex Information and Education Council of the United States. "In the '50s, Donna Reed didn't sleep in the same bed with her husband. A recent 'Cosby' show was about menopause; it ended with the parents making love."

One reason children know more about sex these days is that we want them to. Today's parents believe that innocence can be dangerous. The idea of childhood as a sheltered time, free from adult anxieties, is becoming a nostalgic memory in a world where young people die of AIDS and TV newscasts are filled with stories of child-pornography rings, kidnappings, and the sorrowful faces of abused children. Parents feel the need to arm their kids with more information. As writer Marie Winn points out in her book *Children Without Childhood*, "The Age of Protection has ended. An Age of Preparation has set in."

Many parents now see protection as an impossible goal. As a result of profound societal changes over the past 25 years, parents are simply not as available as they used to be. Most mothers aren't home when their children return from school and can't exert day-to-day control over their children's friends and activities. Single parents, lonely and under stress, often use their children as confidants, making children partners in their own upbringing.

Psychologists say that the result is the breakdown of authority and a loss of faith among children in the wisdom of the adult world. Neil Postman, professor of communications at New York University, believes that many children are robbed of their childhood by being exposed too early to the "secrets" of adulthood—death, illness, violence, sexuality. In the past, he says, children learned these concepts in stages so they could assimilate them. "Now, because of the nature of the electronic media, children have full access to the venality, incompetence, errors and corruption of adults," Postman says. It might be more from necessity than from choice, but modern parents are changing their concept of childhood—and the children are bearing the burden.

Experts say that kids are about two to three years ahead of their counterparts a quarter of a century ago. According to child psychologist David Elkind, recent studies show that 50 percent of 15-year-old girls have had sexual intercourse, as compared with 10 percent in the 1960s. Another study reported that, by the time they were 13, 20 percent of boys had touched a girl's breasts. Dating, which used to begin with adolescence, now often starts a couple of years earlier. Jeffrey, a 13-year-old eighth grader from Long Island, said that of his group of five friends, two are already sleeping with their girlfriends. They are not behaving promiscuously, he states, since these are "long term" relationships— each having lasted for "at least one month."

The sexual acceleration starts early and holds throughout adolescence. A 3-year-old who no longer holds her mother's hand becomes a 6-year old more interested in MTV than in Bambi and a 9-year-old who can discuss homosexuality, AIDS and transexual surgery. Many of these children seem to miss out on their childhood altogether. Kim, a teenager from Phoenix, says her father left her mother for another woman when Kim was 8. "My mother came to me crying and told me everything," Kim says. "It kind of made me uncomfortable and sometimes I kind of felt responsible for her problems too." Kim says she views her mother as her friend. But it's an unequal friendship—a distorted image of the mother-daughter relationship of times past. "I can't tell her lots of stuff because she's too naive," Kim says.

Some observers argue that kids are more sexually advanced for physiological reasons. The average age of menarche (a girl's first period) has gradually lowered from about 14 a century ago to 12.5, and earlier puberty naturally arouses earlier curiosity and sexual exploration. But, as psychologist Elkind points out, the physical acceleration—mostly attributed to better nutrition—was recorded more than a decade ago and hasn't changed since. Today's behavior, he believes, has sociological roots. The children are reflecting a general change in adult values, including a wider acceptance of casual sex, that is reinforced by movies and television. "The teenage vamps on the soaps, the sexually active teenagers in 'Married With Children,' these are a far cry from the Brady Bunch," says Elkind. Many psychologists point out that not all the changes are negative—denial of sexuality is also unhealthy—but that we seem to have swung to the opposite extreme.

American children receive mixed messages about sex. In spite of a more relaxed sexual morality in society, Americans are generally still embarrassed to discuss sex with their children. Traditionally, Americans have left sex education to the family, which often meant that kids learned about sex from each other long before either parent sat down for that birds-and-bees conversation.

Frightened by the prospect of AIDS, parents and educators pressed the schools for help. They were partly successful. In 1980 only three states and the District of Columbia required sex education in public schools. Today 21 states mandate sex education, and 33 states require AIDS education. A 1988 Planned Parenthood poll found that 85 percent of American parents favor some form of sexual education between kindergarten and 12 grade. "To live in the 1990s is to live in a world that is filled with sexual information," says Cathleen Rea, a clinical child psychologist in Newport News, Virginia. The choice is ours whether we attempt to help children vet what they hear or whether we let their innate and very strong sexual impulses make sense of it for themselves.

But children don't need to learn everything all at once. In their zeal to prepare their children, some parents are telling them more than they can assimilate. Anne Bernstein, author of *The Flight of the Stork: What Children Really Want to Know About Sex and How to Tell Them*, tells a joke to illustrate the point. A young boy asks: "Mom, where did Billy next door come from?" The mother launches into a tortuous tale of human sexual response and reproduction. "Oh," replies the puzzled child. "I heard he was from Detroit."

Bernstein suggests that a child can understand only as much about sex as he or she is developmentally capable of grasping at a certain age—no matter how much information is doled out. "Different information will be taken in at different times and have different meanings at different times," says Bernstein, a clinical psychologist in Berkeley, California. Most parents know this intuitively—all they have to do is watch an 8-year-old during the kissing scenes in a movie. "Ugh" is the usual response. By 12, however, children are more able to deal with the different aspects and repercussions of sex, Bernstein says.

Maybe parents worry too much about preparing their children for danger and not enough about their responsibility for protecting them. Elkind believes it is important to teach young children basic facts about their bodies, but parents shouldn't pass on their own anxieties about sexual dangers by telling their children too much too early. Preparing kids, Elkind says, should not be an attempt to shift responsibility for their well-being from the parents to the children. "Some programs that prepare children to deal with child abuse might give the implicit message that it's the children's job to protect themselves," he says. "Children then feel guilty if something happens. It's the parents who need to be more vigilant."

Being vigilant is more than protecting a child from sexual abuse. It means monitoring TV as much as possible and trying to preserve for young children a few precious years of innocence. Psychologists say that the period from 9 to 12 is very important for developing same-sex friendships that prepare children for later heterosexual relationships. A strong sense of privacy emerges in the preteen years, and children begin sharing confidences with friends with whom they feel comfortable. It's easier to do that with people who are more like them and less mysterious than members of the opposite sex. By sharing intimacies with "chums," children prepare themselves for later intimacy with the opposite sex.

When children start dating at 10, they skip the "chum-ship" stage—a gap that research shows doesn't bode well for later relationships.

Still children remain more innocent than they appear. "It is vital to remember," Elkind says, "that children's language ability far outstrips their cognitive ability." A recent incident illustrates his point. An 8-year-old told his mother that he had attended an AIDS project at school. She asked him what he had learned and he replied authoritatively: "Oh, that's easy. Don't have intersections and buy condominiums."

Word count: 1682

4. ANIMALS

"A dog is a man's best friend," someone once observed. Others would say the same thing about their cats or birds or hamsters.

However, not all animals are pets. Many are still living in the wilds, some are in zoos, and still others are used for scientific research. There is particular controversy today surrounding the use of animals for scientific research. Some think animal research is in the interest of both man and animal; others claim that such research is cruel.

In this section you will read about a very special pet dog, animals and fish that may not exist except in legends and myths, and the benefit of zoos.

18. WHEN ANIMALS OPEN WIDE
by Catherine Cremer
from *International Wildlife*

What does a yawn mean? Fatigue? Possibly, but for many animals it is only one of many reasons.

lethargic   "...rushes blood to **lethargic** muscles..."
Meaning: sluggish

ominously   "Many bears and wolves **ominously** bare their teeth before an attack."
Meaning: threateningly

ensues   "The thrashing combat which **ensues**..."
Meaning: follows

estrus   "...female in **estrus**..."
Meaning: period of sexual excitement; in heat

ponderous   "...some crocodiles will spread their **ponderous** jaws..."
Meaning: massive, huge

In the stifling heat of a summer afternoon in Kenya's Masai Marca Game Reserve, a panting lioness rests in the sparse shade of an acacia tree. Flies buzz around the big animal's eyes as she stretches, then opens her jaws, baring a cavern of tongue and teeth. The Queen of Beasts has yawned.

Javelinas do it, birds do it. So do turtles, hyenas and people. Yawning is a reflex action which starts a fatigued body percolating again. But things aren't always what they seem. In fact, the conventional yawn is only one of many open-mouth behaviors. When an animal opens wide, it may actually be courting or threatening, warning or keeping order. A creature that appears tired may really be communicating anything from "I'm boss" to "Watch out."

In the usual sense, though, a yawn occurs when breathing slows down because of fatigue, inactivity or sleep. The sudden intake of air sends oxygenated blood to the heart. The heart, in turn, rushes blood to lethargic muscles, reviving a sluggish system. To further invigorate itself, an animal may stretch by arching its back and extending its legs. During sleep or inactivity, carbon dioxide builds up the blood, and a stretch squeezes veins and the lymphatic system, speeding up the blood's trip to the heart for reoxygenation.

Javelinas are a case in point. Their yawns help to rejuvenate them after resting spells. According to Jerry Day, a research biologist with the Arizona Game and Fish Department, the creatures emit wide, gaping yawns nearly every time they leave the shallow depressions, or bed grounds, in the desert where they sleep. This gears them up for more active hours ahead.

One form of open-mouth display that looks like a yawn but isn't has more to do with aggression than with "tired blood." Often, the seriousness of the situation is underscored by a growl or roar. In territorial or other disagreements, a facial threat can communicate a hostile message and make the creature look more dangerous to its opponent. Lizards and fish commonly threaten intruders with open mouths. Many bears and wolves ominously bare their teeth before an attack.

One of the most spectacular displays of this type comes when hippopotamuses engage in territorial battles. Standing head-to-head with an intruder, the hippo delivers an enormous, toothy show of hostility. Oversized canine teeth up to two feet long are flashed. The thrashing combat which ensues may last up to several hours. The hippos attempt to slash one another until the issue is settled—usually without permanent injury to either combatant.

Another reason for "threat yawning" is the establishment of pecking orders among animal groups. A classic example is the baboon, which, upon the slightest provocation, displays one of the most awesome arrays of sharp pointed teeth this side of the great white shark in the movie *Jaws*. Predictably, lesser members of the group beat a hasty retreat. According to John Fletemeyer of Nova University in Florida, the baboon's exposed teeth ensure dominance when a choice food patch or female in estrus is at stake. "The yawn constitutes a higher-level threat than a raised eyebrow or a stare," explains Fletemeyer, who studied the interactions of these highly social creatures. Yawnlike expressions can also serve to maintain order. "Lions will use a yawn to calm tensions within a group by redirecting aggression to some other context or mood," says Randall Eaton, a professor of animal behavior at Western Wyoming College. When a lioness returns to the pride with her six-to-eight week old babies, she is nervous about protecting them from males. In order to distract potential aggressors, she and other nearby females will yawn frequently, almost in unison.

A number of mammals, fish, and other animals open wide to invite parasitic creatures in for a "free meal." For example, some crocodiles will spread their ponderous jaws, which allows certain birds to dine on the food left on the big reptiles' teeth. Because crocs can't move their tongues efficiently to clean their teeth themselves, this practice turns out to be a mutually beneficial arrangement.

Courtship is still another reason for "yawning"—but presumably not out of boredom. It's not too uncommon among birds, such as when two Adelie penguins woo by facing each other, beaks parted and pointed majestically toward the sky, in their aptly named "ecstatic display."

It's no wonder that animals, with so many different types of yawns at their disposal, have evolved some fascinating ways of making their messages perfectly clear. A zebra will open its mouth wider and wider as its message becomes more intense. If its ears are laid back onto its head, the message is a hostile one. But if the ears are pointed upward, the message is simply a greeting to another zebra. And when a lion stretches its jaws, its motives are unmistakable—at least to another lion or a trained human observer. Researcher Randall Eaton explains that a lion's reflex yawn almost always has the following characteristics: the eyes are closed, the head is lifted up and back, the ears are in the normal position or laid back, and the tongue covers the floor of the mouth and lower canines. On the other hand, a snarl is easily distinguished: the cat simultaneously wrinkles its muzzle, retracts its tongue and growls.

Sometimes, it pays to hide an innocent yawn, lest it be misinterpreted as a hostile gesture. Lions, baboons and other creatures that live in groups have perfected the technique. "If an animal seems concerned about its yawn being perceived as a threat," says lion researcher Eaton, "it can look away, or it can yawn without exposing its teeth by covering them with its lips." Eaton says that, when yawning, lower-ranking lions often turn their heads from higher-ranking ones.

Therein, perhaps in our own distant past, may well lie the primal reason why a human versed in the social graces will try to stifle a yawn or delicately raise a hand to mask it and his own weariness—or boredom.

Word count: 1008

19. OPEN FOR SOURDOUGH, PLEASE
by Eileen and Darwin Lambert
from *Reader's Digest*

> Did you ever have a special pet? Do you have one now? At times, do you feel your pet is almost human? If you have never owned one, perhaps this story will shed light on the reasons why man has kept pets since prehistoric times.
>
> **gleaning**   "...even **gleaning** fallen seeds beside him..."
> *Meaning:* collecting, picking up what has fallen
>
> **suet**   "...supplemented by **suet** tied on a tree branch..."
> *Meaning:* a hard fatty tissue around the loins and kidneys of the ox, sheep, etc., used in cooking

The farmer who took care of lost or unwanted dogs for the rural Virginia county gave us two strangers a friendly welcome. We told him we had a vacancy that only a special dog would fill. We'd moved into an isolated mountain place, where we planned to raise our own food and make the rest of our living by writing about nature. The right dog, we hoped, could guard our garden and young fruit trees, announcing intruders yet not chase away the wild creatures we wanted to study and photograph.

"Tough job," the farmer said as he led us to a fence in back of his house. An eager assortment of dogs came crowding and whining, and he began speculating on their qualifications. He did not mention the longhaired puppy standing aloof farther back. The puppy, maybe ten weeks old, began walking toward the gate with a certain dignity.

We felt pulled toward the gate and we reached it at the same time the puppy did. One of us picked the puppy up. His big, brown eyes held ours. Those wise eyes, plus a hint of yeasty milk in the rich puppy smell, suggested the name Sourdough.

"You're our dog, aren't you, Sourdough?" one of us said. The tail wagged agreement.

Settling In

We showed Sourdough around our three-acre clearing and the brambly orchard. He moved ahead in short rushes but returned often to give us nose touches. This doggy habit of following out front would last through his energetic years, except when we insisted that he heel.

The high time of Sourdough's day became the walk through the woods to our mailbox, a mile down-hollow. His adventuring helped show us many wild creatures—woodchuck, wood rat, snake, even beaver. Rabbits mystified him. He rushed after them with high-pitched yelps, promptly lost them, and then spy-hopped trying to find them again. Once, when he left the road we heard a startled "oops" and he came back smelling distinctly unlike a rose.

The oak rocking chair between kitchen and dining room became the petting chair. Anybody sitting there could expect a suggestive nose-nudge from Sourdough. If he failed to get a petting, he'd walk toward the door, always with such dignified faith that the nearest person felt honored to open it for him. When ready at last to come in, he'd start that confident walk toward the door, and one of us would be there to welcome him. We tried to persuade him to give a yip when he wanted in or out, but he steadfastly declined. His silent method worked. Why change?

One favorite lie-down place was beside the bird feeder. We told him, "No, Sourdough. This is the birds' place." He wouldn't stop lying by the feeder, but he didn't totally defy our wishes. His solution was to ignore the birds completely. When we realized the birds were ignoring him, coming and feeding, even gleaning fallen seeds beside him, we had to agree that he'd won the argument.

His dense fur glowed like silk, and kept growing deeper and harder to untangle. He was black above, red-gold below, white on the chest. At maturity he weighed 60 pounds. He played hide-and-seek with our kitten, and once let her persuade him to catch a meadow mouse. When he realized he'd killed it with his teeth, he dropped it instantly as if ashamed. His responsibilities grew too heavy for frivolous play, but he continued to enjoy the cat's walking massage along his spine and let her catnap there.

Tag With Bears

We still recall the forceful barking of his first real chase of a deer. We tapped on the kitchen window and yelled, "No, Sourdough, no!" He faltered, so we knew he had heard, but he resumed speed and disappeared into the forest.

When we got him back, we told him we wanted to watch the deer, that they were welcome to the windfalls. Only the young fruit trees we'd showed him needed his protection now. His plume of a tail at half-mast, he crawled into the house we'd built for him as if putting temptation behind him.

Yet when the deer came again, he chased it again. Our scolding got stronger and stronger; his tail drooped lower ("tail of woe," one of us called it). One chase started when we were upstairs. Window-tapping stopped him, and he slunk back toward his house. He declined dinner; all the next day he wouldn't eat.

The following day we watched him watch deer. His muscles twitched, but something held him back. The temptation, days later, won again. Hot in pursuit of a spread whitetail, he failed to see a second deer in the brambles. It leaped to follow the first—and came down with all four feet on or beside the racing dog. Although Sourdough wasn't injured, he sulked for days. He never chased deer again.

But there were bears. Despite repeated warnings that the swat of a bear's claws could kill him, he kept chasing the bears into the forest with furious barking. Some bears would turn and chase him back to the house. Then it was his turn to chase again. The contest might continue for several rounds. We came to admire Sourdough's bravery with bears, and it netted us unusual pictures.

We also loved him for his contrasting kindness with non-bears. A bowl of his food left unfinished on the lawn, supplemented by suet tied on a tree branch for birds, launched us into fruitful years of watching gray foxes, raccoons, opossums and skunks. If awake outside when such creatures came, Sourdough made his announcements softly, and then lay still—a wildlife-watcher's friend for sure. When the strain got too severe, he sneaked quietly around the house where he couldn't see.

Playing Keep-Away

In some parts of our world, our sensitive dog was reduced to groping, as we were in parts of his. When we started our gardens, he wanted to dig too. We repeatedly told him, "No. Keep out." We explained that plants are tender, that they had to grow for us to eat. He looked wise but didn't stay off. We lifted him bodily, carried him to the lawn edge and put him down firmly. After several such evictions, he slunk off hurt, tail of woe showing.

Months passed before, suddenly in a late-summer drought, heavy rabbit and deer nibbling began. When we brought Sourdough to ask his help, he wouldn't set foot or thrust nose off the lawn edge. He trembled with tension when we urged him. How could wrong, avoided for months, all at once become right?

We watched for garden bandits by day and listened at night, and we lost sleep. Once, at 2 a.m., three does stubbornly continued to chomp our Swiss chard. We woke Sourdough—"Come on now. We'll show you what we want you to do." Barking vigorously, we charged around the house and out into the garden. He watched from the house corner—embarrassed, we guess, by our lack of dignity. As for the deer, they only briefly interrupted their feeding.

Raccoons began stealing our corn. We set up our tent by the garden. Sourdough showed signs of pleasure and settled down by the tent when we slept inside of it. But when bandits came, his heavy breathing and snoring covered the sounds. He tripped us in the dark when we ran to confront a masked marvel holding an ear of corn in it paws. "Sourdough!" we yelled. "If you can't help us, go away."

He disappeared into the forest. We scolded ourselves. Hadn't he learned, at our urging, to stay out of forbidden places and to accept non-bears? Didn't he risk his life to protect us from fearful black monsters? How much could we ask? We called and searched, and at last we saw him in our flashlight's beam. We embraced him and tried to reassure him of our love. Nobody's perfect, we tried to tell him, but you're much closer than we are.

Training a Successor

In his 13th year Sourdough began falling behind, instead of leading the parade, on our walks to the mailbox. In August he declined to follow us from the yard. The vet suspected arthritis.

Sourdough still enjoyed our yard time, however. In spring he let titmice land on his back, merely rolling his eyes to check what they were, and then let them pull strands of his fur for their nests. If awake when bears came, he still chased them. But he slept deeply. Sometimes a bear would look him over, even sniffed him, and went on by.

One day while he was asleep out front, we heard crying in the woods back of the house. A German Shepherd puppy was lost, desperately hungry for cuddling and food. The puppy was a promising little guy, maybe, we guiltily half-thought, one that we'd be wanting—but not yet. How could we confront dear old Sourdough with a likely successor?

Both of us at once became aware of Sourdough approaching. Never had we knowingly failed his silent asking. We opened the door. His ears and nose led him to the puppy. The two noses touched. No sound at all from either. Sourdough's dimming eyes looked up at us. His heavy tail half-wagged.

We sought the puppy's owner, but without result. Sourdough let the pup snuggle with him. He showed no resentment when the pup started with us on the mail walk. What he couldn't do was play. He'd tolerate a few puppy nibbles, and then look to us for relief.

So we decided not to keep the pup. But before we could do anything, friends came over, bringing their husky boxer whom Sourdough had always gotten along with. Energetically curious, the boxer bowled over the puppy, who screamed in fear. Sourdough overcame his arthritis in an angry lunge that sent the boxer fleeing. He comforted the pup—his pup now—with a soothing tongue.

It soon became obvious that Sourdough was training his successor. When deer and other non-bears were suspected, master and apprentice barked the announcement together. Sourdough wouldn't let him chase. There was trouble keeping the pup out of garden plots, yet Sourdough persisted. Instant retreats from skunks and snakes were practiced.

A bear opportunity came, too, on the front lawn. Sourdough raced and roared with energy so astounding that the bear climbed the nearest tree, while the pup watched in worshipful admiration. Then, limping, but with proud dignity, Sourdough shepherded the pup back to the house. His apprentice was almost trained now.

We tried to keep Sourdough in the house when winter came, but he would continually struggle to the door. We'd open, and he'd start toward one of his forest-edge beds.

On Christmas Eve we felt him approaching the door. We opened and helped him in to his rug. For the first time in months he seemed content there, mostly sleeping but occasionally finding our eyes. He left quietly just before midnight. At the early light of Christmas dawn we buried the body beneath his favorite bed, where the bushes and vines grew tangled under a pine tree. His young successor joined us, singing a wolflike farewell to help him on his journey.

"Someone, wherever he's going," one of us whispered, "must open for him when he comes."

Word count: 1905

20. FRANK SEARLE'S PATIENT STALK OF THE BEASTIE
by Lawrence A. Cenotto
from *Tacoma News Tribune*

> Before reading "Frank Searle's Patient Stalk of the Beastie," read and think about the title. Then consider your feelings about dinosaurs and other prehistoric monsters. Did they die out long before modern man's existence? At least one man is certain that the Loch Ness Monster is alive and well in Scotland.
>
> **elusive**   "...the **elusive** creature local folk call the 'Beastie.' "
> *Meaning:* hard to understand or explain
>
> **Loch**   "...on the **Loch's** shores one-and-a-half miles from the highland capital..."
> *Meaning:* lake
>
> **silt**   "The wind and wave action whips up peat moss and **silt**..."
> *Meaning:* very fine sand
>
> **indisputable**   "...his efforts to establish **indisputable** proof of the Beastie's existence."
> *Meaning:* cannot be argued or questioned
>
> **fjords**   "...skeletons have been found in the shallow North Sea outside the Loch, and in **fjords** in Sweden, Norway..."
> *Meaning:* a long, narrow bays of the sea bordered by steep cliffs
>
> **accrues**   "...I only hope some credit **accrues** to the efforts..."
> *Meaning:* accumulates; arises as a growth or result

Sure as daffodils bloom in the spring, yet another attempt is being made to verify the existence of Scotland's Loch Ness Monster.

The Associated Press has reported that a British scientist, Adrian Shine, has recorded more than 40 sonar contacts with large living objects that could be the elusive creature local folk call the "Beastie."

Frank Searle, wherever he is, would be greatly amused.

Searle, a retired British Army Sergeant, had by the spring of 1974 accumulated over 15,000 hours on the choppy waters of Loch Ness in search of the legendary monster. His efforts had not gone unrewarded.

It was nine years ago that I met Searle while touring the Scottish Highlands. As a guest at his camp on the Loch's shores one-and-a-half miles from the highland capital of Inverness, I was fortunate to learn first-hand of his efforts to establish indisputable proof of the Beastie's existence.

About 350 days out of the year, Searle said, he would take his small motorboat onto the Loch and hunt for the "monster" film which would bring worldwide fame. His weaponry: a 35mm camera with a 400mm zoom lens. In addition, a movie camera was mounted machine-gun style on the prow of his skiff.

At the time of my visit Searle claimed to have seen the Beastie 23 times and photographed it 10 times. The closest he had ever come to her was about 400 yards. I remember asking him why, if he's seen the monster so often (only a handful claimed to have seen it more than once), he hadn't gotten more photos.

Searle laughed. "The Beastie is only out of the water for ten seconds or so at a time," he said. "When it comes up you are so dumbstruck with awe that it takes quite a presence of mind just to remember the cameras."

He described the Beastie as dinosaur-like, about 30 to 35 feet long, having an elongated neck, a pair of flippers on each side.

Had he been spending too much time at the local pubs? Searle broke out his photos.

"There's really no mystery to it," he pointed out. "This creature is a Plesiosaurus (a prehistoric reptile). Until 7,000 years ago, the Loch opened up to the North Sea. But then a volcano sealed the Loch's mouth and whatever was inside became a permanent resident." Searle added that Plesiosaurus skeletons have been found in the shallow North Sea outside the Loch, and in fjords in Sweden, Norway and the Soviet Union.

When asked whether the Loch Ness Monster Legend wasn't perhaps a good-natured local spoof meant to promote tourism, Searle stood adamantly by his theory. "If that were so, it would have to be the world's greatest ongoing conspiracy," he said. "These things have been sighted for over 1,500 years and the descriptions are always the same—even by outsiders who couldn't possibly have known how to describe it without a sighting."

Searle was quick to point out that by "things" he meant more than one Beastie. Scientists had advised, he noted, that a minimum of 16 creatures would be required to carry on the Plesiosaurus population over the last 70 centuries.

Why, then, had no living proof or Beastie remains been found to verify the legend? Searle's answer focused on the characteristics of Loch Ness, rather than the Beastie.

For one thing, he said, the Loch is notorious for "never giving up its dead." Due to its cold, deep waters and their unique chemical properties, corpses sink rather than float as in other bodies of water.

Another factor cited by Searle was that the Loch—30 miles long but only one mile wide and over 1,500 feet deep—has very limited underwater visibility.

"The wind and wave action whips up peat moss and silt on the rocky shelves off each shoreline. Divers and even Japanese mini-subs have attempted to search the Loch's depths but 30 feet below the surface you can't see a thing," he said.

Other attempts have been made to verify the monster's existence. Several years ago, underwater cameras with sonar-activated strobe lights were placed in some of the Loch's shallower areas. One of them resulted in a fairly clear photo of a massive flipper, lending substance to the Plesiosaurus theory. Another, with the aid of computer enhancement, revealed a long, curving neck attached to a small, ugly head—quite similar to Searle's description and photos.

These, and a dusty 1933 photo said by Inverness locals to show a beastie that had come ashore and trampled a man to death, are the only "monster" photos I've heard of, apart from Searle's remarkable collection.

So if the legend is shortly to be brought to light in a manner acceptable to scientist and highland locals alike, I only hope some credit accrues to the efforts and lenses of ex-Sergeant Frank Searle. Assuming he is still shadowing the monster, he has earned a unique claim to fame.

Word count: 814

21. MANY HOOKED ON TALES OF GIANT CATFISH
by John Harold Brunvand
from *The Spokesman-Review*

> John Harold Brunvand is a Utah professor who studies modern folk tales—what he calls urban legends. Examples of urban legends, Brunvand says, are "bizarre but believable stories about mice in coke bottles, spiders in hairdos, etc." In this article he writes about tales of giant catfish.
>
> **gaff** — "It was dragged into the boat with a pole and a **gaff**..."
> *Meaning*: a large, strong hook on a pole, used in landing large fish
>
> **leviathan** — "The **leviathan** catfish of American folklore..."
> *Meaning*: anything huge of its kind
>
> **reservoir** — "The divers are supposedly involved in...work on a **reservoir**."
> *Meaning*: a lake in which water is collected and stored for use
>
> **gargantuan** — "...one of these **gargantuan** fish grabs hold of a diver's leg..."
> *Meaning*: gigantic; huge
>
> **pseudotechnological** — "Add some **pseudotechnological** details..."
> *Meaning*: pretending to be scientific or mechanical
>
> **foraging** — "...lurking shapes...**foraging** for food."
> *Meaning*: searching or rummaging, especially for food

The amazing stories told about gigantic catfish living in Midwestern and Southern reservoirs are remarkably similar, and often they sound like country cousins of the urban legend about alligators in New York City's sewers. Add some pseudotechnological details about dams and turbines, and you have a modern legend—if not exactly an urban one.

Not that catfish are puny; in fact, they grow pretty darn big. The world record for an American blue or flathead catfish caught on rod and reel ran a bit over 90 pounds. The record blue recorded as "caught by any method" was a whopping 117-pound, 5-foot-3 inch monster that got itself tangled onto a troutline set in 1964 by Azel Goans of Lowry City, Mo., in the Osage River. It was dragged into the boat with a pole and gaff before it was able to drag the boat itself away.

Even more monstrous catfish species exist in Southeast Asia, and others were reported in 19th-century Europe; in both places they ran to six or eight feet long and weighed up to 400 pounds. But we are not merely telling fish stories here, ladies and gentlemen; we are looking for creatures of legend.

The leviathan catfish of American folklore—spoken of from Texas up to South Dakota and from Tennessee out to New Mexico—do more than merely grow big. They also grow mean, hungry and dangerous, especially to divers.

The divers are supposedly involved in some repair or maintenance work on a reservoir. Since the water is extremely murky at the face of the dam, the divers have to get in really close to find the cause of trouble. Then they suddenly see those huge, dim, lurking shapes moving slowly back and forth in the water, foraging for food. Giant catfish! They're as big as a dog, or a man, or a calf!

In one variation, the divers are searching for a wrecked Volkswagen Beetle in the deep water, and they approach what looks like the vehicle with its hood up. But the hood appears to be opening and closing rhythmically. Of course, it turns out upon closer inspection to be the gaping mouth of a giant catfish.

In some stories, one of these gargantuan fish grabs hold of a diver's leg or arm, but the man frantically frees himself. Both divers rush back to the surface, pale and shaking. They vow never to dive again. Overnight, their hair turns snowy white from the shock. The presence of monster catfish in reservoirs is attributed to such factors as higher water temperatures near a dam's face, or "electricity in the water" from a dam's generators, or super-rich nutrients settling out near the dam, or to the tasty minced, chopped, and sliced bodies of lesser fish mangled by the blades of the power turbines.

Super-sized catfish are an article of faith among many mid-American fishermen. And a surprising number of people who usually are more truthful than fishermen seem willing to repeat a story that no medical authority I know of has ever gone along with—that someone's hair can turn white in a single night. But it happens all the time in folklore.

For an authoritative comment, I consulted fisheries biologist Jon M. Graznak of Columbia, Missouri. Remembering giant catfish in the folklore of his native Alabama, he set out some years ago to collect as many stories about them as possible.

After talking to nearly 40 superintendents of reservoir powerhouses, most of whom had heard similar catfish tales, Graznak found that "None claimed to have firsthand knowledge, and only two had ever been in a powerhouse where any type of underwater maintenance was even required."

In all of his conversations with workers aware of diver/catfish confrontations, Graznak met only one man who claimed to have been one of the actual divers. "However," remarked Graznak, "this individual was remarkably drunk at the time, and I believe that if I had continued the conversation, he might well have claimed to be the fish."

Word count: 667

226   *Read and Respond*

22. JUST TOO BEASTLY FOR WORDS
by Jesse Birnbaum
from *Time*

Are animal zoos good because they help preserve certain species of animals, or are they cruel environments? This article presents widely differing opinions on this issue, with the author favoring properly-managed zoos.

gawkers
"...designed for the amusement of mindless **gawkers**."
Meaning: people who stare stupidly

precepts
"They are taking human moral **precepts** and trying to apply them to animals."
Meaning: laws or principles

plight
"...and even on the **plight** of laboratory animals..."
Meaning: a difficult situation

incarceration
"...**incarceration** in a penned environment..."
Meaning: locked up; jailed

Homo sapiens
"...all to provide diversion for **Homo sapiens**."
Meaning: technical term for humans

zoophobes
"...some **zoophobes** suggest that the extinction of endangered species..."
Meaning: people afraid of, or against, zoos

agrarian
"For third world **agrarian** economies especially..."
Meaning: farming

demographic
"...competition for space and resources will grow during this '**demographic** winter'..."
Meaning: dealing with human populations relative to size, growth, density, etc.

wrought
"...which has already **wrought** remarkable success."
Meaning: brought about; made

History's first zoo keeper must have been one very busy conservationist, but at least he was spared the burdensome barbs of animal-rights activists, possibly because they were engaged in self-preservation. All Noah had to do was tend his passengers for 40 days and then turn them loose.

Today Noah would be plowing heavier seas. Not only are zoo managers concerned with the care of their charges, they are also concerned that the zoo, as an institution for research, education and preservation, is becoming as endangered as some of the animals it houses. Financial support has dropped, and costs keep climbing. Rising too is a clamor from critics who claim that zoos are no better than prisons, designed for the amusement of mindless gawkers. The more militant activists want to shut zoos down altogether.

Such is their zeal that a delegation from People for the Ethical Treatment of Animals (PETA) dropped into Washington's National Zoo last Christmas bearing gifts of exotic fruits to remind the beasts of the good old days back home. They serenaded the inmates with heartfelt renditions of *God Rest Ye All the Animals* and *Let 'em Go* (to the tune of *Let It Snow*).

Warthogwash! Michael Hutchins, director of conversation and science for the American Association of Zoological Parks and Aquariums, says the activists are "unrealistic and biologically naive; they are taking human moral precepts and trying to apply them to animals." That view, he adds, may have some merit when it is focused on domestic and farm creatures and even on the plight of laboratory animals, but it has no place in wildlife conservation. "We're trying to save animals from extinction," he says of the AAZPA, which includes 158 of the nation's best known, most prestigious and carefully regulated zoos and aquariums. "If we were to follow the animal-rights ethic to the letter, it would be a disaster. It would lead to species extinction." Where the activists may have a point, he says, concerns conditions at 1,400 roadside menageries, traveling shows, and petting zoos around the country, many of which are substandard and, rightly, ought to be shuttered.

But no such distinctions exist for many activists, who believe zoo keepers are guilty of "speciesism," the movement's politically correct counterpart to racism. Animals, PETA insists, are no different from people and should be treated accordingly. "There is really no rational reason for saying a human being has special rights," says PETA cofounder Ingrid Newkirk, whose credo is "A rat is a pig is a dog is a boy."

This means, among other things, that incarceration in a penned environment—or even an unpenned one, in the most modern and progressive of zoos—inflicts unacceptable psychological and even physical harm on animals, all to provide diversion for Homo sapiens. Such treatment, say activists, cannot be justified by any beneficial services that zoos perform.

At the extreme, the zoophobes suggest that the extinction of endangered species is preferable to confinement. In the essay "Against Zoos," University of Colorado philosopher Dale Jamieson asks, "Is it really better to confine a few hapless Mountain Gorillas in a zoo than to permit the species to become extinct?... If it is true that we are inevitably moving toward a world in which Mountain Gorillas can survive only in zoos, then we must ask whether it is really better for them to live in artificial environments of our design than not to be born at all."

The answer is yes, it is better. The globe is losing valuable species day by day; 20 percent to 50 percent of the world's biological diversity may be gone before the end of the next century, and the irony is that human beings will have contributed overwhelmingly to that loss. The human population is expected to nearly double within the next few decades. For Third World agrarian economies especially, the competition for space and resources will grow during this "demographic winter," and the loser will be wild animals.

In fact, what was once called the wild hardly exists anymore. Even some of the great African game preserves are little more than fenced megazoos. The vast spaces required by such predatory species as leopards, for example, have been reduced to fragments occupied by ever smaller animal populations. This often leads to a loss of genetic diversity of species and an increase in infant mortality.

The response to this depletion, argue the zoo managers, is controlled breeding in captivity, which has already wrought remarkable success. The London Zoo has bred the rare Père David's deer of China and the Arabian Oryx and reintroduced them to their native habitats. The San

Diego Zoo, which houses more than 150 species on the endangered list and has returned a dozen of them to the wild, recently produced triplet Sumatran tigers. Working with the Los Angeles Zoo, San Diego has also had spectacular results with the rare California condor. The sparse flock of 16 has grown to 50, and some may be returned this fall to the mountains near Ventura.

That's not good enough for the activists. They suggest that folks who want to see animals should instead visit the wild places. San Diego Zoo spokesman Jeff Jouatt did that very thing earlier this year. In Kenya he saw five rhinoceroses snuffling about in a game park. They were surrounded by 10 vans filled with tourists. That wasn't so bad, he was told. Usually the rhinos perform for 50 vans. God rest ye merry, rhinos.

Word count: 905

5. HEROES

Sometimes we confuse heroes with celebrities. Unlike people who are merely famous, heroes are usually defined as people who exemplify distinguished behavior. They selflessly help others and embody the best traits of human beings.

The articles in this section support the belief that heroes need not be famous to be heroic. Among others, you will read about a man who fights for consumer rights and the first woman to lead an American Indian nation.

23. SOUL OF A HERO
from *Time*

> We often read accounts of people who only stand by and watch while another person is attacked or in trouble. This article relates the story of someone who reacted instinctively to a life-or-death situation.
>
> **gash**   "...bleeding from a **gash** in his head..."
> *Meaning:* a long deep cut
>
> **hoisted**   "...they could be **hoisted** to safety..."
> *Meaning:* lifted up
>
> **toppled**   "...he **toppled** onto the tracks..."
> *Meaning:* fell forward
>
> **anonymous**   "...an **anonymous** donor sent Andrews a $3,000 bank check..."
> *Meaning:* with no name given

As the subway roared into the 14th Street station to take him back to his sparsely furnished Harlem walk-up, Reginald Andrews, 29, was deep in thought. Except for occasional work unloading produce, the father of eight had been unemployed for a year, and he was not optimistic about the job interview he had had that morning at Jamac Frozen Foods, a Manhattan food delivery company.

Suddenly someone else's troubles grabbed Andrew's attention. Trying to board a train, David Schnair, 75, blind from an injury suffered in combat during World War II, was tapping a metal cane to identify an open door. But when he mistook a space between the two cars for a door, he toppled onto the tracks. The train was about to pull out. "My mind left Jamac and Christmas for the kids," recalled Andrews. "I knew what I had to do."

Andrews jumped under the train and dragged Schnair, bleeding from a gash in his head, to a narrow cubbyhole beneath the platform out of the way of the wheels. The train began moving, but then screeched to a halt when a screaming bystander implored the conductor to stop the train.

Andrews and Schnair huddled in the crawl space until the power was cut off and they could be hoisted to safety.

President Reagan, after reading a newspaper account of the rescue, telephoned his congratulations. "At first I thought it was Rich Little," said Andrews, who took the call in a storefront church next door because his own phone had been shut off for nonpayment. No less startled was Jamac Foods Vice President Edward Marbach. He also received a phone call from Reagan, who wanted to put in a good word for Andrews with a Jamac official. "I told him I'd already given him the job in my mind," recalled Marbach. (Andrews reported for work for his new $10,500-a-year truck-loader's position as soon as his knee ligaments, torn during the rescue, healed.)

Three days after the incident, an anonymous donor sent Andrews a $3,000 bank check to wipe out his debts. Andrews has a special sympathy for the blind; his sister lost her eyesight in a New York City subway robbery over four years ago. "If it had been my sister there," said Andrews, "I wouldn't want anyone to just stand around." Said Philip Mottley, a friend of Andrews: "It was not his body that saved that man's life. It was his soul."

Word count: 406

24. COMMEMORATING A HEROIC ACT
from *Time*

> The next time you hear nursery rhymes sung by children, you might question the origin of them. This selection mentions such a rhyme and recounts the noble, unselfish efforts of one man.
>
> **nosegays**   "...the **nosegays** that people carried..."
> *Meaning:* flowers or ornaments in the shape of flowers
>
> **quarantine**   "...he exhorted them to **quarantine** themselves..."
> *Meaning:* to isolate to prevent spreading of disease
>
> **eloquence**   "...the **eloquence** of the 28-year-old rector..."
> *Meaning:* graceful speech, able to persuade
>
> **anti-Semitism**   "...savage flare-ups of **anti-Semitism**..."
> *Meaning:* hostile or prejudiced to Jews
>
> **Flagellants**   "...by groups of **Flagellants**..."
> *Meaning:* people who whip; in this case people who whip themselves as part of their religion

Gerald Phizackerley, an Anglican archdeacon, stood near a rocky outcrop, surrounded by the heath-clad hills and moors of the English Midlands, reciting a nursery rhyme.

Ring-a-ring of roses
A pocketful of posies
Atishoo! Atishoo!
We all fall down.

There was no laughter from the congregation of 600 gathered in the field outside the village of Eyam. Some worshippers seemed close to tears, for this was a service to commemorate a rare act of heroism at the time of the Great Plague that struck England more than 300 years ago. The rhyme's four bitter lines refer to the rosy mark on the chest of plague victims, the nosegays that people carried thinking to prevent infection, convulsive sneezing—and then death.

The plague, caused by bacteria usually spread by fleas carried on rats, raged through London in the summer of 1665, killing 68,500 people, a sixth of the city's population. Two-thirds fled the city, carrying the disease with them. Tiny and remote, Eyam seemed safe. But that September a village tailor received an infested bolt of cloth from London. Within a few days the tailor died. Soon dozens of others were seized by raging fever, vomiting, giddiness and excruciating buboes (swollen glands). But by the end of May the pestilence seemed to have run it course, with only 77 dead.

Then in the late spring of 1666, the plague erupted again in Eyam. By then the few townfolk rich enough to have homes elsewhere were long gone. Not even the common folk, most with nowhere to go, decided to flee town.

It was then that Village Rector William Mompesson spoke up. Knowing that the departing villagers would spread the disease, he exhorted them to quarantine themselves in Eyam to save the rest of Derbyshire. Such was the authority of the clergy, the power of faith, and the eloquence of the 28-year-old rector that the people of Eyam agreed. The Earl of Devonshire agreed to provide most of the necessary food and other goods, which outsiders left nervously at the perimeter every week.

Figuring that indoor meetings were dangerous, Mompesson moved Sunday worship into a nearby field. When pious townspeople gathered to pray for deliverance, they stood at some distance from each other. The rector and the nonconformist minister were the only visitors to console the sick, grieving, and terrified residents.

By the time the plague had run its course, 259 of the 350 villagers had died. One of the last victims was Mompesson's wife Catherine. Assuming he was also destined to die, he wrote a farewell letter: "I thank God I am content to shake hands with all the world, and I have many comfortable assurances that God will accept me." To avoid contamination, he dictated the letter by shouting on the moor to a visiting clergyman. Mompesson did not die. Three years after the plague subsided, he was reassigned to the village of Eakring, where the residents at first feared that he might infect them.

Successive waves of plague, which swept across Europe starting in the mid-14th century, produced much human cruelty, in addition to tens of millions of deaths. There were hysterical and savage flare-ups of anti-Semitism, frenzied self-lacerations by groups of Flagellants who thought the end of the world had come, and countless acts of terrified selfishness. But each year pilgrims from all over England still gather in the same field where Mompesson preached, to honor a priest and people who, as the service notes, "counted not their lives dear to themselves, but laid them down for their friends."

Word count: 591

25. LY TONG'S LONG TREK TO FREEDOM
by Anthony Paul
from *Reader's Digest*

Have you ever wondered what it is like to escape from an unfriendly country? Perhaps you played war games when you were young, trying to escape from the enemy prison. The following story describes the hardships of escaping from a real enemy.

queued "...prisoners **queued** for a 15-minute talk..."
Meaning: lined up

plummeting "At night, **plummeting** temperatures..."
Meaning: falling rapidly

yoke "...the guards tied Ly Tong in a **yoke**..."
Meaning: a frame fitting the neck and shoulder of a person or animal

cannibalizing "...had kept only a handful of planes in the air by **cannibalizing** those on the ground."
Meaning: to repair by the use of parts of other abandoned vehicles

genocidal vengeance "...followed by some three years of **genocidal vengeance**..."
Meaning: to seek revenge by killing certain racial or cultural groups

mustered "Soon drum-beating soldiers **mustered** the area's villagers..."
Meaning: gathered together

consigned "...Ly Tong was **consigned** by a Thai colonel..."
Meaning: entrusted to; put in care of

causeway "...the checkpoint at the Malaysian end of the **causeway**..."
Meaning: a raised roadway, usually over water

berth "Giving the immediate area wide **berth**, he detoured..."
Meaning: a space allowed for safety or convenience between two points

More than one million Vietnamese—primarily "boat people" who risked the South China Sea—are estimated to have fled their country since the end of the Vietnam war in April 1975. Hundreds of thousands have died in the attempt.

For five years, former South Vietnamese jet pilot Ly Tong was an inmate of various prisoner-of-war camps. During that time he often defied his captors and risked his life in abortive escapes. Eventually he managed to flee overland, and for 17 months he walked, rode, swam and crawled through five countries. His flight has become one of the great sagas of our time.

The way his friend died convinced 27-year-old Ly Tong that he had to escape. It was visitors' day in the summer of 1975, and Ly Tong was watching as married prisoners queued for a 15-minute talk with their families waiting outside the camp's barbed-wire fence. Excited by the sight of his wife and family, his friend broke line and stepped toward the fence. A North Vietnamese guard opened fire, and Ly Tong's friend died instantly, under the eyes of his horrified family.

A couple of months later, Ly Tong and a fellow prisoner escaped from a lightly guarded wood-chopping detail. On their second evening at large, a roadblock guard demanded to see identification. Ly Tong's companion panicked and blurted out the story of their escape.

I must go alone, Ly Tong told himself as they were taken back to camp. A bachelor with both parents deceased, he was responsible only for himself. *I will turn these circumstances into a strength.*

And strength he needed immediately. Hauled before a "people's court," he was ordered to kneel as the charges were read. Ly Tong refused and was sentenced to "conex" imprisonment.

Once simple jargon for a type of freight compartment, conex has become a most feared word in Vietnamese prison vocabulary. The metal boxes are now used as solitary-confinement cells. For six months, Ly Tong existed in an eight-foot-high by 4½-foot-wide conex. Interior daytime temperatures exceeded 100 degrees Fahrenheit. At night, plummeting temperatures stiffened Ly Tong's limbs. Stones thrown against the conex boomed like out-of-tune drums and denied him sleep. Air, food—handfuls of rice and salt—and Ly Tong's own wastes passed through the same few holes in a side of the box.

Though he was finally released from the conex, the Communists did not forgive Ly Tong's "bad attitude." After a year, he was transferred to one of Vietnam's worst camps.

As the story of his defiance became legion, his continued refusal to kneel to his captors strengthened their resolve to break him. Guards at Camp 52 knocked him down and jeered, "Not on your knees here. On your face. How do you feel now?"

"Honorable!" y Tong spat back. "Six men treat me like an animal. But who is the animal, who the man?"

He was ordered to construct a scaffold and to dig a grave. "When I gut you with this knife, how happy I'll feel," one guard taunted. Eventually tiring of their sport, the guards tied Ly Tong in a yoke and left him in it for two weeks.

As soon as he was released from the yoke, Ly Tong began planning his next escape. To toughen himself, he put aside what meager comforts camp life provided. In cold weather he would sleep without a blanket. On the hottest day, he worked without head-covering.

Ready to Try

On July 12, 1960, at Camp A30 in Phu Khanh Province, some 240 miles northeast of Ho Chi Minh City (Saigon), he made his move. After ten days of laboriously working a nail to loosen the bar on a toilet-hut window, he crawled out and inched his way across the prison yard. With small pilfered scissors, he broke through the strands of two barbed-wire fences, and then walked all night to Tuy Hoa, the nearest big city. There a friend gave him money, and he finally hailed a bus headed for Nha Trang.

"You're from A30 prison, aren't you?" asked the conductor, spotting Ly Tong's hunted look. "Then you've got trouble. There's a control post dead ahead. Get off and walk through with a crowd of local people. They seldom check all ID cards. I'll wait for you on the road beyond."

Once in Nha Trang, Ly Tong got in touch with an old girlfriend, who furnished him with clothes, cash and a train ticket to Ho Chi Minh City.

There Ly Tong joined the new Saigon's shadow world of Vietnamese in flight from communism's controls. Until September 1981 he lived by selling fake identity cards, so desperately needed by "shadows" like himself. A plan to escape in a boat fell through. Then a new idea formed: *I'm a pilot. Why not steal a plane?*

Ly Tong had once been based at Tan Son Nhut airport. But when he penetrated the base, he found no suitable aircraft. Cut off from U.S.-made spare parts, Vietnamese mechanics had kept only a handful of planes in the air by cannibalizing those on the ground.

Reluctantly, Ly Tong concluded that he must escape overland. With just 150 dong ($7.50 on the black market), he took a bus to the Kampuchean (Cambodian) border, where he crossed by foot on smugglers' tracks.

The country in which Ly Tong would spend the next five months had endured a bloody five-year civil war ending in 1975, followed by some three years of genocidal vengeance by Communist Pol Pot's victorious forces and invasion by Vietnam in 1978-79. Although the Vietnamese occupation army had pacified main population centers and most highways, guerrilla war still raged in much of the countryside.

"Catch Him!"

Roadblocks constantly halted travelers, but as long as Ly Tong was on foot or in a crowded bus, he was relatively safe. It was in a bus that he reached Phnom Penh, the national capital.

There he bought a train ticket to Batdambang, close to the Thailand border, but a Kampuchean station guard took a second look at him. Once again, Ly Tong was under arrest.

The police locked him in a small room. Outside the door a guard settled with a machine gun and a guitar. As the Kampuchean plucked out a tune, Ly Tong squeezed through the small, solitary window. But he had not run more than 100 yards when he heard warning shots and had to surrender.

This time he was handed to the Vietnamese police, who threw him into Phnom Penh's 7708 jail, a notorious prison camp. In a few weeks, he was told, he would be transported back to Vietnam.

By now, however, Ly Tong had confidence in his jail-breaking ability. Here the weakest spot was his dormitory window, a wooden frame with six iron bars. Before dawn one morning, with guards drowsing, he tested the bars. After three hours of tugging—and using the first-freed bar as a lever—the last bar came loose. Ly Tong crawled through.

For the next four months, he moved northwest across Kampuchea, following the mighty Mekong River. At one river village near Kampong Chhang, he worked for three months clearing fishing traps and earned about 1500 riels ($75 on the black market)—enough for a bicycle, food, and clothes. Then it was time to move north again.

The jungle and rice paddies surrounding Sisophon, the last major town on Ly Tong's route to Thailand, harbor one of Asia's nastiest guerrilla wars. To avoid danger, Ly Tong carted his bicycle into the jungle. Reaching a river, he asked some fishermen to help him cross, but they shook their heads.

Their unfriendliness bothered Ly Tong—and for good reason. Suddenly, an armed Kampuchean soldier on a motorbike barred his way. "So you're the man with the bike and the funny accent," he said. "Follow me!" As they passed a dense section of jungle, Ly Tong leaped from his bike and scrambled into the undergrowth. The soldier opened fire, missed, and then roared off in search of help.

The Phantom

Now in his path lay many creeks and large ponds. So often was he forced to strip for a swim that after a while he went naked, holding his clothes in a bag on his head. His strange appearance may have saved him. As he walked along a riverbank, he saw four young soldiers coming his way, speaking Vietnamese. Unable to avoid them, he crouched beside the water. When they spotted him, he leaped into the air with an unearthly yell: "WHOOOOO!" Though armed, the youths fled.

Ly Tong ran in the opposite direction—straight into a Vietnamese camp! All around him stood two-story huts housing sleeping soldiers. He could hear soldiers scouring the riverbank for a "phantom." By inching himself on his stomach through the darkness, he finally cleared the compound.

After walking for several more hours, he thought: *By now, Thailand must be very close, probably under my feet already.* With the sunrise came a feeling of elation until he spotted a camouflaged sniper on a platform high in a tree. *I haven't crossed the border.* And ahead lay great danger: mines.

From his mine-clearing labors as a prisoner, he remembered that the Hanoi army is taught to place small anti-personnel mines wherever a man might take cover: beside a tree trunk or boulder, under a bush. *Avoid cover,* he told himself. *And move only by night.*

For two days Ly Tong hadn't eaten. There was no water. Half-crazed by thirst, he lost track of time. Then, suddenly, he heard the sound of barking. For more than seven years of famine, Kampucheans had been eating their dogs. *Dogs mean a food surplus,* he reasoned. *This must be Thailand!*

And it was. Creeping to within earshot of a peasant's hut, he could hear a language that was neither Kampuchean nor Vietnamese. Following the sound of traffic to a highway, he waved down a passing motorcyclist and asked to be taken to the Red Cross.

Into Prison

But Ly Tong's troubles were not over. To deter an endless stream of refugees, and because Hanoi often "seeds" new waves of refugees with subversives, Thai police first jail and interrogate border-crossing Indochinese. For ten months, despite repeated protests and a hunger strike, Ly Tong was kept in prison in the Thai border town of Aranyaprathet. Finally, his story reached United States consular officials in Singapore, who confirmed Ly Tong's air force service.

Instead of passage to the United States, however, Ly Tong was consigned by a Thai colonel, whom he had offended during one of his protests, to a sprawling refugee settlement at Nong Samet, on the Kampuchean side of the border. It was time, yet again, to escape.

For months Ly Tong had been studying English and questioning refugee-relief workers about conditions in countries west and south of Aranyaprathet. Now he planned to escape across south Thailand and Malaysia to Singapore—perhaps 1,400 miles and three more borders.

On February 1, 1983, Ly Tong climbed over his camp's fence, picked his way through a minefield, swam five creeks, pushed through jungle and headed for Aranyaprathet, 15 miles to the southwest.

The next morning, however, at the first Thai roadside checkpoint, he ignored an order to halt, and the soldiers began shooting. He managed to race ahead of them to a field where he hid in a clump of tall grass. Some minutes later, he heard soldiers run up and then the sound of a cigarette lighter, as one of them tried to set fire to the grass.

For 15 years Ly Tong had not wept. Now, crying softly to himself, he began to pray. *With your help I have come so far. If I am no longer worthy, kill me now! Don't let me fall into enemy hands.* When the grass failed to catch fire, the soldiers finally walked away. *I believe in God,* Ly Tong told himself. *I cannot die anymore.*

The next day Ly Tong reached the house of a young woman he had met when she visited the Nong Samet settlement. Despite the risk to her own life, she had offered help, and now the pair set out for Bangkok by bus, passing themselves off as husband and wife. At the Bangkok railroad station, she handed him money for a train heading south.

Ly Tong left the train at Hat Yai, Thailand's southernmost large town, reasoning that it would be better to cross the border on foot than to face guards and immigration officials at the regular checkpoint. He followed the railroad tracks until night fell and he saw lights, trucks, uniforms. *The Malaysian border!*

Giving the immediate area wide berth, he detoured through the jungle and, doubling back to the highway, saw the sun rise on Kanger, the first town in side the border.

Ly Tong had no trouble catching a bus to Kuala Lumpur, and then another to his last border, Malaysia-Singapore. At about 8 p.m., the bus reached the checkpoint at the Malaysian end of the causeway to Singapore, across the Jonore Strait. Ly Tong slipped away into the darkness and walked about two miles west along the seaside.

Winds whipped the channel. Tying his clothes in a bundle on his back, he entered the water. Singapore's lights beckoned, and at the halfway point of the nearly two-mile swim came a fresh surge of energy. Soon there was sand beneath his feet.

After a few hours' sleep in a seaside park, Ly Tong made his way to the United States embassy. "I'm a Vietnamese," he explained to an official, "and I've just swum the Strait from Malaysia."

"In last night's weather?" said the American. "Impossible."

It was February 10, 1983. Behind Ly Tong were almost 2,000 miles of land and water, five countries, four border crossings, a half-dozen escapes from custody.

"If you've got a moment," said Ly Tong, "Let me tell you my story...."

Reader's Digest Editor's Note: After six months in a refugee-processing center, Ly Tong flew to the United States. He is now living in Texas and has just finished a book about his escape. He hopes to qualify soon for a scholarship to study political science, "to prepare me for the day my country is free again."

Word count: 2374

26. THE CHILD I COULDN'T FORGET
by Lisa Strick
from *Good Housekeeping*

> A young army nurse worked long hours in the emergency room and intensive-care units in Vietnam. She was awarded the Bronze Star for her heroic service. Still, she was not prepared for the bad memories which haunted her later in life.
>
> **drastic**   "Wade Dickinson worried about his wife's **drastic** personality change..."
> *Meaning:* severe; large
>
> **escalated**   "...and nearby fighting **escalated**."
> *Meaning:* increased
>
> **traumatic**   "...in which **traumatic** feelings a person has buried surface to haunt him or her..."
> *Meaning:* emotionally shocking
>
> **marvels**   "...she **marvels** at the way the pain she felt in Vietnam stayed with her."
> *Meaning:* admires; views with wonder

On a winter afternoon two years ago, Mary Dickinson stood in her New Jersey kitchen shaking for no reason, feeling surrounded by danger. Recently she'd had several of these strange panic attacks, which she could neither control nor explain. She'd also experienced terrifying, violent nightmares.

Normally Mary was cheerful and easygoing, very much the "organizer" in a family that included two teenage daughters and a preschool son. When not working with her husband of 16 years, Wade, in his propane-gas and appliance business, Mary was active in community youth activities.

"There was nothing *wrong* to cause these terrible feelings," she says. Still, she suddenly found herself fearing for the safety of her children, especially Wade Junior, her four-year-old son. "I'd be watching him at home or at play outside and feel convinced that something awful was about to happen to him. I wanted to just grab him and run someplace safe."

Soon Mary found herself breaking into tears at unpredictable, even embarrassing moments—at work, out shopping, washing dishes. Wade Dickinson worried about his wife's drastic personality change, and Mary could not reassure him. She was even more frightened than he was.

"The only explanation I could think of," Mary says, "was that I was losing my mind."

She racked her brain for a clue as to what could be causing her feelings of terror. "Then I remembered the newspaper article and the telephone call," she says. "The attacks had started then. I wondered: Could what I was going through have something to do with Vietnam?

"A friend and I joined the Army in 1966," Mary says. "We were 21 years old, one year out of nursing school, and we were looking for adventure, a chance to travel, a challenge. I was so naive—I had no idea what I was getting into."

She was shipped to Vietnam in March of 1967 and assigned to the Ninety-First Evacuation Hospital at Tuy Hoa, near the South China Sea. For Mary, a waking nightmare had begun.

She worked 12-hour shifts, six days a week—and longer hours when casualties were heavy. Because she served in the emergency room and intensive-care unit, she saw the most severe cases.

Mary remembers trying to comfort soldiers she knew were going to die. "They were so young," she says. "That made it worse."

Soldiers weren't the only casualties the nurses tried to help. "We'd get these little Vietnamese kids," Mary remembers, "babies torn apart by bombs, toddlers with bullet wounds and burns. When I look back, it's those children who stick in my mind. They hadn't done anything to anybody."

Out of necessity, Mary learned to deal with fatigue—and with the feelings of hopelessness that came from too many patients lost, too many young bodies damaged beyond repair. "You had to shut down emotionally or you couldn't survive it," she says.

Still, as the months passed, Mary found the atmosphere at Tuy Hoa increasingly hard to take, and she asked for a transfer. In the autumn of 1967, she was sent north to serve in the orthopedic ward of the Seventy-First Evacuation Hospital at Pleiku, near the Cambodian border.

Within weeks of her arrival, Pleiku became a combat zone. Enemy troops were less than a mile away. Mary had to deal not only with a heavy stream of casualties, but also with enemy rockets.

On the night of January 20, 1968, Mary's ward took a direct rocket hit. Suddenly, the ward was on fire.

"We had to get everybody out of there before the fire reached our oxygen tanks and *they* blew up," Mary remembers. Finally, when Mary believed that all the patients had been carried to safety, she broke down in tears.

From then on, rocket attacks became even more frequent, and nearby fighting escalated. "I stuffed my fear down, along with my other emotions, and kept working," Mary says.

She survived the final weeks of her duty in Vietnam in a state of numbed exhaustion, and she was awarded a Bronze Star (with "V" for valor) for her service at Pleiku.

"There were times I doubted I'd ever see home again," she says. "When I finally did get home, the only thing I wanted to do was forget Vietnam."

After her discharge from the Army, Mary moved from her hometown of Philadelphia to the most peaceful place she knew: the south New Jersey shore. She worked at the community hospital, and one day when Wade Dickinson delivered a tank of propane gas for the mobile home she'd bought, she met her future husband. They were engaged within weeks and married in 1971.

Mary told Wade little about her Vietnam service. "I thought he should know I'd been there," she says, "but I had no desire to dredge up painful memories."

Mary did, however, apply for membership in the Veterans of Foreign Wars. But the VFW turned her down—they accepted men only, Mary was told. "The idea then was that there was no such thing as a woman veteran," she says. "I pretty much accepted it."

In 1973, when her daughter Sandra was born, Mary decided to leave nursing and work with Wade. Their second daughter, Carolyn, was born in 1974. By the time Wade Junior was born in 1982, Mary hadn't thought about her Vietnam service in years. Then, in January of 1986, she saw an article in her local newspaper about B. J. Rasmussen, another Vietnam-veteran Army nurse.

"What struck me first was how similar B. J.'s life was to mine," Mary says. "She had served in Vietnam at about the same time I had. She was a nurse at the same hospital where I worked when I first came to South Jersey. She lived fairly near our home. We even had daughters the same age!"

Mary showed the article to Wade, who suggested she write B. J. a note. She did, and a few days later B. J. called her. "We had a short, friendly chat—mostly about our kids."

When the conversation was over, Mary thought no more about it. But soon afterward, the panic attacks, the nightmares, and the tears began. Mary didn't know what had triggered them, but she was determined to find out.

"I gathered up my nerve, called B. J., and told her what was happening to me. She said it sounded to her as if I had something called Post-Traumatic Stress Disorder—PTSD."

PTSD is a psychological disorder, B. J. explained, in which traumatic feelings a person has buried surface to haunt him or her in later years. It is largely associated with veterans of Vietnam. "I'd never heard of it," Mary says, "and I didn't think I could have it, either. After all, I wasn't a combat veteran."

Nevertheless, B. J. urged Mary to seek counseling at her local Vet Center. She told Mary that the services of the Veterans' Administration Outreach Centers are free and confidential and that most of the counselors had served in Vietnam themselves.

Mary decided to give it a chance. One afternoon she drove to the nearest Vet Center, where she requested literature on PTSD. "The receptionist asked if it was for a member of my family," Mary remembers.

"I was embarrassed when I admitted it was for me." But the receptionist convinced Mary to make an appointment for the following week.

Mary's counselor, psychologist Joe Steele, admitted to her that he had never counseled a female vet. But he began to tell Mary about his own Vietnam experience in the Marines. "As he talked, I could feel him reaching out to me," Mary says. "He was telling me he understood what it had been like.

"Joe was kind, and he was a professional, so I put my faith in him. I started to talk. For the first time in years, I forced myself to remember."

It was during her second session with Joe that the source of Mary's panic was dramatically uncovered. "I was telling him about the Vietnamese children," she says. "I talked a lot about one little boy, a five-year old who had been on my ward at Pleiku. Joe asked me what had happened to him. Suddenly I remembered the night the rocket hit."

Mary described the scene: That night, as rockets were exploding nearby and the hospital's sirens began to wail, Mary helped the boy get under his bed, covered him with his mattress for extra protection, and moved on to other patients. But after she turned away, the boy crawled out, panicked, and ran for the door.

"He was nearly there when the rocket hit," Mary said, almost disbelievingly. "It landed right on him." Mary blocked out the memories of the boy's death; instead, she convinced herself that she had seen a medical corpsman carrying him through the flames.

Now other things clicked into place for Mary: The date B. J. had called her, January 20, was the anniversary of that explosion. She also understood the source of her fears for her son. "Wade Junior was almost the same age—and the exact size—of the Vietnamese child who died," she says. "Somehow I'd tied them together in my mind."

That day in counseling with Joe, Mary finally grieved for the lost little boy and realized that there was nothing she could have done to save him. "I also realized that he was not my son," she says softly. My son was *safe*. I returned to reality."

Soon after this, Mary's nightmares and panic attacks stopped, but she continued to meet with Joe for several more weeks. At home, she felt calmer, and to her husband and children she seemed almost her old self.

"But I only felt comfortable talking about Vietnam with Joe, because he'd been there," Mary says.

After three months of individual counseling, Joe suggested that Mary join a Vietnam veterans' "rap group" that met at the Center once a week. "I didn't think the men would accept me," Mary recalls. "I mean, those guys had been in *combat*."

Without telling Mary, Joe checked with the group and afterward assured her that she would be welcome. Mary went to a meeting, and the dozen regular members warmly welcomed her. Several of them had worked in hospitals in Vietnam, one as a lab technician, another as a medical corpsman, a third as a combat medic. Several other members of the group had been inside the war hospitals as patients.

"They remembered the nurses who cared for them and for their buddies," Mary says, "and they went out of their way to make me feel at home."

The men began to talk about their experiences during the war. Although each man's story was different, the emotions each expressed, Mary realized, were much like her own. "The men had felt terror under fire, pain for the injured, grief for the dead."

Like her, some of the men had struggled with PTSD. "Just listening to them talk about it was healing," Mary says. "I understood why Joe had wanted me to come."

The following week, the rap group members invited Mary to go with them to "The Wall," the Vietnam Memorial in Washington, D.C., and she accepted.

At the memorial, she watched her new friends search for the names of buddies who had not come home. "One man spoke softly into a tape recorder as he found the names he was looking for," Mary remembers. "He talked about what each man had been like and how he had died.

"Another man made rubbings of names on The Wall. As he worked, strangers approached him and asked if he would take impressions of the names of their loved ones as well."

Mary herself sought no particular name. "I cried for them all," she says.

Today Mary no longer suffers from PTSD, but she marvels at the way the pain she felt in Vietnam stayed with her. "War is so awful—you have to see it firsthand to know," she says. "I look at my children and pray they will never have to experience it—that none of our children will."

Word count: 2014

27. SHE LEADS A NATION
by Hank Whittemore
from *Parade*

Wilma Mankiller is the first woman to become chief of the Cherokee Indian Nation. Read to see the obstacles she has overcome and some of the reasons she is considered such a good leader.

tenacity
"...we react with a **tenacity** that allows us..."
Meaning: strong grip; perseverance

adversity
"...that allows us to again and again bounce back from **adversity**."
Meaning: unfavorable events; bad times

uncannily
"...her own life **uncannily** reflects the historic struggle of the Cherokee nation itself."
Meaning: unexplained; strange

exodus
"That **exodus** in the winter of 1838-39..."
Meaning: large number of people leaving

trudged
"...some 18,000 Cherokees...**trudged** westward..."
Meaning: walked slowly; plodded

articulate
"...people were saying things I felt but hadn't known how to **articulate**."
Meaning: put into words

procure
"She helped to **procure** grants..."
Meaning: obtain

introspective
"...not yet the calm, **introspective** woman..."
Meaning: self-examining

"My life may be unusual, but not to the Indian world," says Chief Wilma Mankiller, 45, whose name goes back to that of a Cherokee warrior. "My ability to survive personal crises is really a mark of the character of my people. Individually and collectively, we react with a tenacity that allows us again and again to bounce back from adversity."

The first woman to become principal chief of the Cherokee Nation of Oklahoma, she speaks softly but with an undercurrent of urgency and commitment. From the Cherokee capital of Tahlequah in northeast Oklahoma's "green country," where she was born, Wilma Mankiller guides the second-largest Indian nation in the U.S. (only the Navajo Nation is larger), with a population of more than 120,000, an annual budget of $54 million and more than 800 employees spread across 7000 square miles. "It's like running a big corporation and a little country at the same time," she says with a laugh.

Today, wearing an orange blouse and purple skirt in her office at the tribal headquarters, the chief gives no sign of having had a bout with myasthenia gravis after a car accident in 1979, and while her face is puffy from medication following a kidney transplant last year, she radiates health and energy.

Chief Mankiller's rapid rise to Cherokee power—and her accomplishments in economic development, health care and tribal self-governance—already are legendary in the Native American community. She has helped develop new projects from waterlines to nutrition programs, from rural health clinics to a $9 million vocational training center.

Mankiller freely admits, meanwhile, that her people face a continuing crisis in housing, that too many Cherokee youngsters still drop out of high school, that unemployment remains about 15 percent and that decades of low self-esteem cannot be reversed overnight.

"Although we've been affected by a lot of historical factors," she insists, "nobody's going to pull us out but ourselves." In 1975, nearly all Cherokee income came from the federal government, but today more than 50 percent of the tribe's revenues are from its own enterprises, such as an electronics plant.

While leading her tribe to greater self-reliance, Mankiller draws inner strength from the values passed down to her through generations. In many ways, her own life uncannily reflects the historic struggle of the Cherokee Nation itself.

One of 11 children, Mankiller spent her earliest years on "allotted" Oklahoma land amid woodsy hills without electricity or running water.

Her full-blooded Cherokee father, who married a Dutch-Irish woman, was directly related to the tribal members who had been forcibly removed from their original homeland in the southeastern Appalachian states. That exodus in the winter of 1838-39 turned to tragedy as some of 18,000 Cherokees, suffering from hunger and disease, trudged westward and left about 4000 dead on "the trail where they cried," later called the Trail of Tears.

"We knew about it from family stories," Mankiller says, recalling how one of her aunts had a cooking utensil from ancestors on the trail. "Later we learned how our people had left behind their homes and farms, their political and social systems, everything they had known, and how the survivors had come here in disarray—but how, despite all that, they had begun almost immediately to rebuild."

When Mankiller was 12, in 1957, her family was again relocated—in this case, by a federal program designed to "urbanize" rural Indians. Sent from the Oklahoma countryside to a poverty-stricken, high-crime neighborhood in San Francisco, they were jammed into "a very rugged" housing project. Like their ancestors, they were forced to start over.

"My father refused to believe that he had to leave behind his tribal culture to make it in the larger society," Mankiller recalls, "so he retained a strong sense of identity. Our family arguments were never personal but about some social or political idea. That stimulating atmosphere, of reading and debating, set the framework for me."

During the 1960s, Wilma Mankiller got married and had two children. She also studied sociology at San Francisco State University. In 1969, when members of the American Indian Movement took over the former prison at Alcatraz to protest the U.S. government's treatment of Native Americans, she experienced an awakening that, she says, ultimately changed the course of her life.

"I'd never heard anyone actually tell the world that we needed somebody to pay attention to our treaty rights," she explains. "That our people had given up an entire continent, and many lives, in return for basic services like health care and education, but nobody was honoring those agreements. For the first time, people were saying things I felt but hadn't known how to articulate. It was very liberating."

So, in the 1970s, Wilma Mankiller began doing volunteer work among Native Americans in the Bay Area. Learning about tribal governance and its history compelled her to take a fresh look at the Cherokee experience; and what she saw, in terms of broken promises and despair, made her deeply angry.

After the Trail of Tears in 1839, rebuilding by the tribe in Oklahoma proceeded with the creation of a government, courts, newspapers and schools. But this "golden era" ended with the Civil War, followed by the western land rush by settlers who devoured Cherokee holdings. In 1907, Washington gave all remaining Indian territory to the state of Oklahoma and abolished the Cherokees' right to self-government. "We fell into a long decline," Mankiller says, "until, by the 1960s, we had come to feel there was something wrong with being an Indian."

Not until 1975 did U.S. legislation grant Cherokees self-determination. As rebuilding began yet again, Mankiller's own transformation was progressing as well. In 1977, after being divorced, she returned with her children to Oklahoma.

Working in community development, Mankiller saw that the tribe's need for adequate housing, employment, education and health care was staggering. She helped to procure grants and initiate services; but, she says, she was still angry and bitter over conditions—not yet the calm, introspective woman capable of leading the Cherokee Nation.

Then, in the fall of 1979, an oncoming car collided with her station wagon. She regained consciousness in the hospital, with her face crushed, ribs broken and legs shattered. Months of recovery included a series of operations and plastic surgery on her face. Then she developed myasthenia gravis, which sent her nerves out of control. Surgery on her thymus was followed by steroid therapy. Yet, in December 1980—just over a year after the accident—she went back to work.

In a profound way, however, Wilma Mankiller was a different person. "It was a life-changing experience," she says. To sustain herself through recovery, she explains, she drew upon precepts that the Cherokee elders had taught her:

- *"Have a good mind.* No matter what situation you're in, find something good about it, rather than the negative things. And in dealing with other human beings, find the good in them as well.

- *"We are all interdependent.* Do things for others—tribe, family, community—rather than just for yourself.

- *"Look forward.* Turn what has been done into a better path. If you're a leader, think about the impact of your decisions on seven generations into the future."

The same woman who had been immobilized became a bundle of energy relentlessly focused on getting things done. After she helped obtain a grant enabling rural Cherokees to build their own 26-mile waterline, male leaders took notice. By 1983, she was being asked to run for election as deputy chief. Two years after that victory, when Chief Ross Swimmer was named head of the Bureau of Indian Affairs, Mankiller became the principal chief. Then, in the 1987 election, she ran for a full four-year term, becoming the first woman elected as Cherokee chief.

"Wilma is a breath of fresh air in Indian leadership," says Peterson Zah, 58, president of the Navajo Nation and a friend. "She is a visionary who is very aggressive about achieving the goals she has in mind for her people. She truly cares about others."

As chief, Mankiller works 14-hour days filled with meetings in Tahlequah and frequent twin-engine flights to the state capital in Oklahoma City; and she is often in Washington, D.C., lobbying Congress. Her second husband, Charlie Soap, a full-blood Cherokee, keeps up a similar pace developing community programs. "We can't wait until the end of the day," Mankiller says, "to tell each other what went on."

They had long talks before Wilma decided to run for a second full term in June. Her recent kidney transplant was successful (the donor was her oldest brother, Donald Mankiller), but she has yearned to do more "hands on" work in rural communities; and there have been enticing offers to teach.

"Committing to another four years was a big decision," she says. "Basically it came down to the fact that there are so many programs in place that have been started but aren't yet finished."

On June 15—with 83 percent of the vote—Wilma Mankiller was re-elected for four years, beginning August 14.

As she starts her second term, Mankiller sees clearly the depth of problems of her own people, but her vision also includes a national agenda for all Native Americans, whose emerging leadership has heartened her.

One afternoon recently, Mankiller joined other tribal chiefs in Oklahoma City in a meeting with the governor's staff about a plan to tax Indian-owned stores. During a long discussion, Chief Mankiller kept silent; but when she finally spoke up, it was in a way typical of her strong, yet quiet leadership. "I suggest you look at existing tribal contributions to the state," she said in a soft voice, "and decide not to impose any new taxes on us. This is an opportunity for the state to begin a new day, an era of peace and friendship, with the tribes. Deciding against a tax would send a clear signal to the Indian population with long-term, positive impact."

Although the decision was left hanging and has yet to be resolved, in a single stroke Mankiller had elevated the meeting's theme. Then she was off to board a small airplane back to Tahlequah.

Flying over the lush green countryside where her people have lived for a century and a half, she could see the Cherokee Nation spread beneath her.

"We can look back over the 500 years since Columbus stumbled onto this continent and see utter devastation among our people," she says. "But as we approach the 21st century, we are very hopeful. Despite everything, we survive in 1991 as a culturally distinct group. Our tribal institutions are strong. And I think we can be confident that, 500 years from now, someone like Wilma Mankiller will say that our languages and ceremonies from time immemorial still survive."

As her plane descended, some children paused briefly to glance upward before returning to their lives and to the "new day" that Wilma Mankiller was trying to create for them.

The chief was home.

Word count: 1819

28. FOOD FIGHT
by David Grogan and Marilyn Balamaci
from *PEOPLE Weekly*

> David Kessler fights, but not in the army or the boxing ring. Instead, he fights for consumer rights in the arena of food labeling.
>
> **Goliaths** "...by taking food and pharmaceutical **Goliaths** to the mat."
> *Meaning:* giants ("to the mat" here is a way of saying he is fighting them)
>
> **incorruptibility** "Indeed, Kessler has a reputation for **incorruptibility**..."
> *Meaning:* not able to be bribed or influenced to do wrong
>
> **mired** "...the FDA...which recently has been **mired** in scandal."
> *Meaning:* stuck; bogged down
>
> **allegations** "And federal investigators reportedly are checking **allegations**..."
> *Meaning:* charges of wrongdoing

For his 40th birthday last month, David Kessler received a handmade poster from his 6-year-old son, Benjamin. Dad is pictured in a wrestling ring à la Hulk Hogan. His opponent: a large carton of orange juice labeled FRESH.

In real life, Kessler, at 5'11" and 150 lbs., is no Hulk. And his preppy wire rims don't inspire terror either. No matter: Since he became commissioner of the Food and Drug Administration, Kessler has made a name for himself by taking food and pharmaceutical Goliaths to the mat.

Kessler forced the makers of Citrus Hill orange juice and Ragu pasta sauce to stop referring to their processed products as "fresh." A few weeks later he ordered Crisco and Mazola to remove "no cholesterol" claims from their labels. (Though the claims were technically correct, Kessler felt they implied that the pure-fat corn oil products are good for the heart.) He took aim at ice cream, frozen yogurt and other foods that are labeled as more than 90 percent fat free but in fact may derive most of their calories from fat. He also took on pharmaceuticals that promote unapproved uses of their drugs. One target: Retin-A as a wrinkle-prevention ointment.

Some food companies say that Kessler is unfairly singling out individual brands before first giving notice to the entire industry that regulatory action would be taken. Comic Jay Leno, getting in on the act, recently complained that his Bumble Bee tuna contained no bumblebees. Kessler was delighted: "I knew the FDA had hit the big time when Leno included us in his monologue."

Ultimately, Kessler says, he wants labels to contain information about what part of the recommended daily intake of fat, fiber, cholesterol and sodium is provided in a given serving. "Consumers deserve more accurate information," he says.

The wits in Washington, D.C., have already dubbed him "Eliot Knessler," after Eliot Ness of *Untouchables* fame. Indeed, Kessler has a reputation for incorruptibility that is sorely needed at the FDA, which recently has been mired in scandal. The last permanent commissioner, Frank Young, was forced to step down in December 1989 after several agency employees admitted accepting payoffs from generic-drug companies for speeding approval of their drugs. And federal investigators reportedly are checking allegations that a few employees informed stockbrokers about new drug approvals before they were announced.

Kessler seems uniquely qualified to restore credibility to the FDA. After graduating from Amherst College in 1973, he shuttled between schools to earn a law degree from the University of Chicago in 1978 and a medical degree from Harvard a year later. Then, as a resident in pediatrics at Johns Hopkins Hospital in Baltimore, he worked with a Senate committee that was drafting new food-safety legislation. Food-industry attorney and former FDA counsel Peter Barton Hutt used to get late-night phone calls from Kessler from the Johns Hopkins emergency room. "With sirens and people shouting in the background, David would calmly discuss an obscure clause in the law," says Hutt. "He's one of the most hardworking people I've ever met."

Appointed medical director of the hospital of New York City's Albert Einstein College of Medicine in 1984, Kessler taught courses in food-and-drug law at Columbia University and even signed on for weekly duty in the emergency room of a municipal hospital. "In the end, I'm a doc," he says, but adds that he also "really wanted to run a large health-care organization." On top of everything else, he somehow found time to be with his children, Elise, now 8, and Benjamin. "There wasn't a night I missed tucking the kids in," he says. "Then I'd go back to work."

Once stocky, Kessler has lost 55 pounds since he joined the FDA last November. Part of his secret may be that his wife, Paulette, 38, who remained with the kids in Scarsdale, New York, until the end of the school year, hasn't been around to remind him to eat. The family is moving this month to Washington. "Everybody in the agency will be happy when my family arrives," Kessler says. "They hope I'll slow down, so they can go home in the evenings."

Word count: 690

6. THE LAW AND JUSTICE

Two common complaints are aimed at our legal system: 1) the police do not arrest all the criminals, and if they do, judges often let them go with little or no punishment; 2) police and judges do not have enough respect for the rights of the criminal. Whether the legal system is too merciful or too strict with criminals is the topic of many heated discussions.

On the one hand, society aims to protect innocent people; on the other hand, no one likes to read about persons who were granted probation for freedom only to repeat criminal acts. Reading different opinions about the law and justice can lead to a better understanding of the two sides of the issue.

The articles in this section include the story of a prisoner who may be innocent, a look at the pros and cons of seeking out revenge, an account of the mother of a crime victim, and a discussion of your legal rights should you become the victim of crime.

29. YOUR RIGHTS AS A CRIME VICTIM
from *McCall's*

What can you do about harassing phone calls? Is your landlord liable if you are assaulted in your apartment? An attorney answers these and other questions.

vindicate
"However, there are ways that crime victims can **vindicate** their rights..."
Meaning: justify or support a claim

reimbursement
"...write a letter...explaining the circumstances and asking for **reimbursement**."
Meaning: pay back for something taken

redress
"Then it will tell you how to seek legal **redress**..."
Meaning: satisfaction (such as repayment)

immune
"...some states have laws that make them **immune** to this type of suit."
Meaning: exempt; not affected

delinquent
"Were they **delinquent** in not answering the alarm more quickly?"
Meaning: failing to do what is required

thwarted
"...a court might require you to show that the thieves would have been **thwarted** by a speedier police response."
Meaning: prevented from taking place

tumultuous behavior
"...by engaging in **tumultuous behavior**..."
Meaning: noisy or riotous actions

Each year in the United States, there are five million assaults and 20 million thefts—add in other offenses and you have a frightening total of 40 million crimes! Yet aside from calling the police, most of us don't know how to protect our rights when victimized by a crime. This is particularly true when the crime is a so-called lesser offense. Because our courts are so backlogged and district attorneys so overworked, "small" cases tend to be ignored. However, there are ways that crime victims can vindicate their rights and, in some cases, be financially compensated for certain injuries and property losses. Here are seven common situations and advice on the best way to handle them.

STOLEN VALUABLES

What can you do if a repairman or worker steals valuables from your home? The first step is to file a criminal complaint with the police. Even if they fail to take effective action, you'll have an official record of the crime. Next, write a letter to the worker and his employer explaining the circumstances and asking for reimbursement.

If this fails to bring satisfactory results, you then have several options: You can see if your insurance policy covers the theft and accept the settlement; you can refuse to pay the worker's bill (thereby reducing your loss somewhat and putting the burden of suit on his company); or you can file suit against the worker and his employer.

Should you sue, you will be relying on "circumstantial evidence" that the worker committed theft. While such evidence is not conclusive, it could be enough for a court to rule in your favor. You would have a stronger case, however, if the worker's company or the police had a record of past, similar complaints lodged against him—or if you could testify to having seen the stolen item shortly before the worker entered your home, only to find it missing immediately after he left.

HARASSING PHONE CALLS

How can you protect yourself against obscene and harassing telephone calls? Use of a telephone for purposes of harassment is a crime punishable by a fine and/or imprisonment. In addition, it is a violation of civil law and may enable you to recover damages for harassment, intentional infliction of mental suffering and, in certain instances, civil assault.

Your first step should be to contact the Annoyance Call Bureau of your local telephone company, which can be reached by calling the phone company's business office. The bureau can help you determine the identity of your caller through various computer techniques, if his or her identity is unknown. Then it will tell you how to seek legal redress (such as filing criminal charges or a civil complaint) and what evidence you'll need to sustain your claim.

ASSAULT IN AN APARTMENT

If you're assaulted in your apartment, can the landlord be held liable? Quite possibly, yes. While the law leans toward the landlord, a growing number of judges have held that when a landlord fails to take reasonable precautions to protect tenants from crime, he can be held liable for the damage that results.

Keep in mind that the law requires only reasonable standards, such as working locks and adequate lighting. Costs must be in keeping with foreseeable harm. For example, a landlord is not required to hire doormen for what was previously a nondoorman building. However, if a building intercom or front door lock is broken and the landlord fails to make repairs, he is considered negligent and may be held responsible for any crimes that result. (The tenant's case will be strengthened considerably if the landlord received written notice of the defective condition before the crime occurred and failed to fix it.)

In addition to negligence, your landlord might also be liable on grounds of breach of contract. For example, tenants in a doorman building or in a building with a particularly advanced security system are entitled to have these services maintained until the lease expires. Should these services be discontinued, the landlord will have violated the lease, and the tenant will be entitled to damages from any crimes that result.

POLICE FAILING TO RESPOND

Can you recover damages from the police for losses you incur if they fail to answer a burglar alarm in your home promptly? Claims like this involve several obstacles. Most important, some states and municipalities have laws that make them immune to this type of suit. The first thing you should do, therefore, is get in touch with your attorney or local bar association to find out whether authorities in your area can, in fact, be sued at all.

If the answer is yes, you must then prove negligence on the part of the police. Were they delinquent in not answering the alarm more quickly? Maybe not. If, for example, the only police cars on duty that day were actively engaged in lifesaving work (such as rescuing a drowning child), it is hardly reasonable to say that the police should have let the child drown to answer the alarm at your house.

Even if you succeed in proving negligence, a court might require you to show that the thieves would have been thwarted by a speedier police response. After all, it is possible that the alarm was triggered while the thieves were leaving, in which case a quick response would have made no difference.

In short, cases of this nature are hard to win. There is frequently a requirement that authorities be notified of a citizen's intention to sue within a relatively short period of time. Thus, if you would like to sue, it is important that you consult an attorney at once.

VICTIM'S COMPENSATION

How can a crime victim receive compensation if the guilty party isn't caught? In recent years about 40 states have enacted crime-victim compensation laws. For example, the Uniform Crime Victims Reparations Act, which has been adopted by ten states, establishes a state-financed program to compensate those who suffer personal injury. as well as the dependents of persons killed as a result of criminal conduct. The suggested maximum allowance is $50,000 per victim; losses of less than $100 generally are not considered. Reparations are determined by the degree of economic hardship and loss the victim has suffered as a result of the injury. Medical expenses, lost earnings and the cost of replacing services normally provided by the victim (such as child care) are included; property damage is not.

To find out if your state has a crime-victim compensation law, call or write your local attorney general's office. Someone there can ably advise you on how to pursue your case.

COAT-CHECK LIABILITY

What can you do if your coat is stolen from a restaurant checkroom and the restaurant refuses to reimburse you? Laws governing the liability of restaurants for misplaced or stolen items differ from state to state. But certain rules are widely recognized. The most common standard applied to these cases is that a restaurant must exercise "reasonable care" with its checkroom. If, for example, you leave your coat check on the ladies' room floor and someone else picks it up and steals your coat, the restaurant will probably not be held liable. If, however, a checkroom attendant leaves your coat unguarded and it's missing when she returns, the law is on your side.

Compensation is somewhat more difficult to obtain if you live in a state that has a law limiting the liability of restaurants for property stolen from coat checkrooms. These laws are frequently posted on prominently displayed signs that read NO LIABILITY FOR LOST OR STOLEN ITEMS or NO LIABILITY IN EXCESS OF $50. However, even where such laws exist, courts have generally held that a patron may recover the full value of checked property if it has been lost due to the restaurant's gross negligence. For example, if the coat-check attendant gave your coat to another patron who claimed to have lost her check and did not show proper identification, that would be considered gross negligence.

Generally, small-claims court is the best place to pursue a claim of this nature. To make your case as strong as possible. bring the friends who were with you in the restaurant as witnesses, as well as any documents that support your claim. These would include the coat check and any record (such as a bill of sale) that confirms the value of the missing coat.

PUBLIC SEXUAL HARASSMENT

What can you do about men who make obscene comments and gestures to you on the street? They might be breaking the law. In New York, for example, a person is guilty of disorderly conduct when he or she intentionally causes "inconvenience, annoyance or alarm" by engaging in "tumultuous behavior," using "abusive language" or making "an obscene gesture" in a public place. Similarly, almost all states have laws against harassment which encompasses a multitude of acts intended to harass, annoy or alarm another person.

You can lodge a criminal complaint against your tormenter. The courts and the district attorney's office will take it from there. You might also have a civil cause of action for harassment or assault. Civil assault (as opposed to its criminal counterpart) does not require the actual use of physical force. The law is violated if the offender intentionally threatens offensive bodily contact under circumstances that create a reasonable fear in your mind that he will follow through on his threat.

Word count: 1569

30. I CAN'T STOP CRYING
from *Time*

> Do you have faith in our judicial system? Are there innocent people on death row? Are we treating criminals or suspected criminals with too much or too little sympathy? The story of Doug McCray raises questions about these issues.
>
> **recanted**   "An eyewitness...later **recanted**..."
> *Meaning:* changed testimony
>
> **coerced**   "...saying police had coached and **coerced** him."
> *Meaning:* forced or persuaded
>
> **despondent**   "...McCray has grown progressively more **despondent**."
> *Meaning:* dejected, ready to give up

At Dunbar High School in Fort Meyers, Florida, Doug McCray was a triple threat: in football, an all-state wide receiver; in basketball, an all-conference playmaking guard; in track and field, a state champion in the 440-yard run. An honors student, he went on to Edison Community College in Fort Meyers but dropped out after one and a half years to enlist in the Army. He was given a medical discharge after 17 months because of attacks of grand mal epilepsy. He married, fathered a son and went back to college, this time in California. His marriage soured, and he returned to Fort Meyers, where he sank into alcoholism and despair. Sometime between October 13 and 15, 1973, a woman named Margaret Mears, 68, was raped and beaten to death.

Doug McRay, now 32, had been on a drinking binge and could not account for his whereabouts at the time of the crime when police arrested him for murder six weeks later. The FBI matched his palm print with one found in Mear's apartment. Nearly ten years alter, McCray says he still does not know whether he is guilty. He passed two polygraph tests, which prosecutors would not permit in evidence at his trial. An eyewitness who placed McCray in the woman's neighborhood at the time of the slaying later recanted, saying police had coached and coerced him. The physical evidences of rape could not be linked to McCray.

Nevertheless, he now awaits his fate on death row in Florida State Prison at Raifor. McCray looks back in anger: "I feel victimized by the Florida Supreme Court, which waited five and half years to rule on my case, which granted me a new trial and then abruptly took it away. (A 4-3 decision in McCray's favor was reversed six months later when one justice changed his vote without explanation.) I feel victimized by my clemency lawyer, who never even bothered to read the transcript of my trial. I feel victimized by the lawyer who took my mother's few dollars and never came to see me for almost eight years."

Outside observers, including *New York Times* Columnist Anthony Lewis, have rallied to McCray's defense. When a St. Petersburg attorney phoned him and volunteered to help, McCray remembers, "I started to cry. I can't stop crying in this place. It meant so much to me, after all the other things that happened, that this man cared."

McCray lives in a 6-foot by 9-foot cell. He and the other 194 inmates on Florida's death row each have a small black-and-white TV. He uses the light from the set to read constantly. "I've read thousands of books. Prison can be as rewarding as college if you actually have a desire to improve your mind." Yet his thoughts always wheel back to the central mystery that has brought him to this place. "The state says it's convenient for me to say I don't remember. But if it were convenient, I could have plea-bargained or made up some alibi. My girlfriend and one of my brothers say I was with them all that night. I wish I knew, even if it meant knowing that I'd done it. Who would want to live after committing such a terrible crime?" Since last fall, McCray has grown progressively more despondent. He now says he will not seek another stay of execution: "I just wish to die in peace. I will allow the state to do what it may. I am tired."

Word count: 578

Part Two/The Law and Justice   275

31. THEY'VE KILLED MY DAUGHTER TWICE
by Joseph P. Blank
from *Reader's Digest*

We hear a lot about accidents caused by drunk drivers but somehow it all sounds like a jumble of statistics—something that only happens to others. This tragic story about Gail Tietjen makes the horrible consequences of drunk driving more real for all of us.

lacerated — "Gail lay unconscious in a pool of gasoline, her head **lacerated** and bloody."
Meaning: cut and torn, mangled

neurosurgeon — "...the **neurosurgeon** told her parents that he did not know if she'd even survive."
Meaning: doctor who operates on some part of the nervous system

hyperactively — "Gail continued to behave **hyperactively**..."
Meaning: more active than is considered normal

frenetic — "Her **frenetic** movements slowly grew less intense."
Meaning: frantic; wild and out of control

doggedly — "**Doggedly**, she fought and worked her way through college."
Meaning: persistently; not giving up readily

omnivorously — "She read **omnivorously** and developed an astonishing vocabulary."
Meaning: taking in everything

mayhem — "...the dollar cost of this alcohol-induced **mayhem**..."
Meaning: act of intentionally injuring another person's body

Gail Tietjen's young life was just about perfect—until she went driving one night with a friend who was drunk. It took her eight years to fight her way back to health. And then her luck ran out again. It was another drunk-driving accident. Gail Tietjen, 18, was the passenger in her boyfriend's sports car. Bright, pretty, outgoing, she had recently graduated from high school where she had been an honor student, a member of the tennis team, and a homecoming princess. She had been awarded two scholarships to Stanford University, where she planned to study medicine.

About 1:30 a.m., July 25, 1972, her 19-year-old boyfriend was driving her home to Los Altos, southeast of San Francisco, after a family dinner party in his home. He had gotten drunk. Rounding a turn too fast, he lost control and slammed into a tree.

Two hours later, a motorist came upon the wreck and called the police. The traffic officer who arrived found the young man conscious, but suffering from a fractured arm and jaw. Gail lay unconscious in a pool of gasoline, her head lacerated and bloody. Her front teeth had been hammered out of her mouth by the impact, and her chin was deeply cut. The officer assumed she was dead. Then he heard a gurgle in her throat.

Shortly after 4 a.m. the El Camino Hospital telephoned Gail's parents, Betty and Robert Tietjen, and they rushed to the emergency room. Gail was in a coma and thrashing about. When asked the extent of brain damage, the neurosurgeon told her parents that he did not know if she'd even survive.

A blood-alcohol-concentration (BAC) test on the driver registered 0.14 percent; a reading of 0.10 is generally considered "drunk while driving." The young man was subsequently charged with felony drunk driving and causing bodily harm. He was later permitted to plead guilty to a misdemeanor, and he was fined $500.

Gail was unconscious for two weeks, her breathing assisted by a respirator, When she finally emerged from her coma and was moved to a chair, it was obvious that she had suffered severe brain damage.

"She sat there just like a wooden doll," Ann, Gail's older sister, recalls. "Stiff. Staring straight ahead." At other times she rocked for hours, or became so agitated that the nurses had to strap her into the bed. The nurses also had to teach her routine behavior: how to use the toilet, eating utensils, napkin, comb, face cloth.

After three weeks, Betty Tietjen began asking when she could take her daughter home for a visit. The doctors had done what they could, she reasoned. From this point on, a home environment would benefit Gail more than the hospital. On the 32nd day after the accident, Gail's physician issued a weekend pass. But he warned the family that they might not be able to cope with her for more than a day.

Gail didn't recognize home. "This house is in Los Angeles," she insisted. She wanted to go to her real home. And where were her real mother, father, and sister? "I don't know you people." Unable to sit still, she walked constantly throughout the house, her eyes wild.

After Gail went to bed the first night, her parents discussed her condition and decided not to return her to the hospital. Their love and care, they felt, would give her the best chance for improvement. Bob was ill with Parkinson's disease, so Betty took a leave of absence from her job as a secretary to be with her daughter.

Gail continued to behave hyperactively, sometimes to a point of frenzy. During a conversation she would suddenly launch into a series of relentless questions: "Where did you get that container of milk?" "Why?" "Why do you like milk?" "Why that brand?" Ann remembers, "It drove us crazy—until we realized she had to learn all over again about everyday life."

Then, gradually, she began changing. The accident had destroyed some brain cells; it had not destroyed her determination, her spirit, her zest for living. She became aware that she would have to work far harder than those around her to make an independent life for herself.

Gail and her mother went for long walks and played croquet. Her frenetic movements slowly grew less intense. She could sit through a meal without jumping up several times. Although it remained difficult for her to think a problem through, or to utter three sentences in logical sequence, no one in the family hinted that there were things she probably couldn't do.

In September 1973, 14 months after the accident, Gail enrolled at Stanford and moved into a dormitory. She told no one about the effects of the accident; special treatment would have made her cringe with embarrassment.

Knowing she could not cope with demanding pre-med courses, she chose to major in art. She flunked almost every subject in her first year and was threatened with expulsion. University authorities learned of the accident, however, and gave her another chance.

Doggedly, she fought and worked her way through college. "She willed herself to improve," recalls Ann. "At first her drawings and paintings looked like the work of a two-year-old. Then they got better and better, and in a few years she was turning out beautiful things." Homework sometimes took her five times longer to complete than it did the other students, but she never complained. In June 1978, she graduated.

By then, the business world attracted her more than a career in art. Ann's fiance, Tom, offered to help her get a job where he worked. Gail said it was better to do it on her own. Genuine and direct, she was soon hired as a salesperson by a fashionable women's specialty store in Palo Alto. After nearly a year, she took a more challenging position as an office supervisor. When it became apparent that she couldn't handle such a complex assignment, she undertook to learn secretarial skills.

"It was tough for her," remembers Ann. "She had to learn while doing the work of an experienced secretary. She talked to Mom and me and took notes on everything we said. She was slower than other secretaries in her office, so she worked through her lunch hour and after the office closed to make up for it."

Afraid that Gail had taken on too much, Ann and Tom suggested that she look for something less demanding. "No," Gail answered. "That's giving up and I won't do that."

Although mistakes made her feel terrible, they prodded her to improve. One afternoon she called Ann to announce: "I've been through a whole day without making a single mistake. I'm getting there."

And getting there she was. Not only did she grow more proficient at her job, but the extra effort made her mind grow sharper and more capable. She was able to think her way to a reasonable decision. She read omnivorously and developed an astonishing vocabulary. She wanted no sympathy. "I'm doing fine," she told Ann. "I'm probably a stronger person because of what I went through. I'm happy with the way I am."

"She had run her marathon," concludes Ann, "and crossed the finish line."

On the evening of December 18, 1979, Gail met with some friends at a restaurant near Palo Alto. While the others had wine with their food, she had a Coke. Since the accident she never drank alcohol if she was driving and never rode in a car driven by a person who had been drinking.

About 9:30 p.m., the group left the restaurant. Gail got into her 1974 Pinto for the short drive home. She drove down Highway 85, then onto the southbound off-ramp where the highway ended, about one-and-a-half blocks from her apartment.

At the same time, Beth June O'Donnell, a 59-year-old nurse, ignored signs that read "NO LEFT TURN OR U TURN" and "WRONG WAY/DO NOT ENTER," and swung her Pontiac the wrong way onto the off-ramp. She paid no attention to the drivers who flashed their lights and blared their horns to warn her.

A quarter-mile down the ramp, the car immediately in front of Gail's shifted suddenly to the right. She tried to follow, but it was too late. The O'Donnell car smashed into the driver's side of the Pinto.

A sheriff's deputy called to the scene wrote in his report that O'Donnell, who was not injured, told him, " 'I've been a nurse since (age) 35. She's dead, I know a dead body when I see one. I've been drinking and if I go to jail, well, that's the way it goes.' This statement was made freely and voluntarily at approximately 2203 hours. At that time I detected an odor of alcoholic beverage upon the breath of O'Donnell and observed that she was unsteady on her feet." A BAC test given O'Donnell two hours later showed a 0.12 percent alcohol content.

Eighty-four minutes after the collision, Gail Tietjen was pronounced dead. "It's happened again," her mother said when informed by police. "They've killed my daughter twice!"

But the record showed only another drunk-driving accident.

The following are comments from the editors of *Reader's Digest*:

WHY?

Gail Tietjen's tragic fate is painful to think about. Yet, incredibly, it is repeated more than 25,000 times a year. In fact, roughly one half of all fatal highway accidents—which average between 50,000 and 55,000 year after year—involve alcohol. Nor is that all. Consider:

- Six of every ten drivers who kill themselves in single-vehicle accidents are drunk at the time—and besides their own lives they manage to snuff out the lives of thousands of innocent people every year.

- In the 16-to-24 age group alone, alcohol is responsible for 8,000 deaths a year, and for the disfiguring of an additional 40,000 young people.
- Each year, alcohol on the highways results in physical injuries to 125,000 people.
- The National Highway Traffic Safety Administration (NHTSA) conservatively estimates the dollar cost of this alcohol-induced mayhem at $5 billion per year—if a dollar cost can be associated with such massive loss of life.

How can we as a nation allow this to go on, year after year? Why is it that in this country a driver is not considered drunk until his blood-alcohol count goes over 0.10 percent? In Canada the standard is 0.08; in Norway, Sweden, and Denmark, 0.05.

Why is it for every 2,000 drunks on the road at a given time, only one is arrested? And why is it that a lone individual's chances of receiving a stiff fine, revocation or suspension of license, even a jail term, are mathematically insignificant? (September 19, 1980, Beth June O'Donnell was sentenced to eight months in the county jail and four years probation. She had been arrested and convicted of drunken driving in 1977, and fined $190.)

Think about Gail Tietjen. And then think about this: According to the NHTSA, on any given weekend night, one out of every ten drivers on our highways is drunk.

And then ask yourself if it isn't time we got serious about the problem of drunk drivers.

Word count: 1569

32. BATTERED WOMEN WHO KILL: SHOULD THEY RECEIVE CLEMENCY?
from *Glamour*

> The law is usually open for interpretation. Sometimes we feel it is justified to kill someone—in self-defense, for instance. What about battered women? Are they killing in self-defense? Some of the difficulties of this issue are presented in this article.
>
> **traumatic** — "When he was alive, physical beatings were so frequent—and so **traumatic**..."
> *Meaning:* emotionally shocking
>
> **clemency** — "The state's governor granted her **clemency**..."
> *Meaning:* mercy (in the legal sense, usually released from prison)
>
> **mitigate** — "It may **mitigate** the sentence..."
> *Meaning:* to make milder; moderate
>
> **commuted** — "...who recently **commuted** the sentences of eight battered women..."
> *Meaning:* changed a penalty to a lesser one

"It was so peaceful," said Janet Abbott of Ohio. "I had my first night where I could lie down and go to sleep."

Abbott was referring to life after she had her husband killed. When he was alive, physical beatings were so frequent—and so traumatic—that she could barely function.

Abbott was recently released from prison in Ohio after serving almost ten years of a life sentence. The state's governor granted her clemency (along with twenty-four other battered women), arguing that if she had been allowed to introduce evidence of her repeated beatings at the trial, the verdict might have been different. Women who are so thoroughly beaten down, both psychologically and physically, by a vicious mate are now commonly said to be suffering from "battered woman syndrome," which is becoming a controversial topic in many states.

In the past, many judges have refused to allow women accused of murder to testify that they had been beaten by their husbands repeatedly and over a long span of time. They were often only allowed to tell the jury about beatings that had taken place immediately before the murder. Four states—Missouri, Ohio, Louisiana and Maryland—have now passed legislation that explicitly permits battered women to use evidence of their abuse in court cases. At least nine others, including New York, Texas and California, are considering such legislation. In addition, the governors of several states are reconsidering the sentences of battered women already serving time for killing their mates, to determine whether they should be granted clemency.

A number of district attorneys are concerned that letting these women off when they have been beaten may send the wrong message to society. "I can see that being battered by their mates does something to the women," says Sandra Stensaas, an assistant district attorney in Oklahoma who has handled four cases where the defense was battered woman syndrome. "But whether that is sufficient to allow them to kill their husband or boyfriend is another story. It may mitigate the sentence, but it certainly shouldn't excuse the crime."

Some observers are also concerned that the psychological condition hasn't been adequately described in the medical literature so as to be useful in legal circles. "If the psychiatrists cannot agree about whether or not it is a syndrome or a group of symptoms," says Stensaas, "then I don't think that I can accept it either."

"No one is assuming that there is a single scientific definition of what battered woman syndrome is," says Paul Schurick, a spokesman for Governor William Donald Schaefer of Maryland, who recently commuted the sentences of eight battered women in his state's jails. "But if continued psychological and physical abuse leads to a crime, it should have as much weight in a courtroom as a plea of self-defense."

An added concern about governors' commuting past sentences is that they may not be getting the whole story. In Maryland, for instance, *The Baltimore Sun* accused the governor of allowing himself to be misled by one-sided information provided by groups interested in furthering the interests of battered women. One complaint: The attorneys who had originally prosecuted the cases were not consulted before clemency was granted. But the governor has not had second thoughts, and believes he had all the information necessary to make reasonable judgments.

Word count: 554

284   Read and Respond

36. REVENGE IS THE MOTHER OF INVENTION
from *Time*

Do you believe in the death penalty? Does it really prevent people from committing crimes? Does it make the public feel good to get revenge on the criminal? This historical look at how the death penalty has been carried out may give you second thoughts on the subject.

humane "...his execution in 399 B.C. was singularly **humane**."
Meaning: kind; merciful

ingenious "...the only dilemma had been to find the most **ingenious** and cruel methods of execution."
Meaning: showing cleverness of invention

excruciating "A 19th century French traveler described an **excruciating** method in India..."
Meaning: causing intense physical or mental pain

rajahs "...during the rule of the **rajahs**..."
Meaning: princes or chiefs in India

wretch "...which makes the body of the condemned **wretch**..."
Meaning: miserable or unhappy person

incurred "What kinds of crime **incurred** such punishments?"
Meaning: brought about; caused to happen

heretics "...when tens of thousands of convicted **heretics** were burned."
Meaning: people whose beliefs oppose the official beliefs

meted "The English **meted** out the death penalty..."
Meaning: gave out; allotted

curative "...it and the scaffold were believed to have **curative** powers."
Meaning: tending to cure or having the power to cure

arbitrarily "Death sentences were often **arbitrarily** applied."
Meaning: in a manner based on a personal preference or whim rather than democratically or fairly

catharsis "The rituals of execution...**catharsis** and revenge..."
Meaning: a release of emotional tension

Socrates was lucky. Found guilty of heresy and "corruption of the young," he was condemned to drink a cup of hemlock, a relatively honorable and painless death. By standards of history, his execution in 399 B.C. was singularly humane.

Not until the Enlightenment 200 years ago did societies seriously question the state's right to kill. Until then, the only dilemma had been to find the most ingenious and cruel methods of execution. Boiling, choking, beheading, dismembering, impaling, crucifying, stoning, strangling, burning alive—all were in vogue at various times. The crucifixion of Jesus Christ was, for its day, only a routine execution.

In ancient China, an occasional penalty was "death by the thousand cuts," the slow slicing away of bits of the body. A 19th century French traveler described an excruciating method in India during the rule of the rajahs: "The culprit, bound hand and foot, is fastened by a long cord, passed round his wrist, to the elephant's hind leg. The latter is urged into a rapid trot through the streets of the city, and every step gives the cord a violent jerk, which makes the body of the condemned wretch bounce on the pavement.... Then his head is placed upon a stone, and the elephant executioner crushes it beneath his enormous foot."

What kinds of crime incurred such punishments? Murder and treason have almost always ensured death. Under the Mosaic law, capital offenses ranged from gathering sticks on the Sabbath and adultery to the sacrifice of children to the god Molech. A medieval German code decreed: "Should a coiner (counterfeiter) be caught in the act, then let him be stewed in the pan or a caldron."

England's response to the bewildering social evils caused by the Industrial Revolution was unique even in a world long used to such officially sanctioned slaughters as those during the Spanish Inquisition, when tens of thousands of convicted heretics were burned. The English meted out the death penalty for more than 200 offenses, including stealing turnips, associating with gypsies, cutting down a tree or picking pockets. "Hanging days" were public holidays, and in 1807 a crowd of 40,000 became so frenzied at an execution that nearly a hundred were trampled to death. Frequently both victims and executioner were drunk, and occasionally the job was botched, with the condemned man being hanged two or even three times. Afterward the crowds surged toward the corpse, because it and the scaffold were believed to have curative powers.

Death sentences were often arbitrarily applied. The social standing, sex, citizenship or religion of the victims usually determined the degree of horror they would suffer. Death alone was rarely considered a sufficient penalty unless it was preceded by terror, torture, and humiliation, preferably in public. One of history's most spectacular executions was that of Damiens, the unsuccessful assassin of Louis XV, in Paris in 1757. His flesh was torn with red-hot pincers, his right hand was burned with sulfur, his wounds were drenched with molten lead, his body was drawn and quartered by four horses, his parts were set afire and his ashes scattered to the winds. His execution was accomplished before a large crowd.

"The more public the punishments are, the greater the effect they will produce upon the reformation of others," declared Seneca in ancient Rome. Over the centuries, many societies came to believe otherwise. The rituals of execution, rooted perhaps in a primitive need for sacrifice, catharsis and revenge, seemed less to cast out the evils of humanity than to feed its blood lust. By the late 18th century, a reform movement had taken hold in Europe, aided by the invention of such "humane" devices as the hanging machine and the guillotine.

Today the death penalty has been abolished in Canada, at least officially in much of Latin America, and in most of Western Europe. In Eastern Europe only Albania has abandoned capital punishment, and it remains in force throughout Asia and the Islamic world. In 1982, the world leader in announced executions was Iran, with more than 600.

Word count: 667

7. THE SEXES

Do you want to start an argument? Simply make a remark about either men or women being the superior sex. Although some people joke about the "battle of the sexes," it is a subject taken very seriously by many people.

In this section you can read a light-hearted commentary about women in sports, serious articles on romantic love and marriage, and take a look at how women are in some ways superior to men.

290   *Read and Respond*

34. MARRIAGES MADE TO LAST
by Jeanette and Robert Lauer
from *Psychology Today*

> What is the secret to a lasting marriage? What keeps married partners together? The authors of this article asked these questions of several couples who have had a long-lasting marriage. The answers may surprise you.
>
> **colleagues**   "Through **colleagues** and students, we located..."
> *Meaning:* co-workers in the same profession
>
> **trite**   "It may seem almost **trite** to say..."
> *Meaning:* overused and commonplace, insignificant
>
> **inexorably**   "They saw it not as a chain that **inexorably** binds people together..."
> *Meaning:* unyielding, firmly
>
> **incongruous**   "...the high value...strikes us as **incongruous** with infidelity."
> *Meaning:* disagreeing
>
> **catharsis**   "...aggression is a **catharsis** that gets rid of hostility..."
> *Meaning:* something which purifies
>
> **egalitarian**   "...the value of an **egalitarian** relationship."
> *Meaning:* promoting equal rights

Americans are keenly aware of the high marital breakup in this country. More than a million couples a year now end their expectations of bliss in divorce; the average duration of a marriage in the United States is 9.4 years. The traditional nuclear family of husband, wife, and children in less and less common. Indeed, it seems at times that no one out there is happily married. But in the midst of such facts and figures, another group tends to be overlooked: those couples who somehow manage to stay together, who allow nothing less than death itself to break them up.

Social scientists have long been concerned about the causes of marital disruption. There are numerous works that tell us why people break up. But as J.H. Wallis wrote in his 1970 book, *Marriage Observed*, "we have still not quite come to grips with what it is that makes marriages last, and enables them to survive." His conclusion remains valid. The books that tell couples how to construct a lasting and meaningful marriage tend to be based either upon the clinical experiences of those who have counseled troubled and dissolving marriages, or upon the speculations of those who believe that they have found the formula for success.

We recently completed a survey of couples with enduring marriages to explore how marriages survive and satisfy in this turbulent world. Through colleagues and students, we located and questioned 351 couples married for 15 years or more.

Of the 351 couples, 300 said they were happily married, 19 said they were unhappily married (but were staying together for a variety of reasons, including "the sake of the children"); and among the remaining 32 couples only one partner said he or she was unhappy in the marriage.

Each husband and wife responded individually to our questionnaire, which included 39 statements and questions about marriage—ranging from agreement about sex, money and goals in life to attitudes toward spouses and marriage in general. We asked couples to select from their answers the ones that best explained why their marriages had lasted. Men and women showed remarkable agreement on the keys to an enduring relationship (see list at end of article).

The most frequently named reason for an enduring and happy marriage was having a generally positive attitude toward one's spouse: viewing one's partner as one's best friend and liking him or her "as a person."

As one wife summed it up, "I feel that liking a person in marriage is as important as loving that person. Friends enjoy each other's company. We spend an unusually large amount of time together. We work at the same institution, offices just a few feet apart. But we still have things to do and say to each other on a positive note after being together through the day."

It may seem almost trite to say that "my spouse is my best friend," but the couples in our survey underscored the importance of feeling that way. Moreover, they told us some specific things that they liked about their mates—why, as one woman said, "I would want to have him as a friend even if I weren't married to him." For one thing, many happily married people said that their mates become more interesting in time. A man married for 30 years said that it was almost like being married to a series of different women: "I have watched her grow and shared with her both the pain and the exhilaration of her journey. I find her more fascinating now than when we were first married."

A common theme among couples in our study was that the things they really liked in each other were qualities of caring, giving, integrity and a sense of humor. In essence, they said, "I am married to someone who cares about me, who is concerned for my well-being, who gives as much or more than he or she gets, who is open and trustworthy and who is not mired down in a somber, bleak outlook on life." The redemption of difficult people through selfless devotion may make good fiction, but the happily married people in our sample expressed no such sense of mission. Rather, they said, they are grateful to have married someone who is basically appealing and likable.

Are lovers blind to other's faults? No, according to our findings. They are aware of the flaws in their mates and acknowledge the rough times, but they believe that the likable qualities are more important than the deficiencies and the difficulties. "She isn't perfect," said a husband of 24 years. "But I don't worry about her weak points, which are very few. Her strong points overcome them too much."

A second key to a lasting marriage was a belief in marriage as a long-term commitment and a sacred institution. Many of our respondents thought that the present generation takes the vow "till death us do part" too lightly and is unwilling to work through difficult times. Successful couples viewed marriage as a task that sometimes demands that you grit your teeth and plunge ahead in spite of the difficulties. "I'll tell you why we've stayed together," said a Texas woman married for 18 years. "I'm just too damned stubborn to give up."

Some of the people in the survey indicated that they would stay together no matter what. Divorce was simply not an option. Others viewed commitment somewhat differently. They saw it not as a chain that inexorably binds people together despite intense misery but rather as a determination to work through difficult times. "You can't run home to mother when the first sign of trouble appears," said a woman married for 35 years.

"Commitment means a willingness to be unhappy for a while," said a man married for more than 20 years. "I wouldn't go on for years and years being wretched in my marriage. But you can't avoid troubled times. You're not going to be happy with each other all the time. That's when commitment is really important."

In addition to sharing attitudes toward the spouse and toward marriage, our respondents indicated that agreement about aims and goals in life, the desire to make the marriage succeed, and laughing together were all important. One surprising result was that agreement about sex was far down the list of reasons for a happy marriage. Fewer than 10 percent of the spouses thought that good sexual relations kept their marriage together. Is sex relatively unimportant to a happy marriage? Yes and no.

Although not many happily married respondents listed it as a major reason for their happiness, most were still generally satisfied with their sex lives. Seventy percent said that they always or almost always agreed about sex. And indeed for many, "satisfied" seems too mild a term. A woman married for 19 years said: "Our sexual desire is strong, and we are very much in love." One man said that sex with his wife was like "a revival of youth." Another noted that for various reasons he and his wife did not have sex as frequently as they would like to, but when they do "it is a beautiful act of giving and sharing as deeply emotional as it is physical."

While some reported a diminishing sex life, others described a relatively stable pattern and a number indicated improvement over time. "Thank God, the passion hasn't died," a wife said. "In fact, it has gotten more intense. The only thing that has died is the element of doubt or uncertainly that one experiences while dating or in the beginning of a marriage."

On the other hand, some couples said they were satisfied despite a less-than-ideal sex life. A number of people told us that they were happy with their marriage even though they did not have sex as frequently as they would like. Generally men complained of this more than women, although a number of wives desired sex more than did their husbands. There were various reasons for having less sex than desired, generally involving one partner's exhaustion from work or family circumstances ("We are very busy and very involved," reported a husband, "and have a teenager who stays up late. So we don't make love as often as we would like to").

Does this dissatisfaction with sex life lead to affairs? We did not ask about infidelity directly, but the high value that most of our subjects placed on friendship and commitment strikes us as incongruous with infidelity. And in fact only two of those we questioned volunteered that they had had brief affairs. One husband's view might explain the faithfulness of the group: "I get tempted when we don't have sex. But I don't think I could ever have an affair. I would feel like a traitor."

Such treason, in fact, may be the one taboo in enduring relationships. A wife of 27 years said that although she could work out almost any problem with her husband given enough time, infidelity "would probably not be something I could forget and forgive." The couples in our sample appear to take their commitment to each other seriously.

Those with a less-than-ideal sex life talked about adjusting to it rather than seeking relief in an affair. A woman married 25 years rated her marriage as extremely happy even though she and her husband had had no sexual relations for the past 10 years. "I was married once before and the marriage was almost totally sex and little else," she said. "So I suppose a kind of trade-off exists here—I like absolutely everything else about my current marriage."

Many others agreed that they would rather be married to their spouse and have a less-than-ideal sex life than be married to someone else and have a better sex life. As one wife put it, "I feel marriages can survive and flourish without today's emphasis on sex. I had a much stronger sex drive than my husband and it was a point of weakness in our marriage. However, it was not as important as friendship, understanding and respect. That we had lots of, and still do."

We found some beliefs and practices among our couples that contradict what some therapists believe is important to a marriage. One involves conflict. Some marriage counselors stress the importance of expressing feelings with abandon—spouses should freely vent their anger with each other, letting out all the stops short of physical violence. According to them, aggression is a catharsis that gets rid of hostility and restores harmony in the marital relationship. But some social scientists argue that intense expressions of anger, resentment, and dislike tend to corrode the relationship and increase the likelihood of future aggression.

Happily married couples in our survey came down squarely on the side of those who emphasize the damaging effects of intensely expressed anger. A salesman with a 36-year marriage advised, "Discuss your problems in a normal voice. If a voice is raised, stop. Return after a short period of time. Start again. After a period of time both parties will be able to deal with their problems and not say things that they will be sorry about later."

Only one couple said that they typically yelled at each other. The rest emphasized the importance of restraint. They felt that a certain calmness is necessary in dealing constructively with conflict.

Another commonly held belief that contradicts conventional wisdom concerns equality in marriage. Most social scientists note the value of an egalitarian relationship. But according to the couples in our sample, the attitude that marriage is a 50-50 proposition can be damaging. One husband said that a successful marriage demands that you "give 60 percent of the time. You have to be willing to put in more than you take out." A wife happily married for 44 years said she would advise all young couples "to be willing to give 70 percent and expect 30 percent."

In the long run, the giving and taking should balance out. If either partner enters a marriage determined that all transactions must be equal, the marriage will suffer. As one husband put it, "Sometimes I give far more than I receive, and sometimes I receive far more than I give. But my wife does the same. If we weren't willing to do that, we would have broken up long ago."

Finally, some marriage experts have strongly advocated that spouses maintain separate as well as shared interests. It is important, they argue, to avoid the merging of identities. But those in our survey with enduring, happy marriages disagree. They try to spend as much time together and share as many activities as possible. "Jen is just the best friend I have," said a husband who rated his marriage as extremely happy. "I would rather spend time with her, talk to her, be with her, than with anyone else."

"We try to share everything," said another. "We even work together now. In spite of that, we often feel that we have too little time together."

We did not detect any loss of individuality in these people. In fact, they disagreed to some extent on many of the questions. Their intense intimacy—their preference for shared rather than separate activities— seems to reflect a richness and fulfillment in the relationship rather than a loss of identity. "On occasion, she has something else to do and I enjoy the time alone. But it strikes me that I can enjoy it because I know that soon she will be home, and we will be together again."

Our results seem to underscore Leo Tolstoy's observation that "Happy families are all alike." Those who have long-term, happy marriages share a number of attitudes and behavioral patterns that combine to create an enduring relationship. For them, "till death us do part" is not a binding clause but a gratifying reality.

What keeps a marriage going?

Here are the top reasons respondents gave, listed in order of frequency.

MEN	WOMEN
My spouse is my best friend.	My spouse is my best friend.
I like my spouse as a person.	I like my spouse as a person.
Marriage is a long-term commitment.	Marriage is a long-term commitment.
Marriage is sacred.	Marriage is sacred.
We agree on aims and goals.	We agree on aims and goals.
My spouse has grown more interesting.	My spouse has grown more interesting.
I want the relationship to succeed.	I want the relationship to succeed.
An enduring marriage is important to social stability.	We laugh together.
We laugh together.	We agree on a philosophy of life.
I am proud of my spouse's achievements.	We agree on how and how often to show affection.
We agree on a philosophy of life.	An enduring marriage is important to social stability.
We agree about our sex life.	We have a stimulating exchange of ideas.
We agree on how and how often to show affection.	We agree about our sex life.
I confide in my spouse.	I am proud of my spouse's achievements.
We share outside hobbies and interests.	

Word count: 2496

35. THE MYTH OF ROMANTIC LOVE
from *The Road Less Traveled*
by M. Scott Peck, M.D.

> You hear about people who marry their high school sweetheart and how fifty years later they are still married. You also hear about the high divorce rate and wonder why things go wrong with so many people who thought they were in love. Is it dangerous to believe in the ideal of "living happily ever after?" Read on to see what one person has to say about this subject.
>
> **illusion** "...the **illusion** that the experience will last forever..."
> *Meaning:* image or idea that is not true
>
> **embody** "...they represent and **embody** greater universal truths..."
> *Meaning:* to give a concrete form to
>
> **ghastly** "...the **ghastly** confusion and suffering..."
> *Meaning:* dreadful; terrifying
>
> **subjugates** "Mrs. A. **subjugates** herself absurdly..."
> *Meaning:* to make submissive
>
> **psychosomatic** "...can't believe they are **psychosomatic**."
> *Meaning:* a physical disorder brought on by an emotional state
>
> **rampant** "...by mutual **rampant** infidelity..."
> *Meaning:* widespread; unchecked

To serve as effectively as it does to trap us into marriage, the experience of falling in love probably must have as one of its characteristics the illusion that the experience will last forever. This illusion is fostered in our culture by the commonly held myth of romantic love, which has its origins in our favorite childhood fairy tales, wherein the prince and the princess, once united, live happily forever after. The myth of romantic love tells us, in effect, that for every young man in the world there is a young woman and only one woman for a man and this has been predetermined "in the stars." When we meet the person for whom we are intended, recognition comes through the fact that we fall in love. We have met the person for whom all the heavens intended us, and since the match is perfect, we will then be able to satisfy all of each other's needs forever and ever, and therefore live happily forever after in perfect union and harmony. Should it come to pass, however, that we do not satisfy or meet all of each other's needs and friction arises and we fall out of love, then it is clear that a dreadful mistake was made: We misread the stars; we did not hook up with our one and only perfect match; what we thought was love was not real or "true" love; and nothing can be done about the situation except to live unhappily ever after or get divorced.

While I generally find that great myths are great precisely because they represent and embody great universal truths, the myth of romantic love is a dreadful lie. Perhaps it is a necessary lie in that it ensures the survival of the species by its encouragement and seeming validation of the falling-in-love experience that traps us into marriage. But as a psychiatrist I weep in my heart almost daily for the ghastly confusion and suffering that this myth fosters. Millions of people waste vast amounts of energy desperately and futilely attempting to make the reality of their lives conform to the unreality of the myth. Mrs. A. subjugates herself absurdly to her husband out of a feeling of guilt. "I didn't really love my husband when we married," she says, "I pretended I did. I guess I tricked him into it, so I have no right to complain about him, and I owe it to him to do whatever he wants." Mr. B. laments: "I regret I didn't marry Miss C. I think we could have had a good marriage. But I didn't fall head over heels in love with her, so I assumed she couldn't be the right person for me." Mrs. D., married for two years, becomes severely depressed without apparent cause, and enters therapy stating: "I don't know what's wrong. I've got everything I need, including a perfect marriage." Only months later can she accept the fact that she has fallen out of love with her husband but that this does not mean that she made a horrible mistake. Mr. E., also married two years, begins to suffer intense headaches in the evenings and can't believe they are psychosomatic. "My home life is fine. I love my wife as much as the day I married her. She's everything I ever wanted," he says. But his headaches don't leave him until a year later, when he is able to admit, "She bugs the hell out of me the way she is always wanting, wanting things without regard to my salary," and then is able to confront her with her extravagance. Mr. and Mrs. F. acknowledge to each other that they have fallen out of love and then proceed to make each other miserable by mutual rampant infidelity as they each search for the one "true love," not realizing that their very acknowledgment could mark the beginning of the work of their marriage instead of its end.

Even when couples have acknowledged that the honeymoon is over, that they are no longer romantically in love with each other and are able still to be committed to their relationship, they still cling to the myth and attempt to conform their lives to it. "Even though we have fallen out of love, if we act by sheer will power as if we still were in love, then maybe romantic love will return to our lives," their thinking goes. These couples prize togetherness. When they enter couples group therapy (which is the setting in which my wife and I and our close colleagues conduct most serious marriage counseling), they sit together, speak for each other, defend each other's faults and seek to present to the rest of the group a united front, believing this unit to be a sign of the relative health of their marriage and a prerequisite for its improvement.

Sooner or later, and usually sooner, we must tell most couples that they are too much married, too closely coupled, and that they need to establish some psychological distance from each other before they can even begin to work constructively on their problems. Sometimes it is actually necessary to physically separate them, directing them to sit apart from each other in the group circle. It is always necessary to ask them to refrain from speaking for each other or defending each other against the group. Over and over again we must say, "Let Mary speak for herself, John," and "John can defend himself, Mary; he's strong enough." Ultimately, if they stay in therapy, all couples learn that a true acceptance of their own and each other's individuality and separateness is the only foundation upon which a mature marriage can be based and real love can grow.

Word count: 961

36. WHY ISN'T A NICE PERSON LIKE YOU MARRIED?
by Elsie Bliss

> What are the advantages of being married? What are the advantages of being single? Some people react to single people as if something is wrong with them. This article expresses a viewpoint that is often ignored—the idea that some people may prefer single life to married life.
>
> **inordinately**   "...but for some who have stayed single for an **inordinately** long time..."
> *Meaning:* exceeding ordinary limits
>
> **candidly**   "...and if they respond **candidly**..."
> *Meaning:* openly, honestly
>
> **C'est moi**   "If the definition is a protective, assertive, overly sensitive,...person, then hallelujah! **C'est moi!**"
> *Meaning:* that is me [French]
>
> **angst**   "Probably what causes the greatest **angst** among single people is someone looking at us with a mixture of wonder and pity..."
> *Meaning:* a feeling of of anxiety or depression
>
> **twinge**   "...plus the occasional **twinge** of being left out as you observe hand-holding couples..."
> *Meaning:* a sudden, sharp physical or emotional pain (in this case, emotional)

I am asked THE QUESTION by friends at every wedding reception. Also at every party and family gathering by well-meaning relatives and sometimes strangers. If it were not for this question and my creative response, some of the people I meet wouldn't find anything to say to me. But the time it hurts most is that moment when an eligible man I've just met wonders aloud, "Gee, it's a wonder you aren't married."

Am I supposed to admit that I am very insecure yet demanding? That no one I have ever met who was available was sufficiently desirable to justify giving up my precious independence? That no matter how I searched (while appearing not be searching) there has not been anyone who met my rather rigid list of criteria? Am I expected to actually unload this emotional baggage on some poor schnook who might himself prove to be truly desirable? Of course not. Because then I would frighten him off.

Speaking for many nice, attractive, loving and desirable single people, I'd like to climb up on my soapbox and explain a few things. What I say may not hold true for all single people, but for some who have stayed single for an inordinately long time...

Being single is quite respectable. It is a valid way of life. It is not a tragedy or a handicap. It is being the boss; the captain of your ship. I quite like it, even though I readily admit that I frequently miss what married people have when their marriage is going well, just as they miss the freedom I have to decide my own goals and priorities.

I am sorry to say that statistics are against their marriages going well, unfortunately. Marriage in the 20th century is in trouble. Single is not in trouble, despite its bad press and your Aunt Sophie's opinion. Single has a lot going for it.

If you took a poll of your friends and their feelings about marriage, and if they responded candidly, you'd find that (as some brilliant mind once noted) marriage is like a besieged fortress; those who are inside want to get out and those who are outside want to get in. Perhaps the question should be put to married people, "Why is a nice person like you married?"

Some day I may find a partner who will allow me to be me and who will even respect and admire my need to be myself. He won't criticize my liking health foods or tell me I'm uptight because I won't go to a nude beach. He'll think I am fine, quirks and all even though I love sitcoms and hate game shows and violent movies. If I am lucky, he will have the same desire for himself, and I'll respect and love him for it. Our two selves may join and become a couple of happy individuals. Note, I did not say we would become ONE, but a couple of individuals. Where did that myth originate that you become part of another? Better half, indeed.

Until that happens, no matter how long it takes (maybe never), I will not be categorized as a liberated woman or a Jewish Mother or anything else. I am all of these and none of them. I am the product of years of development and growth including experiences of joy and sorrow. I am like fine chocolate—bitter-sweet. I was liberated long before it was fashionable and I was a Jewish Mother type as a ten year old child. You don't have to be Jewish or a mother or even a female to be a J.M. If the definition is a protective, assertive, overly sensitive, deeply involved, demonstrative person, then hallelujah! C'est moi!

Probably what causes the greatest angst among single people is someone looking at us with a mixture of wonder and pity and saying, "You are so attractive, it's a shame you aren't married."

Would I gaze at anyone and say, "You are such an attractive person; it's a shame you are overweight"? Or, "How come a couple like you who argue so much are not divorced?" Or, "You seem so nice; why can't you find a good job?"

Of course no civilized person would ask these things. But there are those who consider being single a national dilemma and one that permits constant probing into the single person's psyche to learn the causes.

As with most things, being single is a trade-off. It is a mixed blessing of being private with time of your own to use as you see fit plus the occasional twinge of being left out as you observe hand-holding couples strolling down life's road together.

To some single people, the fear of failure is a great deterrent to marriage, especially if they have feelings of insecurity born of being the children of perfectionist parents. This can color all decision-making for them.

If you are single, and none of the above applies to you, then you will have no trouble replying easily when you hear that ageless question, "Why isn't a nice person like you married?" You'll smile sweetly at Aunt Minnie and say, "Gee, I've been too busy to notice it, but gosh, you're right, I'm not married; I didn't realize. I'll give it some thought and get back to you."

Word count: 894

37. LOVE AND ROMANCE MAKE A COMEBACK
by Gabriel García Márquez
from *World Press Review*

Read the views of a celebrated author who welcomes the return of love and romance, which he claims is definitely making a comeback.

indelible   "...one of those **indelible** markers..."
Meaning: permanent; cannot be erased

graffiti   "...that are used in the guerrilla warfare of political **graffiti**..."
Meaning: writing, scratching, or drawing on walls or other public surfaces

blasé   "...no matter how **blasé** she is..."
Meaning: not affected; unemotional

frenzy   "This is attributed to the sexual **frenzy** of the 1970s..."
Meaning: violence or madness; agitation

erotic   "...humanity went through all of its **erotic** reserves."
Meaning: concerning sexual desire

chastity   "...the first signs of pressure on **chastity** began to appear..."
Meaning: purity; virginity

medieval   "...something was changing in that **medieval** society..."
Meaning: pertaining to the Middle Ages

heyday   "...we were living in the **heyday** of venereal disease."
Meaning: period of great strength or power

boleros   "**boleros**, danced cheek-to-cheek..."
Meaning: romantic Spanish dances

unadulterated   "...swept away by the whirlwind of **unadulterated** sex."
Meaning: by itself; not mixed with anything

I woke up recently to find an enormous sign written on the long white wall across the street from my home in Mexico City: "Peggy, give me a kiss," it said. It had been written with one of those indelible markers that are used in the guerilla warfare of political graffiti, and one could see in it the tension and intensity of the slogans written late at night, with your heart racing and while your comrades were keeping a lookout at the corner.

The sign is outside the parts of the city where these shadow wars usually take place. But it is big enough so that Peggy will see it when she walks by, no matter how much she has on her mind, no matter how blasé she is, and it is desperate enough to melt a heart of stone.

I discovered it when I had finished reading the papers, which, in this day and age, is like taking castor oil before breakfast. Things looked so bad that it was a great relief to discover that there was someone, right around the corner, whose only problem in the world was that Peggy would not give him a kiss.

Panorama, the Italian weekly, recently published an article based on the idea that sex is going out of style and old-fashioned love is returning to its place. It was filled with the results of surveys that showed that men and women are having sex less and less often and even claiming that there are couples who have stopped entirely, yet remain happy. This is attributed to the sexual frenzy of the 1970s, during which, it seems, humanity went through all of its erotic reserves.

Throughout my life, I have watched the process of sexual liberation take place in two countries where it seemed least likely: Columbia and Spain. In the latter, the first signs of pressure on chastity began to appear even long before Franco died. For me, the first signal that something was changing in that medieval society was the closing of a hotel, famous for its short-term occupancy, that shut down for lack of business. My children, whose grade school was next door to this secret paradise, loved to climb to the top of the wall between the two buildings during recess, to watch events on the other side. The most entertaining thing that happened, in reality, was that the maids put covers over the license plates of every car as it arrived, so that other clients would not be able to identify them.

When I arrived in Bogatá, Colombia, in the 1940s from the Caribbean coast, I was 13 years old and had already lost my virginity, as was common in the region I came from. My mother, like all mothers, warned me against the two most serious threats that awaited us at Bogatá's high altitude: pneumonia and shotgun marriages.

The threat of forced marriage was not the worst thing that could happen, for we were living in the heyday of venereal disease. In streetcars, in public toilets, everywhere, were signs reminding us: "If you do not fear God, fear syphilis." So the only recourse against solitude was the Saturday night dance, which provided the only sanctioned expressions of love: boleros, danced cheek-to-cheek, dates made for after mass the next day, perfumed letters, dark movie houses, pillows soaked with tears, and poetry. All of this disappeared in the 1970s, swept away by the whirlwind of unadulterated sex. I do not regret it. To the contrary, I have always believed that we were born with our pleasures numbered, and what we do not use, we lose. But the best thing is sex with all that goes with it, meaning total love. This is undoubtedly what is coming now, to judge by the personal ads. Love stories have taken over the fiction shelves once again, and couples are once again kissing on the streets.

A few days ago, my 18-year-old son asked his mother to teach him the bolero, which has made a comeback. In the cities of Latin America and Spain, dimly lit discos are opening to experience it anew. I have always believed that love would save the human race, and these signs, which might seem regressive, are not; they are rays of hope. That is why I am hoping that Peggy will read the message that someone has written across the street from my house. Please, Peggy, give him a kiss.

Word count: 748

38. WOMEN STILL FACE LONG JOURNEY TO SPORTS FANATICISM
by Dave Barry
from *The Spokesman-Review*

Do females place less importance than males on athletics? Dave Barry is well known for his humorous writing. In this selection, he pokes fun at the men as well as the women in sports.

obnoxious	"...but is certainly one of the most **obnoxious**..."
	Meaning: rude, disgusting
leatheroid	"...special **leatheroid** racquetball gloves..."
	Meaning: leather-like, imitation leather

Mankind's yearning to engage in sports is older than recorded history, dating back to the time, millions of years ago, when the first primitive man picked up a crude club and a round rock, tossed the rock into the air and whomped the club into the sloping forehead of the first primitive umpire.

What inner force drove this first athlete? Your guess is as good as mine. Better, probably, because you haven't had four beers. All I know is, whatever the reason, Mankind is still nuts about sports. As Howard Cosell, who may not be the most likable person in the world, but is certainly the most obnoxious, put it: "In terms of Mankind and sports, blah blah blah blah the 1954 Brooklyn Dodgers."

Notice that Howard and I both use the term "Mankind." Womankind really isn't into sports the same way. Oh, I realize things have changed since my high school days, when sports were considered unfeminine and your average girls' gym class consisted of six girls in those gym outfits colored digestive enzyme green running around waving field hockey sticks and squealing, and 127 girls standing on the side lines in civilian clothing, claiming it was That Time of the Month. I realize that today you have a number of top female athletes such as Martina Navratilova, who can run like a deer and bench-press Chevrolet pickup trucks. But to be brutally frank, women as a group have a long way to go before they reach the level of intensity and dedication to sports that enables men to be such incredible jerks about it.

If you don't believe me, go to your local racquetball club and observe the difference between the way men and women play. Where I play, the women tend to gather on the court in groups of random sizes—sometimes three, sometimes five, as if it were a Jane Fonda workout. One of them will hit the ball at the wall, and the rest of them will admire the shot and compliment her quite sincerely, and then they all sort of relax, as if they're thinking, well, thank goodness THAT's over with, and they always seem very surprised when the ball comes BACK. If one of them has the presence of mind to take another swing, and if she actually hits the ball, everybody is VERY complimentary. If she misses it, the others all tell her what a GOOD try she made, really, then they all laugh and act very relieved because they know they have some time to talk before the ball comes bouncing off that darned wall again.

Meanwhile, over in the next court, you will have two males wearing various knee braces and wrist bands and special leatheroid racquetball gloves, hurling themselves into the walls like musk oxen on Dexedrine, and after every single point one of them will yell in the self-reproving tone of voice you might use if you had just accidentally shot your grandmother. American men tend to take their sports more seriously than they take family matters or Asia.

This is why it's usually a mistake for men and women to play on teams together. I sometimes play in a coed slow-pitch softball league, where the rules say you have to have at least two women on the field. The teams always have one of the women play catcher because in slow-pitch the batters hit just about every pitch, so it wouldn't really hurt you much if you had a deceased person as catcher.

Our team usually puts the other woman at second base, where the maximum possible number of males can get there on short notice to help out in case of emergency. As far as I can tell, our second basewoman is a pretty good baseball player, better than I am, anyway, but there's no way to know for sure because if the ball gets anywhere near her, a male comes barging over from, say, right field, to deal with it. She's been on the team for three seasons now, but the males still don't trust her. They know, deep in their souls, that if she had to choose between a fly ball and saving an infant's life, she would probably elect to save the infant's life, without even considering whether there were men on base.

The difference in attitude between men and women carries over to the area of talking about sports, especially sporting events that took place long ago. Take the 1960 World Series. If we were to look at it objectively, we would have to agree that the outcome of the 1960 World Series no longer matters. You could make a fairly strong case that it didn't really matter in 1960. Women know this, which is why you almost never hear them mention the 1960 World Series; whereas you take virtually any male older than 35, even if he can't remember which of his children have diabetes, he can remember exactly how Pirates shortstop Bill Mazeroski hit the ninth-inning home run that beat the Yankees, and he will take every available opportunity to discuss it at length with other males.

See that? Out there in Readerland, you females just read right through that last sentence, nodding in agreement, but you males leaped from your chairs and shouted: "Mazeroski wasn't a SHORTSTOP! Mazeroski played SECOND BASE!"

Every male in America has millions of perfectly good brain cells devoted to information like this. We can't help it. We have no perspective. I have a friend named Buzz, a successful businessman and the most rational person you ever want to meet, and the high point of his entire life is the time he got Hubie Brown, the coach of the New York Knicks, to look directly at him during a professional basketball game and make a very personal remark rhyming with "duck shoe." I should explain that Buzz and I have season tickets to the Philadelphia 76ers, so naturally we hate the Knicks a great deal. It was a great honor when Hubie Brown singled Buzz out of the crowd for recognition. The rest of us males congratulated Buzz as if he'd won a Nobel Prize for physics.

It's silly, really, this male lack of perspective, and it can lead to unnecessary tragedy, such as soccer riot deaths at the University of Texas. What is even more tragic is that women are losing perspective, too. Even as you read these words, women are writing vicious letters to the editor, expressing great fury at me for suggesting they don't take their racquetball seriously. Soon they will be droning on about the importance of relief pitching.

Word count: 1106

39. SUPER WOMEN
by Edward Dolnick
from *Health*

Women have often been called the "weaker sex." According to Edward Dolnick, this description is highly inaccurate.

swaddled "...at row upon row of **swaddled** babies."
Meaning: wrapped in blankets or strips of cloth

trundling "...the 60-year-olds **trundling** off the bus..."
Meaning: moving as if on wheels, shuffling

epidemiologist "...Deborah Wingard, an **epidemiologist**..."
Meaning: a doctor who specializes in diseases which are widespread

satirizing "Mark Twain once devoted a bitter essay to **satirizing** the workmanship of a Creator..."
Meaning: to criticize or expose, using humor, ridicule, sarcasm, etc.

lamented "...Twain **lamented** in his old age."
Meaning: complained; regretted

resilient "In bad times, women may also be psychologically more **resilient** than men."
Meaning: able to recover

acute "Women have more **acute** hearing than men..."
Meaning: sharp or keen

conscientious "...any **conscientious** manufacturer would have issued a product recall."
Meaning: careful

innate "Women seem to have an **innate** health advantage."
Meaning: inborn; natural

panache "Breadwinning in earlier years may have had more **panache**..."
Meaning: flair; swagger; style

camaraderie "...provides women with feelings of self-esteem, responsibility, and **camaraderie**..."
Meaning: friendship; good will

Look at a school photo of a fifth-grade class, the boys in their coolest T-shirts, the girls just starting to grow gangly. Look at the nursery in a big-city hospital, at row upon row of swaddled babies. Look at the teenagers working at McDonald's or at the 60-year-olds trundling off the bus behind their tour guide a the Washington Monument.

Then look again in a few years. In every case, if you tried to put together a reunion, you'd find that more males than females had died. If you could take an immense group snapshot of everyone in the United States today, females would outnumber males by 6 million. In this country, women outlive men by about seven years, and the figure is close to that in all industrialized nations.

Throughout the modern world, cultures are different, diets are different, ways of life and causes of death are different, but one thing is the same: Women outlive men.

It starts even before birth. At conception male fetuses actually outnumber females by about 115 to 100; at birth, the ratio has already fallen to about 105 boys to every 100 girls. By about age 30, there are only enough men left to match the number of women. And from there on, women start building a lead that just grows and grows. Beyond age 80, there are twice as many women as men.

"What's dramatic," says Deborah Wingard, an epidemiologist a the University of California at San Diego, "is that if you look at the top 10 or 12 causes of death, EVERY SINGLE ONE kills more men." She runs a finger down this melancholy Top 10 and rattles off one affliction after another—heart disease and lung cancer and homicide and cirrhosis of the liver and pneumonia. Each kills men at roughly twice the rate it does women.

"Diabetes," Wingard resumes after catching her breath , "is the only one that even comes close to being"—she pauses, in search of a non-judgmental word—"to being equitable."

Women's superiority extends far beyond merely living longer. Women are better than men at distinguishing colors. They have a sharper sense of taste and a better sense of smell. Would any child, confronted with a dubious-looking glass of milk, be so foolish as to give it to his father, rather than his mother, to sample?

The differences between men's and women's sexual capacities are much too familiar to need repeating here. Mark Twain once devoted a bitter essay to satirizing the workmanship of a creator who had come up with two such mismatched creatures. "After 50, a man's performance is of poor quality, the intervals between are wide, and its satisfactions of no great value to either party," Twain lamented in his old age. "Whereas his great-grandmother is as good as new."

In outdoor athletics, women aren't a match for men. But one trend is worth noting: The more a competition requires stamina, the better women fare. The first woman to win a mixed-sex national championship did so in a 24-hour endurance race. Ann Trason ran 143 miles' worth of circles around a track, four miles more than the (male) runner-up. Helen Klein, a 68-year-old who considers a 50-mile race routine, holds all the "ultramarathon" records in her age group. Women win so many long-distance dogsled races that one musher has designed a "Save the Males" T-shirt.

In real-life ordeals, too, women seem at least as durable as men. One man trapped in the Warsaw Ghetto by the Nazis kept a journal in which he recorded the growing misery of his fellow Jews.

"At 14 Ostrowska Street is a house where there are only women and children," he wrote in the cold and hungry winter of 1942. "All the menfolk have died. In general, men have a markedly higher mortality—the reason being that men have less endurance, work harder, and so forth." Six miserable months later, the diarist continued to marvel at "the courage and endurance of our women" who were now " coming forward to replace the men, who fall out exhausted."

In bad times, women may also be psychologically more resilient than men. A study of areas of London heavily bombed during World War II, for example, found that 70 percent more men than women became psychiatric casualties. The study's (male) author summarized its findings: "It may be true that women are more emotional than men in romance, but they are less so in air raids."

Women have more acute hearing than men, and keep their hearing longer. Women have colder hands and feet than men, and keep their hearing longer. Women have colder hands and feet than men, but complain and suffer less when exposed to bitter cold.

Are you beginning to detect a pattern?

Men out-stutter women 4 to 1. Men go bald, and sprout hair from their ears to make up for it. They're more likely to be color-blind, 16 to 1, and are especially prey to ulcers and hernias and back problems. Faced with such a list of defects, any conscientious manufacturer would have issued a product recall.

Why are men so puny? A century ago, the question would have made no sense. In 19th-century America, men outnumbered and outlived women. This situation presented no challenge to conventional wisdom. Women were, authorities from the Bible to Shakespeare agreed, "the weaker vessel."

God was in his heaven, all was right with the world. But in the 20th century, the trend reversed itself. Women began living longer than men, primarily because pregnancy and childbirth had become less dangerous. The gap grew steadily through the decades. In 1950, for the first time ever in the United States, females outnumbered males.

That made for some wrinkled brows. If men were so strong, why were they all dying? Part of the damage turned out to be self-inflicted.
Overall, statisticians figure that one-third of the longevity gap can be attributed to the ways men act. Men smoke more than women, drink more and take more life-threatening chances.

Men are murdered (usually by other men) three times as often as women are. Overall, they commit suicide at a rate two or three times higher than that of women. This fact holds for every age group, without exception, whether you compare teenagers or the middle-aged or the elderly. If men don't have guns or knives, they make do with cars. Men have twice as many fatal accidents per mile driven as women do. Men are more likely to drive through an intersection when the light is yellow or red, less likely to signal a turn, more likely to drive after drinking. Men drivers!

But behavior doesn't explain away the longevity gap. Women seem to have an innate health advantage. Even among people who have never smoked regularly, for example, the death rates from heart disease, lung cancer and emphysema are between two and four times higher for men than women.

As the '50s drew to an end, conventional wisdom finally came up with an explanation. Men's problem wasn't biology so much as a newly discovered killer called stress. Heart disease was claiming more and more male victims, and the reason, according to the new way of thinking, was that stress lurked in office buildings and corporate boardrooms, the very places men spent their days.

Breadwinning in earlier eras may have had more panache—slaying a lion with a spear called for a certain flair—but earning a living in the modern workplace was portrayed as just as dangerous. A popular book called "Stress and Your Heart," published in 1961, summed it all up: "It seems that being the breadwinner—whether man or woman—is a difficult job. Tension is inevitable. The job of homemaker, on the other hand, gives the woman some time—if she desires it—to relax and let some things go."

Let women be so foolish as to venture out of the home and into the line of fire, the good doctors thundered, and they would begin dying at the same rate as men. But a funny thing happened on the way to the funeral. Between 1950 and 1985, the percentage of employed women in the United States nearly doubled. Those working women, study after study has found, are as healthy as women at home. And where differences between the two groups have been reported, the advantage has gone to the working women.

The doomsayers had predicted that employed women would collapse under the stress of "role overload," as they tried to juggle work, children and homemaking. The extra stress is there, surveys confirm, but it hasn't brought ill health along with it. The reason, it seems, is that paid work provides women with feelings of self-esteem, responsibility, and camaraderie that outweigh its drawbacks. Work is no picnic—that's why they call it work—but it appears to beat staying home.

Word count: 1475

320 *Read and Respond*

HOW TO APPROACH DIFFERENT TYPES OF READING:
Reading Textbooks and Narrative Articles

APPENDIX A
READING TEXTBOOKS

Textbooks present special reading problems. Very often they include vocabulary such as technical and specialized terms that are difficult to spell, pronounce, and remember. The chapters are sometimes lengthy, and the relationships between the chapters may be unclear. Despite these difficulties, you have to remember much of the material at test time, sometimes weeks after you have read it.

However there is good news! There are methods you can use to help you understand and remember textbook material better than you have before. The basic rule to remember is this: Do not *read* textbooks—*study* them. Most students read a textbook just as they would a novel or magazine article. However, viewing a textbook as a source of information, much like a dictionary or encyclopedia, will lead to other approaches that are more effective.

Use Textbook Aids

Most textbooks have special features such as boldface headings (sometimes in different-sized type and color), pictures, charts, graphs, study questions, and glossaries to help you understand and remember the subject matter. Sometimes you can gain a better understanding of a concept by studying a picture or graph than you would from just reading an explanation.

Preview the Entire Textbook

When you first get a textbook, spend some time *previewing* or looking over the entire book to get an overall idea of the subject you will be studying. Take a few minutes to examine any of these features that your textbook contains:

- The *preface* (sometimes titled "To the Student" or "Forward") is found before the table of contents and provides you with the author's perspective on the subject. In this section, the author often explains his/her philosophy about the subject as well as way the book is organized. Reread the "To the Student" section in this book as an example of this book feature.
- The *table of contents*, found at the front of the book, lists the book's chapters. By studying the chapter titles, you can get an idea of what each section of the book is about and how the topics relate to each other.
- The *index*, located at the end of the book, is an alphabetical listing of the topics, terms, and names mentioned in the book. Use this section to find the page where a particular concept or person is discussed.
- The *glossary* is a list of technical and specialized words and their definitions. A glossary may be found in a number of places in a textbook such as at the end of a chapter, the end of the book, or in the margins of the text, near where the word is used.
- The *appendix* presents additional information that can be helpful to your understanding of the book's subject matter. Found near the back of the book, an appendix may include charts, graphs, special documents, or alternate views and approaches to the subject. The appendix that you are now reading is an example.
- *Questions, problems or exercises*, typically found at the end of a chapter, provide practical application of the ideas in the chapter or things to look for as you read.

Preview the Chapter

Before you read a chapter, consider your own knowledge and experience. Give yourself credit for what you already know about the subject. For example, suppose you are studying a textbook chapter entitled "Ways Animals Protect Themselves." Since you already know that some animals defend themselves with their claws and teeth, you won't have to take extensive notes on it when you find the place in the chapter where the author mentions this information. Likewise, you won't have to spend much time reviewing it before a test. However, when you encounter information that is new to you, such as the fact that some animals defend themselves with speed and camouflage, you should write it down or mark it in your book and study it.

TEXTBOOK STUDY-READING SYSTEMS

What is a Study-Reading System?

A study-reading system is a step-by-step procedure for reading a textbook chapter. Using such a system will help you concentrate on, understand, and remember what you read. Keep in mind that textbooks should not simply be read—they are to be studied as well.

Study-reading systems work. Research studies show that students who are taught to use a study-reading system understand and remember what they read much better than do students who have not been taught to use such a system.

There are several textbook study systems you may want to investigate or ask your instructor about. The SQ3R method, created by Francis Robinson, is one of the best known of these.

THE SQ3R SYSTEM

The 5 steps of the SQ3R study system are:

> Step One: **Survey**
> Step Two: **Question**
> Step Three: **Read**
> Step Four: **Recite**
> Step Five: **Review**

HOW TO APPLY THE SQ3R SYSTEM

Step One: Survey

To survey means to look over what you are going to read before you begin reading it closely. The survey step helps you plan your time, shows you the chapter's organization, focuses your attention on what the chapter is about, and aids in learning the material.

Procedure for surveying a chapter:

A. Read the chapter title and think about what it suggests.

B. Determine how many pages there are in the chapter and how many major topics are covered (to determine this, count the number of main headings, usually set in larger or darker type).

C. Read the summary (if there is one).

D. Glance at any illustrations, graphs, charts, etc. These will give you a clearer understanding of what the chapter is about.

Step Two: Question

A. Find the first heading of the chapter (*not* the chapter title) and *write* it as a question.

Main headings and subheadings indicate the most important topics in the chapter and can be quickly changed from statements into questions. For example, the main heading "The Endocrine System" becomes "What is the Endocrine System?" This is obviously the most important question to ask, but you might also ask, "Where is the endocrine system located in the body?" Another heading example might be "Activation Theory." Again, the most obvious question is, "What is the Activation Theory?" Other important questions, though, might be "Who thought up the activation theory?" and "When was it developed?"

Be sure to write your question down. This is necessary to complete the later steps of the SQ3R system.

B. Treat each section separately. That is, after you write the heading as a question, *complete Steps Three and Four before going on to the next heading.*

C. If the chapter has subheadings, complete steps Two, Three, and Four for each subheading as well.

D. Unfamiliar terms—often italicized—should prompt you to ask questions such as "What does this word mean?" and "How is it related to the main topic?"

Step Three: Read

Read the section to find the answer to the questions you have written. (Reading to answer a question gives you a purpose and a sense of direction.) Read extra carefully all the underlined, italicized, or bold printed words and phrases. You will often find the answer to your question in the first paragraph after the heading. You may not have to read carefully beyond that, but be sure to skim all the material to see that you have not missed something important.

Step Four: Recite

In this case, to recite means to answer the question you have asked. First, try to write your answer without looking at the book. Then, check the book to see if your answer is correct. Add anything that you have left out, and correct any errors. *Whenever possible, answer in your own words.* Simply copying sentences from the text does not insure your understanding of the subject matter. Answers do not have to be in complete sentences, but should be clear readable notes. Be sure to write your answers down under the questions they apply to.

When you have completed Steps Two, Three and Four for each major and minor heading in the chapter, you are ready for the final step.

Step Five: Review

The review is the most important step to help you remember what you have learned.

A. After you finish a chapter, go over the material *immediately*. Cover your answers and ask yourself the questions you have written down. Then look at the answers to see if you were right and to remind yourself of the ones you did not know.

B. Plan a second review within 48 hours. The timing of your reviews is almost as important as the method you use. Research has shown that forgetting most often occurs within a day or two after initial learning. Frequent, brief reviews are more effective than infrequent, long ones, so schedule several of them before the test rather than one long session near the test time.

This procedure may take a little extra time until you get used to it. With practice, however, you will not spend any more time studying than you did with other methods (or with no method). Also, you will remember more and will probably get better grades on exams.

Many students underline or highlight important items in a textbook, but a study-reading method is a vastly superior approach to studying. Simply underlining or highlighting does not require comprehension, and it provides you with nothing to review from except the textbook. On the other hand, an effective study method insures thorough learning, makes reviewing simple and effective, and helps eliminate last-minute cramming for tests.

Remember that the SQ3R study-reading method is a system, and all the steps in the process are necessary. Survey before questioning, and be sure to write down your questions and answers. Surveying prepares you to learn, reciting gives you a chance to test yourself before the instructor does, and reviewing is essential to remembering what you've learned.

APPENDIX B
READING NARRATIVE AND EXPOSITORY PROSE

Authors write for four main purposes: 1) to tell a story, 2) to describe, 3) to argue or persuade, 4) to explain. In many articles two or more of these purposes are combined. Articles that tell a story (narratives) are usually accompanied by description, and articles that explain something (exposition) are often written to persuade the reader. As a reader, you should determine whether you are reading a story or an explanation, since each type of article calls for a different approach.

How to Approach a Narrative Article

A narrative, or story, is organized by *time*. The classic beginning of a fairy tale is "Once upon a time..." When you approach a story in order to summarize it, it is important to look for time markers. It makes no difference whether the story records actual events (non-fiction) or is made up (fiction).

Suppose you read a story about an adventure in the wilderness. It begins with the main character eating breakfast by a campfire on Saturday morning. After breakfast the character sees a wild animal and goes in pursuit of it. An hour later, snow begins to fall and the character suddenly realizes he is lost. He spends the afternoon looking for camp in hopes of reaching it before dark. As evening approaches, the character looks for shelter in order to survive the storm.

Keep in mind two points while reading this type of writing. First, in order to remember the details, run a "movie" of the story in your head. Picture, in your mind, the character as he eats his breakfast, goes in search of the animal, or wanders around in the snow. In other words, visualize the characters, setting, and action using descriptive details provided by the author and your own imagination.

Second, divide the story into time segments. Look for words indicating a specific time ("10:30," "Saturday morning," or "noon"), or words that signal the passage of time, such as "later," "after that," or "soon." This will help you identify major plot events which are the major details of the story.

How to Approach Expository Articles

An expository article is organized logically rather than chronologically (by time). Because of this, it may be impossible to visualize or divide this kind of article into time segments. All of the articles in Part One and most of those in Part Two are expository articles.

When you approach this type of article in order to summarize it, you should look for the main idea in the manner described in Chapter Two. You'll also want to look for the article's major details, which support and clarify the main idea. See Chapter Three for examples of this approach.

INDEX OF ARTICLES AND PARAGRAPHS

Battered Women Who Kill: Should They Receive Clemency? 281
Buying a New Car 101
Commemorating a Heroic Act 235
Daylight Saving Time 21
Dealing With the Angry Child 195
Diet and Exercise Dangers 153
Diets of Champs 161
Discipline 104
Do the Facts Ever Lie? 11
Driving in Europe 19, 37
Facing the Test 173
Family Pet: For the Birds 183
Food Fight 261
Frank Searle's Patient Stalk of the Beastie 219
Hitting the Road 181
Houseplants 20
How to Improve Your Vocabulary 129
How to Keep Your Legs Young 167
How to Preview a Textbook 41, 71
How to Read Faster 25, 59
How to Spell 125
How to Take Good Notes 49
I Can't Stop Crying 273
Improving Your Memory 51
Just Too Beastly for Words 227
Love and Romance Make a Comeback 307
Ly Tong's Trek to Freedom 239
Many Hooked on Strange Tales of Giant Catfish 223
Marriages Made to Last 291
Open for Sourdough, Please 213
Part-time Jobs/Big-time Money 121
Pressure: How to Keep Going When the Going Gets Tough 141
Re-entry Students 5
Repairing Your Car 9, 75

Revenge is the Mother of Invention 285
Revitalize Your Memory 135
School Age Parents: The Challenge of Three-Generation Living 191
She Leads a Nation 255
Soul of a Hero 233
Speedwalk 149
Super Women 315
Taking Tests 22, 39
Test Anxiety 45
The Child I Couldn't Forget 247
The End of Innocence 201
The Importance of Childhood Memories 54, 79
The Key to Good Memory 7
The Myth of Romantic Love 299
The Shakers 73
The Value of a Speed Reading Course 23
They've Killed My Daughter Twice 275
Washington State's Economy 42
When Animals Open Wide 209
When Staying Thin is a Sickness 157
Why Isn't a Nice Person Like You Married? 303
Why Take Good Notes? 47
Women Still Face Long Journey to Sports Fanaticism 311
Wool...The Living Fiber 88
Your Child's Self-Esteem 187
Your Rights as a Crime Victim 267